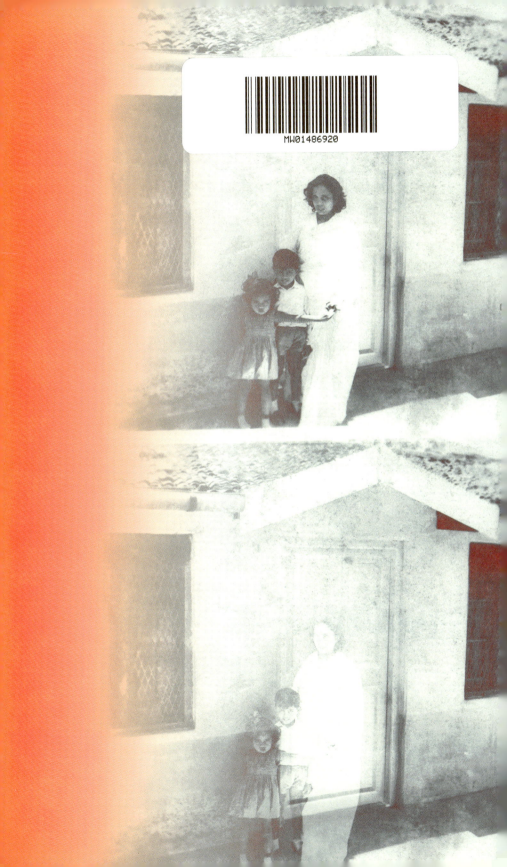

ALSO BY ARUNDHATI ROY

Novels

*The God of Small Things*

*The Ministry of Utmost Happiness*

Nonfiction

*Walking with the Comrades*

*Capitalism: A Ghost Story*

*Field Notes on Democracy: Listening to Grasshoppers*

*Things That Can and Cannot Be Said: Essays and Conversations*
(with John Cusack)

*The End of Imagination*

*The Doctor and the Saint: Caste, Race, and the Annihilation of Caste*

*My Seditious Heart: Collected Nonfiction*

*Azadi: Fascism, Fiction, and Freedom in the Time of the Virus*

*The Architecture of Modern Empire: Conversations with David Barsamian*

# MOTHER MARY COMES TO ME

## Arundhati Roy

SCRIBNER

New York   Amsterdam/Antwerp   London
Toronto   Sydney/Melbourne   New Delhi

Scribner
An Imprint of Simon & Schuster, LLC
1230 Avenue of the Americas
New York, NY 10020

For LKC
Together we made it to the shore

For Mary Roy
Who never said Let It Be

*The guests as they left*
*kissed the crown of her head*
*and she knew them*
*by their voices*

—John Berger

# Contents

# Contents

# Contents

MOTHER MARY COMES TO ME

# Gangster

She chose September, that most excellent month, to make her move. The monsoon had receded, leaving Kerala gleaming like an emerald strip between the mountains and the sea. As the plane banked to land, and the earth rose to greet us, I couldn't believe that topography could cause such palpable, physical pain. I had never known that beloved landscape, never imagined it, never evoked it, without her being part of it. I couldn't think of those hills and trees, the green rivers, the shrinking, cemented-over rice fields with giant billboards rising out of them advertising awful wedding saris and even worse jewelry, without thinking of her. She was woven through it all, taller in my mind than any billboard, more perilous than any river in spate, more relentless than the rain, more present than the sea itself. How could this have happened? *How?* She checked out with no advance notice. Typically unpredictable.

The church didn't want her. She didn't want the church. (There was savage history there, nothing to do with God.) So given her standing in our town, and given our town, we had to fashion a fitting funeral for her. The local papers reported her passing on their front pages,

1

most national papers mentioned it, too. The internet lit up with an outpouring of love from generations of students who had studied in the school she founded, whose lives she had transformed, and from others who knew of the legendary legal battle she had waged and won for equal inheritance rights for Christian women in Kerala. The deluge of obituaries made it even more crucial that we do the right thing and send her off the way she deserved. But what was that right thing? Fortunately, on the day she died the school was closed and the children had gone home. The campus was ours. It was a huge relief. Perhaps she had planned that, too.

Conversations about her death and its consequences for us, especially me, had begun when I was three years old. She was thirty then, debilitated by asthma, dead broke (her only asset was a bachelor's degree in education), and she had just walked out on her husband—my father, I should say, although somehow that comes out sounding strange. She was almost eighty-nine when she died, so we had sixty years to discuss her imminent death and her latest will and testament, which, given her preoccupation with inheritance and wills, she rewrote almost every other week. The number of false alarms, close shaves, and great escapes that she racked up would have given Houdini pause for thought. They lulled us into a sort of catastrophe complacency. I truly believed she would outlive me. When she didn't, I was wrecked, heart-smashed. I am puzzled and more than a little ashamed by the intensity of my response.

My brother put his finger sharply on that nerve. "I don't understand your reaction. She treated nobody as badly as she treated you." He could be right, although according to me, it was he who held that trophy. I can understand him feeling that I was humiliating myself by not acknowledging what had happened to us as children. But I had put that behind me a long time ago. I have seen and written about such sorrow, such systemic deprivation, such unmitigated wickedness, such diverse iterations of hell, that I can only count myself among the most fortunate. I have thought of my own life as a footnote to the things that really matter. Never tragic, often hilarious. Or perhaps this is the lie I tell myself. Maybe I pitched my tent where the wind blows strongest hoping it would blow my heart clean out of my body. Perhaps what I am about to write is a betrayal of my younger self by the person I have become. If so, it's no small sin. But I'm in no position to be the judge of that.

*     *     *

I left home—stopped going home, or what passed as home—after I turned eighteen. I had just entered my third year at the School of Architecture in Delhi.

In those days we finished high school at sixteen. That's how old I was in the summer of 1976 when I first arrived at Nizamuddin Station, alone, without even a working knowledge of Hindi, to take the entrance exam for the School of Architecture. I was terrified and had a knife in my bag. Delhi was three days and two nights away by train from Cochin, which is a three-hour drive from our town, Kottayam, which in turn is a few miles away from our village, Ayemenem, where I spent my early childhood. In other words, for me Delhi was a different country altogether. Different language, different food, different climate, different everything. The scale of the city was beyond my comprehension. I came from a place where everybody knew where everyone lived. Pathetically, I asked an auto-rickshaw driver if he could take me to the home of my mother's older sister, Mrs. Joseph. I assumed he knew where she lived. He took a deep drag of his bidi and turned away, looking bored. Two years later I was the one smoking bidis and cultivating that peerless look of bored disdain. In time I traded in my knife for a good supply of hashish and some big-city attitude. I had emigrated.

I left my mother not because I didn't love her, but to be able to continue to love her. Staying would have made that impossible. Once I left, I didn't see or speak to her for years. She never looked for me. She never asked me why I left. There was no need for that. We both knew. We settled on a lie. A good one. I crafted it—"She loved me enough to let me go." That's what I said at the front of my first novel, *The God of Small Things*, which I dedicated to her. She quoted it often, as though it were God's truth. My brother jokes that it's the only piece of real fiction in the book. To the end of her days, she never asked me how I managed during those seven years when I was a runaway. She never asked where I lived, how I completed my course of study and took my degree. I never told her. I managed well enough.

After our brittle, tentative reunion, I returned to her, visiting her regularly over the years as an independent adult, a qualified architect, a production designer, a writer, but most of all as a woman watching another with love and admiration—and a fair amount of disquiet—not just for her great qualities, but the opposite, too. In that conservative, stifling little South Indian town, where, in those days, women were only allowed the option of cloying virtue—or its affectation—my mother conducted herself with the edginess of a gangster. I watched her unleash all of herself—her genius, her eccentricity, her radical kindness, her militant courage, her ruthlessness, her generosity, her cruelty, her bullying, her head for business, and her wild, unpredictable temper—with complete abandon on our tiny, insular Syrian Christian society, which, because of its education and relative wealth, was sequestered from the swirling violence and debilitating poverty in the rest of the country. I watched her make space for the whole of herself, for all her selves, in that little world. It was nothing short of a miracle—a terror and a wonder to behold.

Once I learned to protect myself (somewhat) from its soul-crushing meanness, I even grew fascinated by her wrath against motherhood itself. Sometimes the barefaced nakedness of it made me laugh. Not the laughing-out-loud kind of laughter, but the kind that comes upon you when you are alone. When you surgically excise an incident from its circumstances and look at it dispassionately, shorn of context. As though she were someone else's mother and as though it were not I but someone else who was the object of her wrath.

*            *            *

As a child I loved her irrationally, helplessly, fearfully, completely, as children do. As an adult I tried to love her coolly, rationally, and from a safe distance. I often failed. Sometimes miserably. I wrote versions of her in my books, but I never wrote *her*. She liked those versions though and embraced the character of Ammu in *The God of Small Things*, whom she would refer to as "I" and "me." She wanted to be Ammu because she knew very well that she wasn't. When a mischievous journalist asked her whether she had indeed had a tragic love affair as Ammu did in the book, she looked him in the eye and said, "Why? Aren't I sexy enough?" She was in her sixties by then, a diva of her own making. She could say what she liked.

When the book came out, she was worried about what secrets it might reveal. To be safe, she checked herself into hospital. There she read it hurriedly and was greatly relieved that it wasn't any kind of exposé. At first, she said she couldn't understand what the fuss was all about. Then she studied it closely. After her third or fourth reading— she was home by then—she summoned me to her bedside. It was a bright afternoon and the light that filtered through her curtains was bordello red. Her eyes were shut. She said that she thought it was a good book. Well written. She wanted to know about a particular passage, one in which Ammu's seven-year-old twins, Esthappen and Rahel, remembered their parents fighting. How they grew huge, like giants, and pushed the children from one to the other, saying, "You take them, I don't want them."

"Who told you about this? You were too young to remember."

"It's fiction."

"No, it's not."

And she turned to the wall.

I have never felt the weight or the sorrow of this memory. I really believed it was fiction. I learned that day that most of us are a living, breathing soup of memory and imagination—and that we may not be the best arbiters of which is which. So read this book as you would a novel. It makes no larger claim. But then, there can *be* no larger claim. Fiction is that strange, smoky thing that writers don't entirely own, even if they think they do. Where does it come from? Our past, our present, our reading, our imagination—yes. But perhaps from premonitions of our future, too? How else can it be that like the characters in my second novel, *The Ministry of Utmost Happiness*, I too, am now the caretaker of a sort of grave in the grounds of a sort of guesthouse? It's outlandish. It keeps me awake at night. But then I ask myself, Why should we know everything?

\*          \*          \*

In my effort to fathom my mother, to see things from her perspective, to accommodate her, to understand what hurt her, what made her do the things she did and to predict what she may or may not do next, I turned into a maze, a labyrinth of pathways that zigzag underground and surface in strange places, hoping to gain a vantage point for a perspective other than my own. Seeing her through lenses that were not entirely colored by my own experience of her made me value her for the woman she was. It made me a writer. A novelist. Because that's what novelists are—labyrinths. And now this labyrinth must make sense of its labyrinthine self without her.

To bridge the chasm between the legacy of love she left for those whose lives she touched and the thorns she set down for me, like little floaters in my bloodstream—fishhooks that still catch on soft tissue as my blood makes its way to and from my heart—is why I write this book. It is as hard to write as it is not to.

Perhaps even more than a daughter mourning the passing of her mother, I mourn her as a writer who has lost her most enthralling subject. In these pages, my mother, my gangster, shall live. She was my shelter and my storm.

# Fugitives

A teacher was what she had always wanted to be, what she was qualified to be. During the years she was married and living with our father, who had a job as an assistant manager on a remote tea estate in Assam, the dream of pursuing a career of any kind atrophied and fell away. It was rekindled (as nightmare more than dream) when she realized that her husband, like many young men who worked on lonely tea estates, was hopelessly addicted to alcohol.

When war broke out between India and China in October 1962, women and children were evacuated from border districts. We moved to Calcutta. Once we got there, my mother decided that she would not return to Assam. From Calcutta we traveled across the country, all the way south to Ootacamund—Ooty—a small hill station in the state of Tamil Nadu. My brother, LKC—Lalith Kumar Christopher Roy—was four and a half years old, and I was a month away from my third birthday. We did not see or hear from our father again until we were in our twenties.

In Ooty we lived in one-half of a "holiday" cottage that belonged to our maternal grandfather, who had retired as a senior government servant—an Imperial Entomologist—with the British government in Delhi. He and my grandmother were estranged. He had severed links with her and his children years ago. He died the year I was born.

I don't know how we got into that cottage. Maybe the tenant who lived in the other half had a key. Maybe we broke in. My mother seemed familiar with the house. And the town. Perhaps she had been there as a child, with her parents. The cottage was dank and gloomy with cold, cracked cement floors and an asbestos ceiling. A plywood partition separated our half from rooms that were occupied by the tenant. She was an old English lady called Mrs. Patmore. She wore her hair in a high, puffy style, which made us wonder what was hidden inside it. Wasps, we thought, my brother and I. At night she had bad dreams and would scream and moan. I'm not sure if she paid any rent. She might not have known whom to pay it to. We, certainly, paid no rent. We were squatters, interlopers—not tenants. We lived like fugitives amid huge wooden trunks packed full of the dead Imperial Entomologist's opulent clothes—silk ties, dress shirts, three-piece suits. We found an old biscuit tin full of cuff links. (Obviously he was an enthusiastic collaborator with the colonial government and took the Imperial part of his professional designation seriously.) Later, when my brother and I were old enough to understand, we would be told the legendary family stories about him: about his vanity (he had a portrait of himself taken in a Hollywood photo studio) and his violence (he whipped his children, turned them out of the house regularly, and split my grandmother's scalp open with a brass vase). It was to get away from him, our mother told us, that she married the first man who proposed to her.

Quite soon after we arrived, she got a teaching job at a local school called Breeks. Ooty was, at the time, swarming with schools, some of them run by British missionaries who had chosen to stay on in India after Independence. She became friends with a group of them who taught at an all-white school called Lushington, which catered to the children of British missionaries working in India. She managed to persuade them to let her sit in on their classes when she had time off from her job. She hungrily absorbed their innovative teaching methods for primary schoolchildren (flash cards for reading and phonetics, colored wooden Cuisenaire rods for math), while being simultaneously disturbed by their kindly, well-meaning racism toward Indians and India. When she was away at work, she left us for a few hours with a sullen woman and occasionally with neighbors.

A few months into our fugitive life, my grandmother (the entomologist's widow) and her oldest son—my mother's older brother, G. Isaac—arrived from Kerala to evict us. I hadn't seen either of them before. They told my mother that under the Travancore Christian Succession Act, daughters had no right to their father's property and that we were to leave the house immediately. It didn't seem to matter to them that we had nowhere to go. My grandmother didn't say much, but she scared me. She had conical corneas and wore opaque sunglasses. I remember my mother, my brother, and me holding hands, running through the town in panic, trying to find a lawyer. In my memory it was night, and the streets were dark. But it couldn't have been. Because we did manage to find a lawyer, who told us that the Travancore Act applied only in the state of Kerala, not Tamil Nadu, and that even squatters had rights. He said that if anyone tried to evict us, we could call the police. We returned to the cottage shaking but triumphant. My brother and I were too young to understand what the adults were saying. But we more than understood the emotions at play: intimidation, fear, anger, panic, reassurance, relief, triumph.

Our uncle G. Isaac could not have known then that by trying to evict his younger sister from their father's cottage, he was laying the ground for his own downfall. It would be years before my mother had the means and the standing to challenge the Travancore Christian Succession Act and demand an equal share of her father's property in Kerala. Until then, she would shield and safeguard this memory of her mortification as though it were a precious family heirloom, which, in a way, it was.

*           *           *

After our legal coup we expanded into the cottage, made ourselves some space. My mother gave away the Imperial Entomologist's suits and cuff links to taxi drivers at the taxi stand near the market, and for a while Ooty had the best-dressed taxi drivers in the world.

Despite our hard-won but still-tentative sense of security, things didn't go our way. The cold, wet climate in Ooty aggravated my mother's asthma. She would lie under a thick metallic-pink quilt on a high iron cot, breathing great, heaving breaths, bedridden for days on end. We thought she was going to die. She didn't like us standing around staring at her and would order us out of her room. So, my brother and I would go off to find something else to stare at. Mostly, we swung on the low, rickety gate at the corner of the triangular compound, watching newlywed couples on their honeymoon holding hands and walking past our home on their way to romance each other in Ooty's famous botanical gardens. Sometimes they stopped and talked to us. They gave us sweets and peanuts. A man gave us a catapult. We spent days perfecting our aim. We made friends with strangers. Once one of them grabbed my hand and marched me back into the house. He told my mother sternly that her daughter had chicken pox. He made me show her the blister on my stomach, which I had been showing off to anybody who cared to examine it. My mother was furious. After he left, she smacked me hard on my cheek and told me I was never to lift my dress and show my stomach to strangers. Especially men.

It could have been her illness, or the medication, but she became extremely bad-tempered and began to hit us often. When she did this, my brother would run away and only come home after dark. He was a quiet boy. He never cried. When he was upset, he would put his head down on the dining table and pretend to be asleep. When he was happy, which wasn't often, he would dance around me boxing the air, saying he was Cassius Clay. I don't know how he knew who Cassius Clay was, I didn't. Maybe our father told him.

I think those years in Ooty were harder for him than for me because he remembered things. He remembered a better life. He remembered our father and the big house we had lived in on the tea estate. He remembered being loved. Fortunately, I didn't.

My brother started school before me. He went to Lushington, the white people's school, for a few months. (It must have been a favor to my mother from the missionaries.) But when he began to call local children like ourselves "those Indian children," she pulled him out and enrolled him in Breeks, the school that she taught in. When I turned five, she put me into a nursery school (for Indian children) that was run by a frightening-looking Australian missionary called Miss Mitten. She was a cruel woman with freckles on her arms. She had a slit for a mouth. No lips. She made it clear that she didn't like me. Our classroom was a shed on the edge of a patchy meadow where a few thin cows with prominent hip bones grazed.

On days when her asthma was really bad, my mother would write out a shopping list of vegetables and provisions, put it into a basket, and send us into town with it. Ooty was a safe, small town then, with little traffic. The policemen knew us. The shopkeepers were always kind and sometimes even gave us credit. The kindest of them all was a lady called Kurussammal, who worked in the Knitting Shop. She knitted two polo-neck sweaters for us. Bottle green for my brother. Plum for me.

When my mother became completely bedridden for a few weeks, Kurussammal moved in with us. Our edgy lifestyle came to an end. It was Kurussammal who taught us what love was. What dependability was. What being hugged was. She would cook for us and bathe us outdoors in the bitter Ooty cold with water she boiled in a huge pot on a wood fire. To this day my brother and I need to be almost boiled to feel properly bathed. Before she bathed us, she combed the lice out of our hair and showed us how to kill them. I loved killing them. They made a satisfying sound when I squashed them with my thumbnail. Apart from being a lightning-quick knitter, Kurussammal was a superb cook. She specialized in producing food from almost no ingredients. Even boiled rice with salt and a fresh green chili tasted good when she put it on our plates.

Kurussammal's name meant "mother of the cross" in Tamil. Her husband, who visited us often, was Yesuratnam, "Jesus jewel," "jewel of jewels." He had a goiter on his neck that he hid with his woolen muffler. He, like us, always smelled of woodsmoke.

Eventually my mother grew too sick to hold down her job. Even the massive dose of steroids she was on didn't help. We ran out of money. My brother and I grew undernourished and developed primary tuberculosis.

After a few more grim months of fighting on all fronts, my mother gave up. She decided to swallow her pride and return to Kerala, to Ayemenem, our grandmother's village. By then the heat of her quarrel with her mother and brother had cooled. Even if it hadn't, she was out of options.

I was heartbroken about leaving Kurussammal. But I would meet her again a few years later, when she moved to Kerala to live with us.

# The Cosmopolitans

As our train crossed the border from Tamil Nadu into Kerala, the land turned from brown to green. Everything, including the electric poles, was smothered with plants and creepers. Everything glistened. Almost all the people who slid past the train window, both men and women, wore white and carried black umbrellas.

My heart sang.

And then sank.

We arrived in Ayemenem uninvited and manifestly unwelcome. The house whose doorstep we appeared on with our invisible begging bowl belonged to my grandmother's older sister, Miss Kurien. She would have been in her sixties then. Her thin, wavy gray hair was cut in a style that used to be called a pageboy. She wore starched, papery saris with big, loose blouses. Miss Kurien was far ahead of most women of her time. She was single, held a master's degree in English literature, and had taught at a college in Sri Lanka (then Ceylon). She had a home of her own. She had savings, a pension, and all the sagacity and single-mindedness of an unmarried working woman who knew she had to take care of herself. It's unlikely she could have foreseen how many others she would have to look after, too.

My mother assured her that we would stay only as long as it took for her to find a job. Miss Kurien, who prided herself on being a good Christian, agreed to let us stay, but made no effort to hide her disapproval of us and our situation. She did this by ignoring us and showering her delicate affections on other relatives' children who visited her. She gave them gifts, played her piano, and sang to them in her quavering voice. Even though she made it clear that she did not like us (which made us not like her), she was the one person who helped us out and gave us a roof over our heads when we most needed it.

My grandmother lived with her, too. Her conical corneas had deteriorated and she was almost blind by then. She still wore her dark glasses. Even at night. She had a ridge that ran across her scalp—her famous brass vase scar. Sometimes she let me run my finger over it. And sometimes she allowed me to braid her thin hair into a rat's tail before she went to bed.

Every evening she would sit on the veranda and play her violin.

She was an accomplished violinist and had taken music lessons when her Imperial Entomologist husband was posted in Vienna. When her tutor told him that his wife had the potential to become a concert-class violinist, he stopped the lessons and, in a fit of jealous rage, smashed the first violin she owned.

I was too young to tell how well she played, but as darkness fell in Ayemenem and the sound of crickets swelled, her music made the evenings and the very dark nights more melancholic than they already were.

My uncle G. Isaac lived in an annex attached to the main house. At first, I was terrified of him. I only knew him as the tall, fat, angry

man who had tried to turn us out of our home in Ooty. In Ayemenem, though, I began to see him in a new light. He seemed more
interesting and less intimidating. I grew to love him after he began
to take my brother and me down to the river and teach me to swim
by making me paddle in circles around his stomach.

G. Isaac was one of India's first Rhodes scholars. His subject was
Greek and Roman mythology. At the dining table he would suddenly
say things like "Isn't it wonderful to have a god of wine and ecstasy?"
Everybody would look at him blankly. And he would tell us about
Dionysus, or whoever his god of the day was.

After teaching for a few years in a college in Madras, he gave up
his academic career to return to his roots and start a pickle, jam, and
curry-powder factory with his mother. It was called the Malabar Coast
Products. They ran it out of the Imperial Entomologist's family home
in Kottayam town, which was a short bus ride away. (This was the
house that would become the center of the dispute when my mother
challenged the Travancore Christian Succession Act.) G. Isaac, notwithstanding his keen interest in inheritance and private property,
was a Marxist. He said he had given up his career to start a factory to
promote small industry and generate local employment. Fed up with
his nonsense, his Swedish wife, Cecilia, whom he met in Oxford, left
him and returned to Sweden with their three young sons.

*      *      *

In these strange and manifold ways, this constellation of extraordinary,
eccentric, cosmopolitan people, defeated by life, converged on the
tiny village of Ayemenem.

The hot, humid climate suited my mother better. Her asthma,
although it remained severe and chronic, improved a little. While

she tried to work out what to do with her life, she homeschooled my brother and me. Everyone else mostly ignored us, except occasionally G. Isaac when he was in a good mood.

Life in Ayemenem was like living on a ledge that we could be nudged off at any moment. Even Kochu Maria, the cook, would tell me that we had no right to be living there. She would mutter and grumble about the shamefulness of having fatherless children living under the same roof as decent people. Every few days the Cosmopolitans would quarrel. When they fought, the whole house shook. Plates would be smashed; doors broken down. It was hard to keep track of the relationship between G. Isaac and my mother. Sometimes they were the best of friends and then, suddenly, without warning, mortal enemies. Most of the fights were, unsurprisingly, about money. About how my mother was not contributing to household expenses, not earning her keep. G. Isaac took care not to include my brother and me in those quarrels.

As soon as the shouting began, I would flee. The river was my refuge. It made up for everything that was wrong in my life. I spent hours on its banks and came to be on intimate, first-name terms with the fish, the worms, the birds, and the plants. I became close friends with other children (and some adults) in the village. I picked up Malayalam quickly and was soon able to communicate with everybody quite easily. They inhabited a different universe from mine. Most of them worked in nearby paddy fields and rubber plantations, or in the large compounds of landowning people, picking coconuts or working as house help. They lived in mud and thatch-roofed houses. Many of them belonged to castes that were considered "untouchable." I didn't know much about this horror at the time because everybody in the Ayemenem house was too busy fighting with one another to bother about indoctrinating me.

One young man who lived in Ayemenem but worked in Kottayam in the Malabar Coast Products became my most beloved friend. We spent a lot of time together. He made me a fishing rod out of a culm of bamboo and showed me where to find the best earthworms to use as bait. He taught me to fish, he taught me to stay still and be quiet. He fried the tiny fish I caught, and we ate them together as though we were feasting at a banquet. He was the inspiration for the character called Velutha—Ammu's lover—in *The God of Small Things*. Had I been sixteen years old instead of six, who knows, if I got lucky, he might well have been mine. He was the kindest, most handsome man I had ever seen.

Within months of being in Ayemenem, I turned into a part of its landscape—a wild child with calloused feet who knew every hidden path and shortcut in the village that led to the river. I lived outdoors and went home as seldom as possible. In the nonhuman category, my closest companion was a striped palm squirrel who lived on my shoulder and whispered in my ear. We shared secrets. She wasn't my pet. She had her own life, but chose to share it with me. She would disappear often because she had things to do. At mealtimes she would appear, perch on my plate, and nibble at my food. She loved pineapples most of all. She was constantly watchful, eternally alert to every possibility of looming danger. She taught me things.

Squirrel survival skills were an asset for anybody attempting to navigate the ledge life in Ayemenem.

# "I Love You Double"

My mother unloaded the burden of her quarrels and the daily dose of indignity that she had to endure onto my brother and me. We were the only safe harbor she had. Her temper, already bad, became irrational and uncontrollable. I found it impossible to predict or gauge what would anger her and what would please her. I had to pick my way through that minefield without a map. My feet and fingers and sometimes even my head were often blown off, but after floating around untethered for a while, they would magically reattach themselves.

When she got angry with me, she would mimic my way of speaking. She was a good mimic and made me sound ridiculous to myself. I clearly remember everything about every instance she did that. Even what I was wearing. It felt as though she had cut me out—cut my shape out—of a picture book with a sharp pair of scissors and then torn me up.

The first time it happened was on our way home from Madras, where we had been for two weeks. Her older sister, Mrs. Joseph, had asked if my mother could look after her three children while she and her husband were away on holiday. (The same Mrs. Joseph whose house I would years later ask the auto-rickshaw driver in Delhi to take me to.) My mother agreed. She must have felt that she would—at least nominally—be earning her keep while she was there.

Unlike the quarrelsome Ayemenem Cosmopolitans, Mrs. Joseph had a proper husband, who was a pilot for Indian Airlines, proper children, and a proper house with servants. Mrs. Joseph was acutely conscious of the fact that in these matters she had succeeded where her siblings had failed. She was good-looking, with a high, smug voice that matched her starched, ironed saris and her neat hairstyle. She had a tight, knowing smile and always sounded as though she were confiding in the person she was talking to. There was no resemblance at all, neither physical nor temperamental, between her and my mother.

When Mrs. Joseph came back from her holiday, the sisters had a terrible spat about something. We returned to Kerala the next day by plane. My aunt's pilot husband had a quota of free tickets.

We hadn't been in a plane before. Once we were seated, intending to conduct a reasonable, adult conversation as should be conducted by co-passengers on an airplane, I asked my mother how, if Mrs. Joseph was her real sister, was Mrs. Joseph so thin? My mother turned on me in a rage and mimicked me. I felt myself shrinking from my own skin and draining away, swirling like water down a sink until I was gone. Then she said, "By the time you are my age, you'll be three times my size." I knew I had said something terrible, but I wasn't sure what. (I was too young for "fat" and "thin" to be value judgments.) It was only years later, when the incident played over in my mind as it often does, and when I managed to think about it clearly without dwelling on my own feelings, that I finally realized how hurtful what I said must have been.

The steroids my mother was on had made her suddenly gain weight. She had developed a typical cortisone moon face. Her striking, fine-featured face had disappeared behind puffy cheeks and a double chin. She must have been feeling forlorn and hopeless after her visit to her slimmer sister's perfect home. Her triumphant career was still ahead of her, but there was no sign of it then. (In time she would embrace her size and shape. And she would teach her girl students to do that, too. In her fifties she modeled a bathing suit for a fashion show in the school and showed the children how to sashay.) My question to my mother about her thin sister would have felt like vinegar on an open wound. Careless words from a careless child. So, she turned on me and mimicked my six-year-old's way of speaking. And I turned on myself. I remember the air in the plane—there wasn't any. I remember the color of my dress. Sky blue with polka dots. A perfect hand-me-down from my perfect cousin with straight hair and big doe eyes. I saw that the dress didn't match my knees, which were full of scars and cuts—a comprehensive logbook of my wild, imperfect, fatherless, pilotless life on the banks of the Meenachil River in Ayemenem. I staged an imaginary competition with my perfect cousin, which I won hands down. She had a pilot father. And lovely hair. But I had a green river. (With fish in it, with the sky and trees in it and at night the broken yellow moon in it.) And a squirrel. I looked at my feet and saw that they didn't belong in the sandals they wore.

It was a horrible plane full of horrible people in a horrible sky. I wanted it to crash and for all of us to die. I especially hated the spoiled children with doting parents. I was all for collective punishment. But in a while my mother said, "I'm your mother and your father and I love you double."

And then the plane was all right. The sky was all right. But my feet were still strangers to the sandals they wore. And there were still some unresolved issues:

If I was going to be three times her size, I would need three seats to sit on. So, three free tickets.

Double. Triple. A math class. A sum to solve.

What is double-love divided by triple-my-size multiplied by free tickets divided by careless words? A cold, furry moth on a frightened heart. That moth was my constant companion.

I learned early that the safest place can be the most dangerous. And that even when it isn't, I make it so.

Years later, when I was in my thirties, a grown woman and a published novelist, I visited a friend who had just got married. The happy couple cooed and baby-talked to each other all day, for days. On the third day I nearly ran out of their house into oncoming traffic. I didn't know what had upset me so much. It's only now, as I write this, that I think I understand. They had done nothing terrible—it was me. My old friend the cold moth had paid me a visit unannounced.

(Still, it would be nice for people like me if baby-talking adults came with a statutory warning.)

# The Sliding-Folding School

After that unhappy trip to Mrs. Joseph's home in Madras, we returned to our precarious life on the ledge in Ayemenem.

But then, Redemption came.

It appeared in the stern shape and form of a middle-aged British lady who wore shoes and flowered dresses. Mrs. Mathews was one of the missionaries who had befriended my mother in Ooty. They had remained in touch and had hatched a plan.

Together, in 1967, they started a school in Kottayam. I was seven, my brother eight and a half.

They rented two small halls that belonged to the Kottayam Rotary Club, which the club members used only in the evenings. The school began with seven students, including my brother and me. It sounds simple enough, but my mother couldn't have done it alone. It was Mrs. Mathews's presence—white, virginal Christian missionary—that won the confidence of the first few parents who enrolled their children in the new school. Without her, it's unlikely that anyone in town would have trusted the education of their children to a wayward local woman who had married an outsider and then divorced him.

When I think back now, it's likely that it was G. Isaac who persuaded the Rotary Club to rent its premises to his sister. Because he was a member of the club. It was typical of their brother-sister relationship: help and harm in equal measure.

Every morning Mrs. Mathews, my mother, my brother, and I would take a bus into town to be in time for school. On some days, G. Isaac, my brother, and I would walk, cutting through paddy fields and groves of rubber trees all slanted toward the sun. When the roads were submerged by the monsoon floods, we rowed over them in little boats. We made several flirting stops at the houses of young women who worked in the pickle factory, women G. Isaac was either courting or proposing to. We were his chaperones. Our presence was meant to assure the girls' families that his intentions were honorable.

Once we got to town, he would drop us off at the newly founded school and go on ahead to his factory. On holidays my brother and I would be allowed to work on the assembly line in the factory, packing curry powder and sticking labels on pickle bottles. We wore royal-blue aprons and white headscarves. And we smelled of pickle.

*       *       *

In the Rotary Club my brother and I would help Mrs. Mathews and my mother to sweep up the cigarette butts and clear away the dirty cups and glasses left by the members. (All men, of course. To whom it would never occur to clean or clear away anything.) We would put out a table, a few stools, and a blackboard on a stand. By three o'clock we would have to fold up our school and stack it against the walls and slide away so that we didn't overlap with the club's meetings.

I thought of our new school as a sliding-folding school.

The Rotary Club rooms were located on top of a car garage and workshop that opened onto the main road. The approach to the club was through the workshop and up an open flight of steps. It wasn't a first floor so much as a two-level building set into a steep hillside. The chief garage mechanic had a little house and garden on the same level as the Rotary Club rooms. His name was Anand. He was from Tamil Nadu. I liked him a lot. The grease and grime from his workshop somehow made its way up the staircase and embedded itself in the dusty, coarse, grainy surface of the unfinished concrete floor of the club rooms. As we swept, it rose and blackened our clothes. I sneezed so much I was on a permanent antihistamine, a pretty bloodred capsule.

The school quickly became a success. The number of students began to increase exponentially. Parents of nursery school children requested my mother and Mrs. Mathews to add classes so that their children could continue to study there. My brother and I were the advance party, the lab rats on whom new teachers were tested—"Did you like her?" "Did you understand what she taught you?"

My mother thrived in her new environment. She was soon able to contribute toward the Ayemenem household's expenses. The Cosmopolitans' quarrels became less vicious. As she gained confidence, she started to cultivate her own views on education. The school began to drift away from its Christian-missionary origins and develop a character and creed of its own. Disagreements between my mother and Mrs. Mathews became fraught and not infrequent. The breaking point came when two young classical dancers, Bhavani and her husband, Chellappen, arrived to teach us Bharatanatyam. Through Bharatanatyam we learned the stories and substories of the Ramayana and Mahabharata. We came to know them as well (or as badly) as we knew the Bible. Mrs. Mathews was outraged. She said ChellappenBhavani (we always thought of them as a unit) were the Devil Incarnate. She vehemently objected to the "Vandana," the opening invocation to Lord Shiva, with which every Bharatanatyam performance begins. She said it was heathen, unchristian, and unacceptable to her and that a choice would have to be made between ChellappenBhavani and her.

Sadly, Mrs. Mathews didn't stand a chance against those two exquisite human beings whose every glance was coquetry, and every gesture high art. So, she left as suddenly as she had arrived. It was sad, but somehow inevitable. Her departure did not in any way dampen the enthusiasm or slow down the success of the school.

Within two years it was doing well enough for my mother to be able to rent the rambling old three-bedroom house next door to the Rotary Club and start a hostel for students from out of town. We left Ayemenem and moved into our new hostel-home to begin the next phase of our lives. A man who my mother said was our "landlord" would come on the first of every month to collect the rent. I did not like the way he looked at her, so I tried to make sure I was with her in the room when he came.

As the number of boarders increased, Kurussammal arrived from Ooty to manage the hostel kitchen. I was ecstatic. Apart from her, my mother hired two young women as assistants. If Kurussammal's arrival wasn't enough to make me happy, someone else arrived, too. To make up for the river I had lost, we got a puppy. My mother named her Dido—after Dido, Queen of Carthage, in the Christopher Marlowe play. She replaced my squirrel (who had gone on to mother a squirrel dynasty) as the love of my life.

Two of the bedrooms in the rented house were converted into dormitories. Each had a row of tiny beds covered with checked bedspreads. Bright raincoats hung on wooden pegs. Each boarder had a mug, a toothbrush, and a soap dish of their own. It looked like the home of Snow White and the Seven Dwarfs. Or, more accurately, Mary Roy and the fifteen dwarfs. Two of the fifteen were my brother and me.

My mother became the owner, headmistress, and wild spirit of a unique school in a unique town. A school that would, in time, wage its own unique battles.

# Federico Fellini and
# the Kottayam Santa

I say "my mother," but once she started her school, she was no longer only my mother. The moment children entered the school, she became their mother, too. Not just figuratively, but literally. When her school turned into a residential school, she would put the little ones who were unwell or homesick in her own bed. She would personally supervise their baths. The littlest tadpoles, each only slightly taller than the big iron bucket of hot water they stood next to, thought that screwing their eyes shut and lathering their stomachs in circular strokes was what constituted a bath. They would get a patient tutorial on how to soap themselves, crevices and all. Maybe ours was the only school that had bathing lessons. Later, when they were bigger, the children were taught to wash and clean the school toilets. As a result, all of us are outstanding toilet cleaners.

To ensure that the other children didn't feel that my brother and I were in any way more special than them, we too had to call our mother Mrs. Roy in public. Since public and private were geographically fluid zones, it wasn't always easy to switch. For us school was home and home was school, so we erred often and sometimes she was Mrs. Roy in private, too—"Excuse me, Mrs. Roy . . . " To me she still is more Mrs. Roy than mother. She felt it necessary to demonstrate that she had no favorites, so she was especially punitive with us, her own children. We were often punished for what others had done.

*     *     *

The responsibility of looking after so many children, of managing the food, the accounts, and the increasing numbers of teachers and staff, once again triggered a spike in her asthma. But now, each attack was an event. A piece of theater. It created a flutter in the whole school. People would rush and whisper, flock around her. She was waited upon hand and foot. I think she recognized quickly that ill-health was a good way of controlling people, keeping them on the hop.

She often told me that she might die any day, anytime, from one moment to the next, and then what would I do?

Unless somebody agreed to take me in, which was unlikely, she said, I would end up on the streets. I'd have to take care of myself. I'd have to be prepared, to plan for myself.

But how?

As I watched her struggling to breathe during those attacks of asthma that came without warning, her heaving chest struck terror into me. Unlike in our days in Ooty, I was old enough to understand the idea, the finality, of death and dying. The shadows that collected in the deep hollows that formed near her collarbones were like a confederation of jeering skulls knocking against one another, their mirthless smiles asking, *What will you do now, little girl?* Her wheeze asked the same thing in a higher register: *What will you do now, little girl?* My reply was always *I'll breathe for you, Mama.* I tried to breathe for her. I became her lungs. Her body. I attached myself to her in ways she wasn't aware of. I became one of her valiant organs, a secret operative, breathing my life into hers.

*       *       *

It all became much worse when she finally identified a family who *might* take me in. A slim chance, a sliver of hope for me on an otherwise grim horizon. The family didn't know, of course, it was just speculation on my mother's part, a secret plot between her and her valiant organ-child. The family was a perfect fit in many ways—for the task it didn't know it had been assigned. A young widow who worked in the school. Her children, my friends, a little younger than me, studied there.

They, the chosen ones, lived in a big, airy house. The trouble was their grandfather. Patriarch of the house. Respected senior in the town. Sweaty brown Santa at the Rotary Club Christmas party in a red jumpsuit and a cotton-wool beard and a "Ho! Ho! Ho!" I was sometimes sent to their home for weekends (presumably so that the children could get used to their soon-to-be-permanent sister and vice versa). There, when he caught me alone, which wasn't hard because I was a reading child, the "Ho! Ho! Ho!" turned into a snuffling and a groping between my legs and a rolling down of my underwear. I could tell that what he was doing was wrong and I sensed that it had something to do with having babies. And that I must escape. He was a lumbering, ungainly man and I always managed to get away. But still, it was a hunt, and I was his prey. While everybody else saw the kindly Kottayam Santa—loving, bumbling grandpa—I saw a human-size pig with glasses, a snorting wild boar sitting across the table from me at mealtimes.

I say I got away, and I'm sure I did. But at the time I didn't know what I had got away from. What exactly had to happen to make you have a baby? Had I got away in time? I would think about this while I was sitting in my improvised classroom—just a trestle table and a few low wooden stools in the halls of our sliding-folding Rotary Club school—while some poor teacher that my mother was trying out was attempting to teach me something. Hindi. Malayalam. History. Geography. Was I pregnant? Can children have babies? I'd break out into a cold sweat at the thought. The sweat would trickle down the back of my legs. I was convinced that cold sweat trickling down the back of your legs was a sure sign of pregnancy. The long-stemmed ceiling fan went round and round during those quiet afternoons. It sounded like doom.

I never told my mother about the wild boar, or the hunt. I am not sure why. I was unsure, I suppose. What if I was wrong? What if it was just wild-boar affection? How ungrateful could I be? And who would believe me (bad unchristian girl) and how would my friends feel? In any case I was sure I could fend him off. I made myself some quick, easy rules. Hide in the crowd. Make sure never to be alone, be alert, never read. It was only a question of a day or two at a time. At most.

But what if it wasn't? What if my mother died and I had to live with them?

And then I knew that if she died, I must, too. I'd have to find a way. I wasn't debilitated by the idea, but underneath the sunny hop-scotch moments, that thrum of apprehension was a constant theme, like the background score in a never-ending horror movie. I had to make every effort to keep her alive. Breathe for her.

\*          \*          \*

I kept an eagle eye on all the other children's mothers, hoping to spot a trace of a mother like mine. I never did. It's not that I wanted her to be like my friends' mothers, I didn't. Because they always seemed a little frightened, a little tentative, as though they were perpetually waiting for instructions.

I was once invited to a birthday party at one of their homes. It happened rarely because we were considered outsiders—not sufficiently Christian, not sufficiently Malayali. Not sufficiently wealthy. So, this occasion was special. I was alone. Mrs. Roy wasn't there. My hosts were rich plantation people. They had a grand house with deep verandas, a long driveway, spotted deer in their compound, and many servants.

The mother of the birthday child was plump and safe looking. Her brilliant diamond earrings were like tiny searchlights. It was a children's party, but most of their parents were there, too. A mountain of food was on the table. The mirrors on the wall made it look as though there were many parties and many tables with many mountains of food. The child's father came into the room with an envelope. It looked as though he was many fathers with many envelopes. Or maybe my imagination has turned him into a multitude. He threw the envelope onto the floor. *Edi ninakkoru ezhutthu vannu.* The rudest way of saying, "Woman, there's a letter for you." The safe-looking mother bent down with her diamonds and picked the letter up from the floor. In front of everybody. She looked so alone. I wanted to put my arms around her, but I didn't want a mother like her. And at that moment, I was relieved not to have a father at all. That's a terrible thing to say, I know, but back then fathers seemed like an extremely risky proposition to me.

By this time my brother's and my memory of our own father had completely faded. We only knew him as the mysterious stranger (quite handsome, we thought) in the gray photo album that Mrs. Roy kept locked in her cupboard and allowed us to look at occasionally. There was a photograph of their wedding, too. (Quite Hindu, we thought.) In the album our mother looked as mysterious and as much of a stranger as our father did. There was a picture of her sitting on a wicker chair in the Assam Planters' Club, wearing a sexy sleeveless blouse and smoking a cigarette. She wasn't Mrs. Roy. She was someone else.

Mrs. Roy didn't talk about Assam at all. The only thing she said about her husband was "He was a Nothing Man."

*     *     *

As her school grew from being a primary school into a junior school, Mrs. Roy had to persuade nervous parents that a coeducational school was not the den of vice and sexual profligacy that people in Kottayam made it out to be. She reassured them by imposing strict moral discipline and being excessively vigilant about students flouting the flirting rules. Nevertheless she was defiant in her belief that boys and girls should play and study and grow up together.

In the early years, she was extra-alert. When it was brought to her attention that boys in the hostel had begun to tease the girls about breasts and bras, she held a special assembly. She sent two of the main young bullies to fetch a bra from her cupboard. It was an impressive one, halfway between a bodice and what we now know as a bra. In those days there was only one brand—Maidenform. It looked like a piece of armor. And hers looked sizable in the hands of the two frightened boys. (For this and much else, I must be forgiven for believing, when I first encountered his films, that Federico Fellini was a social realist.) "This is a bra. All women wear them. Your mothers wear them, your sisters will, too, soon enough. If it excites you so much, you are very welcome to keep mine." It was rough, yes. But it was one of those moments that changed the balance of power between boys and girls in the school forever.

Mrs. Roy made it her mission to disabuse boys of their seemingly God-given sense of entitlement. She turned them into considerate, respectful men, the kind the town had rarely seen. In a way she liberated them, too. She freed them of the burden of being what society thought men ought to be. She raised generations of sweet men and sent them out into the world. What she did for her girl students, the spirit she instilled in them, was nothing short of revolutionary. She gave them spines, she gave them wings, she set them free. She bequeathed her unwavering attention and her stern love on them, and they shone back at her.

That revolution, like all revolutions, came at a cost.

# Collateral

Mrs. Roy directed all her fury against men, her idea of men (her father, husband, and brother in particular), on her son. My brother, LKC. From the time he was only six or seven years old, for even the smallest mistake or slipup she would call him a male chauvinist pig. She sent him away to a boarding school when he was nine; I followed two years later. We had outgrown her school by then.

Although the fees in our new boarding school were not exorbitant in the way fees are in private schools today, she still struggled to pay them. For years we never heard the end of how much we owed her for our education—"Speaking as your banker . . . " was the way many conversations went.

I hated being sent away. (How we need our tormentors.) The school we were sent to, where I studied for six years, was in the Nilgiris, the Blue Mountains, quite close to Ooty. It was an overnight journey in a big broad-gauge train and then a three-hour ride on another, smaller train up the steep mountain terrain. On those journeys back to school, surrounded by boisterous, happy fellow students, I came to intimately understand the meaning of desolation, and how never to show my feelings.

Our new school could not have been more different from Mrs. Roy's. It had a grand reputation, an iconic clock tower, and beautiful, rambling grounds. But the first thing that struck me about it was how filthy it was. The dorms were filthy, the kitchen was filthy, and the dining room was full of flies. Filthiest of all were the toilets. For a trained and experienced toilet cleaner such as myself, this was a trauma and an affront.

The school prided itself on being a military school. We spent long hours learning to march around like soldiers with an instructor, an ex-soldier, roaring at us. ("Left, left, left-right-left. Dig your heels and roll your toes. Left, left, left-right-left.") He would bend down low and literally roar at our heels. I worried about stepping on his huge, bushy mustache. There were no bra demonstrations at assembly. The boys were taught to behave like boys. Their school uniform was khaki shorts and a khaki "battle jacket." They had an army band in which my brother played the bugle. They had painting and sculpture classes. We were very few girls. No battle jackets and no army band for us. No painting or sculpture either. Instead, we had old-lady V-necked cardigans, pleated gray skirts, "home science," and needlework.

During midterm weekends I would watch with some fascination the joyful, loving reunions between my classmates and their parents, who took them out for an overnight break and brought them back laden with food, new clothes, and shoes. Mrs. Roy did come sometimes, traveling from Kerala all alone, to take us out. She would be the only single mother in a sea of couples. When I saw her standing among them, my heart would burst with love for her. We would spend the weekend in the Imperial Entomologist's cold cottage. To call those occasions joyful or loving would be untrue. But I still counted the days, the hours, the minutes to when I would be able to see Mrs. Roy again.

There were other students like my brother and me who did not come from wealthy homes and did not always get taken out for weekends. The poorest ones, far poorer than us, were "merit scholars," whose parents could not afford to travel or stay in hotels. They were easily the brightest of us all.

In my mind I had a separate category of humans who I thought of as the Mummydaddy people. I regarded them with a tangential interest that was laced with a faint protective drizzle of cultivated disdain. I believed that I belonged to a completely different species.

The only thing I loved about the school was the athletics track. Even now when I think about what heaven ought to be like, the image that comes to mind is not a writers' heaven. Not a library or a book paradise. It's me sitting under the huge oak tree on the grassy bank that marked off the sports field, lacing up my running shoes. Running was my way of exorcising bleakness. I ran through my meals. I ran through my lessons. I ran in my sleep. I ran even when I was standing stock-still. I think, like Forrest Gump, I could have run forever.

*     *     *

We came home (back to Mrs. Roy's school, that is) twice a year for holidays. We lived in dread of the day our (other) school report cards would arrive in the post. Because our banker made it clear that she expected substantial returns on her investment. If she didn't get them, the consequences were grim.

I feigned sleep the night she came and woke my brother up and took him—little boy sleepwalking—to her room. I followed as quietly as I could and watched through the keyhole as she beat him until the thick wooden ruler broke. "No son of mine comes home with a report that says 'average student.'" She raged at him without raising her voice above a whisper so as not to wake the other children in our hostel-home. The whispering made the whole thing even more terrifying. My brother didn't react. That made her angrier. Finally, she grew tired, and he came back to his bed, quiet as death. I pretended to be asleep. We both knew I was awake. In the morning, she hugged me and said, "You have a brilliant report." I was filled with shame. I hated myself. Since then, for me, all personal achievement comes with a sense of foreboding. On the occasions when I am toasted or applauded, I always feel that someone else, someone quiet, is being beaten in the other room. If you pause to think about it, it's true, someone is.

None of this stopped my brother and me from having our own arguments, fighting physically, almost to the death, almost every day, breaking lamps and other fragile things that came in our way. It changed only when he grew vastly stronger. He then became my great protector. Mrs. Roy did not take kindly to this.

When he was a teenager, she once said to him, "You're ugly and stupid. If I were you, I'd kill myself." He was neither of those things. He was just quiet and unsure of himself because he remembered his father and was marked by the trauma of losing him more than I was. It was remarkable that Mrs. Roy felt able to say these terrible things to her son in this, the land of son-worshippers. The land in which sons must be given more than daughters, more of everything—attention, love, money, education, inheritance, even food. The land of infanticide and female feticide, in which millions of daughters are done away with even before they are born, and some just after. Sometimes my mother behaved as though all of this was my brother's fault. Because he was the only man she could reach, the only man she could punish for the sins of the world. The way she was with him has queered and complicated my view of feminism forever, filled it with caveats.

The corollary to son worship is of course mother worship. Ours is a land of mother-worshippers, too. Or, more accurately, a land that deifies mothers who produce and then deify their sons. My brother and I grew up in the cleft between that syrupy dream and our capricious nightmare, not always knowing which was worse. On balance, if we *had* to choose between the two, I think I'd choose our nightmare, and he, the dream.

# The Naxalites

Compared to her abusive, bullying wrath against my brother, Mrs. Roy's rage against me had an entirely different quality and texture. It was more ambiguous, but no less harsh. Its contours became clearer as I grew older, or perhaps I just became more accustomed to it.

The year before I followed my brother to boarding school, a telephone—our first—was installed in the front room of our hostel-home. It was 1969. I was nine.

It wasn't a good day. I still remember our phone number: 2793. The phone was one of those black Bakelite instruments. Mrs. Roy the Cosmopolitan knew about phones. She had grown up in Delhi, studied in Madras, was married in Calcutta, and had lived in Assam.

But I was, at the time, still a villager. I knew a lot about some things and little about others. I knew how to make an improvised fishing rod, how to fish, where to find the best earthworms for bait, how to raise baby birds and squirrels, but I didn't know a thing about telephones.

We—the rest of the hostelers and I—watched the telephone being installed in silent awe. After the man who installed it left, Mrs. Roy dialed a number. I couldn't believe that my mother was talking to someone who wasn't in the room by holding a black object to her ear. I thought she was talking to herself—pretending, or practicing something. Fascinated by our new acquisition, I pressed down on the twin chrome plunger buttons, and the call was disconnected. Her eyes turned cold. "You bitch," she said. In front of everybody. I didn't know what that meant, but it sounded bad, the way she said it.

Once again, I swirled like water down a sink and disappeared. I have tried hard to forget this moment—more because of the expression in her eyes than the word itself—but clearly, I haven't succeeded. A few years before she died, she asked me if my dogs in Delhi were men or women. So, when she said "bitch" all those years ago, maybe she didn't mean it badly after all. On the other hand, she was merciless with dogs. So maybe she did mean it badly. The story of Dido—my big, beautiful black Alsatian—is hard to tell, but I will, in a while.

Perhaps the reason that the "bitch" incident is lodged so firmly in my mind is because it was a doubly bad day. The day we got our first telephone was also the day the newspapers reported that the Naxalites had beheaded a landlord in a district north of Kottayam. His photograph was in the papers. Blurry black-and-white. The way I remember it, his severed head lay some distance from his body, which was tied to a pole. The earth around him was dark with blood.

The Naxalites were a group of far-left, radical insurgents—Maoists—who had broken away from India's main Marxist parties. They believed that these Marxists, by joining the mainstream and participating in elections, had become bourgeois and betrayed the central tenets of communism. The Naxalites believed in armed revolution. They declared Parliament a "pigsty" and called for the "annihilation of the class enemy." To this end, they committed shocking acts of exhibitionist violence. The mainstream Marxists in Kerala, who had formed the first-ever democratically elected Communist state government in

India in 1957, were hostile to them and called them anarchists and adventurists. The two groups hated each other more than they hated non-communists.

The Naxalite uprising, which began in the village of Naxalbari in West Bengal, ignited the imagination of angry, frustrated students and young people and spread fast across the country. The beheading of the landlord in Kerala took place in Palakkad, where the tea, coffee, and spice plantations were. The papers said the Naxalites had held an impromptu trial, at which they read out the landlord's crimes to him—murder, the exploitation of his workers, and cruelty toward women—before they cut his head off.

A pall of fear hung over us for the next few weeks. Almost all the children in the school, in the hostel especially, were the children of landlords and plantation owners—people the Naxalites considered to be the "class enemy." I worried that they would all be beheaded, and Mrs. Roy, LKC, and me too, by accident, even though we weren't landlords. We monitored the Bakelite telephone closely for threatening calls. The bravest among us picked it up sometimes, even when it didn't ring. We believed that someone was waiting on the other end of the line, permanently. Waiting to threaten us. When Mrs. Roy wasn't watching, we practiced saying, "Hello? Who's speaking?"

The Naxalites announced that the Revolution was coming. Any day it would be upon us, and the world wouldn't be unfair anymore. Revolutions were meant to make the world less unfair, Mrs. Roy explained. The poor would inherit the earth. The rich would be killed.

*       *       *

In church the priests said the same sort of thing about the poor that communists did, but they didn't sound as though they meant it. They were far less extreme about the fate of the rich because their congregations were made up of comparatively well-off people. The really poor, who mostly belonged to castes that were considered "untouchable" and had converted to Christianity relatively recently, hoping to escape the stigma of the Hindu caste system, were not allowed in Syrian Christian churches. Caste pursued them into Christianity. On the subject of caste, the Syrian Christians of Kerala (many of whom like to believe, with no real basis, that their forefathers were Brahmins who had been converted to Christianity by St. Thomas the Apostle when he traveled east after the Crucifixion) and the Hindus in the rest of India are similarly hidebound. The priests in church said it would be as difficult for the rich to go to heaven as it was for a camel to pass through the eye of a needle. I imagined the rich were busy making a gigantic needle with a huge, camel-size eye. If you think about it, that needle has been forged. It exists. And a ceaseless cavalcade of camels passes through it.

I wasn't sure what was to become of us, who were neither rich nor poor. We rarely went to church. Almost never. Even when Mrs. Roy was old and seriously unwell, if a priest or nun visited her—many did and invariably, irritatingly, spoke a little louder and a little slower than necessary—she would say, "Please, can you ask her [or him] to leave?"

\*　　　　\*　　　　\*

Anyhow, it didn't come. The Revolution. The Naxalite movement was quickly crushed, but every now and then it rose (rises) in another part of the country. It's like a dreadful thermometer that takes our temperature from time to time and tells us how sick we are.

I didn't realize then what a deep impression the Naxalites made on me. Their deeds shocked and distressed me, but I understood their rage instinctively. When I wrote *The God of Small Things*, Velutha would be suspected of having joined the Naxalites. He would be mercilessly killed because nothing threatened—and continues to threaten—the Indian elite (Hindus, Christians, Muslims, Sikhs, and many Communists, too) more than when oppressed-caste and working-class rage conjoin. They rarely do.

Forty years after the Day of the Telephone, in 2010, I would spend some of the most intense weeks of my life with Naxalite guerrillas deep inside the Dandakaranya forest in Central India and write a little book called *Walking with the Comrades*.

In those puzzling, unaccountable ways in which we associate particular memories with particular things or smells or songs, I still associate Naxalites with Bakelite telephones.

Mrs. Roy wasn't by any means unsympathetic to communism. For my Class VII school debate (I was eleven and in the military boarding school by then), she came visiting and dressed me up as a Vietcong girl, but in civilian clothes. I wore her flowered yellow sarong, which was folded into two to end just below my knees, and a blouse with a Chinese collar. (In Kerala, we wore our sarongs down to our ankles.) She showed me Vietnam on a map and told me about the war, about the bombing, about Agent Orange and how it burned away miles and miles of trees and plants and poisoned the earth. She told me that the Americans called the Vietnamese "gooks" and how Vietnam was just like Kerala. Full of jungles, rivers, rice fields, and communists. We were gooks, too, she said.

She was eclectic though. She also taught me Shakespeare, Kipling, and A. A. Milne. She read me parts of *The Rise and Fall of the Third Reich*. And the opening passage of *Lolita*. (She called G. Isaac "Humbert Humbert" because of his interest in women much younger than him.) She had a low, strong voice that betrayed no doubt or hesitation.

She sang Paul Robeson's "Ol' Man River" and told me about slavery and the slave boats that sailed up the Mississippi. I loved the word *Mississippi*. And the word *Beirut*. Every three months we would get a parcel of books from a library in Madras that we could read and return. The day the parcel arrived, I would be so excited my stomach would convulse and I'd need to run to the bathroom several times.

For the school debate she made me rehearse my speech. I learned to call counterrevolutionaries and supporters of the American invasion "running dogs of imperialism" while my voice shook with rage. I spoke well enough, but the whole time I was conscious of my legs, which had begun to get a little hairy. And of my wild, curly hair. Very un-Vietnamese. A different type of gook. In Kerala, because we had a Marxist state government, there were huge marches in support of Ho Chi Minh and the North Vietnamese. But we heard little about the Soviet gulag, the famine in Ukraine, or the Great Leap Forward in China, in which millions had perished.

Like most people in the world, then as well as now, we grew up between shouting and silence. Some of us made up our own minds, others had their minds made up for them.

# I'm All for the Unconquered Moon

My brother isn't quiet anymore. We're completely different. He runs his own successful business and drives a BMW. He has a microphone and three electric guitars on stands by his bed. He plays lead and sings rock 'n' roll. The music he makes is loud. Very loud. Very sixties and seventies. Very good. But very white. Creedence Clearwater, Pink Floyd, Deep Purple. He built his life on his own with no help from anybody else. He has the best laugh of anybody that I know. He works in the seafood industry. To tease him I call him a prawnbroker. I envy him his moments of unmitigated delight. I'm not sure that I am capable of those anymore.

When we were children, he and I never spoke about Mrs. Roy to each other. We only referred to her as "she." She hated us having anything to do with each other because she suspected we were conspiring against her. She did everything she could to keep us separated. It's only now, after she's gone, that we meet freely and laugh about things. He didn't pretend to be sad when she died. Not even when she was lying in her coffin. It was different for me. I came undone. If I could understand myself better, I'd probably understand a lot more about the world and certainly about my country, in which so many people seem to revere their persecutors and appear grateful to be subjugated and told what to do, what to wear, what to eat, and how to think. There is something knotty here, something puzzling about the human condition in all of this. But maybe it's best to leave some things un-understood, mysterious. I'm all for the unclimbed mountain. The unconquered moon. I'm weary of endless theories and explanations. I think I have begun to prefer descriptions. Anyway, all this to say that while Mrs. Roy lay in her glass-topped coffin, I was in ruins, but my brother was jovial and warmly welcomed all those who had come to pay their respects to her. People looked at him oddly. He didn't care. I like that about him. He never pretends that what happened to us didn't happen.

It was almost as though for her to shine her light on her students and give them all she had, we—he and I—had to absorb her darkness.

Today, though, I am grateful for that gift of darkness. I learned to keep it close, to map it, to sift through its shades, to stare at it until it gave up its secrets. It turned out to be a route to freedom, too.

# Laurie Baker and the Bald Hill

I was less than two years away from completing high school when Mrs. Roy decided that her sliding-folding school needed to move into a campus of its own.

It was doing remarkably well. But temporary classrooms in the rented halls of the Rotary Club were limiting her stride. There were no playgrounds, no separate classrooms, no proper furniture. And sometimes the debris left behind by the club meetings got in the way of the school.

One morning after the sweeping ritual, a six-year-old student went missing. We eventually found him locked in the toilet, which was a short walk from the main halls. He had collected all the cigarette stubs in a heap and was trying to smoke them. We found out just in time to douse his bonfire. The little man had clearly planned it and come prepared with a matchbox. (He's a Holy Roller now, a soldier of Christ. Doesn't smoke.)

When children fell, they scraped themselves badly on the rough cement floor and their wounds festered. They skittered around like the walking wounded, with daubs of gentian violet or bright red

Mercurochrome announcing the injuries on their knees and elbows. Some of the mishaps were more serious and needed stitches and plaster casts. The worst accident, fortunately, happened to me and not another student.

The Rotary Club, set into a steep hillside, was at a much higher level than our ground-floor hostel-home next door. An iron stepladder with a handrail, bolted into the mossy ten-foot-high laterite retaining wall, connected the grounds of the two compounds. This shortcut allowed staff and provisions to move between the adjacent buildings without having to go out onto the main road. A locked metal gate prevented easy access to the ladder. Children were strictly forbidden to use it. I broke the rule, climbed over the locked gate, and had a terrible fall. I tumbled down the ladder and hit my teeth on a rock. I had to spend weeks with my mouth in a kind of plaster, on a liquid diet. For more than a year I could only eat mashed food. The friendly neighborhood Kottayam dentist re-embedded my front teeth into my gums. He was so proud of his accomplishment that for years after that, like a cattle owner, or a horse buyer, he thought nothing of examining my teeth in public, at social gatherings, to see how they were doing. Despite all his attentions, my two front teeth didn't make it. They fell out after a few years. The ones I have now are fake. They have begun to move sideways and leave an odd gap. (It's annoying, but since it shackles me to my past, I have decided to embrace the gap.)

Mrs. Roy had other reasons for wanting a proper campus for the school. She had developed bigger ambitions for her students. She wanted them to do sports, theater, and art like children in other schools. But all she had were those two small halls with marked-off spaces for different activities. As the school grew, so did the chaos. Animated, eager voices echoed through the halls and bounced off the walls. It wasn't easy for anyone to concentrate on anything.

With each passing day there was new excitement; there were new students, new ideas. Young women in town who might otherwise have lived obedient, housewifey lives picking up things their husbands flung to the floor suddenly had the opportunity to become teachers in this new, experimental school, and to pursue exciting careers of their own. The halls in the Rotary Club were too small to contain the exuberance the school was generating.

Mrs. Roy identified a piece of land a few kilometers out of town. To raise money to buy it, she asked her students' parents for a "caution deposit"—something like an interest-free loan—which would be refunded when the student left the school. The parents gladly agreed. It was 1974. Her school was seven years old. I was fourteen going on fifteen.

\*　　　　\*　　　　\*

The land she bought was three acres of wilderness known as *motta kunnu*, "the bald hill." It wasn't really bald, because nothing in Kerala can be. It had giant jackfruit trees, and dense thickets of towering bamboo that creaked and moaned like people at a funeral. It was covered with thick undergrowth, full of the rustle of skinks, mongoose, and garden lizards. There was a shallow well that had gone dry. People who lived in the little houses around the base of the hill, close to the main road, told us helpfully that the well was lined with the skeletons of birds, snakes, and toads that had been trapped and eaten by a pair of ghosts who lived in it. Nobody dared to go up there at night. Not even vagabonds and drunks. The chirp of crickets and the croaking of frogs covered the hill like a dome of sound, sealing it off from the nearby town. The land was relatively cheap because it was considered too haunted, too steep, and too difficult to build on. Mrs. Roy's next task was to find an architect who would accept the challenge.

One name made its way quickly to the top of her list. Laurence Wilfred Baker, known to most as Laurie Baker, and to his team of expert masons simply as Daddy. Baker was an Englishman, a conscientious objector in the Second World War, who, deeply influenced by a chance encounter with Gandhi, moved to India in 1945, where he began work as an architect for the World Leprosy Mission. He met and married Elizabeth Jacob, a Malayali doctor who also worked there. The young couple then decided to branch out on their own. They traveled from Faizabad to Pithoragarh, a remote town in the foothills of the Himalayas, where they ran a small hospital for villagers in the district who had no access to medical care. After sixteen years in Pithoragarh they began making their way south and eventually settled at the tip of the Indian peninsula, in Trivandrum, the capital of Kerala, about a hundred miles south of Kottayam.

Half a century before it occurred to anybody else, before words like *sustainable* and *organic* became part of everyday conversation, Laurie Baker was already at that station. He developed building techniques using locally available materials and adapted to the local climate. He used cheap kiln-baked bricks and lime mortar instead of cement. As far as possible, instead of windows, which were expensive, he used a range of brick jalis—a kind of latticework that let in air, beautiful patterns of light, and the occasional curious reptile. His greatest innovation was his roofing technique. He called it a filler slab. It was halfway between a concrete roof and a tile roof. The "filler" was a local inexpensive terra-cotta roof tile embedded in the cement slab within a grid of minimal steel reinforcement. It could be cast flat, conical, gabled, it could be a vault—any shape at all. In a climate that required steep-sloped roofs because of the ferocity of monsoon rain, Baker's filler slab liberated the building plan from the geometrical tyranny of a tile-and-rafter roof.

Baker was a genius not just because he built cheaply, but because his buildings had none of the bleakness or unsmiling, heartless mass replication that you might expect with low-cost architecture. Each of his buildings was unique and had soul, playfulness, and a radical irreverence that was part of his personality. (When he died, he left instructions saying he should be cremated immediately, that nobody should weep over his corpse, and that his ashes should be put into an egg timer.) And yet, despite their uniqueness, his buildings had no ego. You could hardly see them because they fused so perfectly—with a wink and a nod—into their environment. He joked that his ambition was not to be a "low-cost architect" but a "no-cost architect." He was acutely conscious that the people he built for had little money and tender dreams. He respected that, and their dreams became his. That is what made him a prodigy. That Mrs. Roy found him and trusted him, literally with her life, without tutoring or encouragement or help from anyone, without a background in architecture, and with no access at all to those exclusively male club meetings in which things like business, taxes, banking, and building are discussed, made her a prodigy, too.

Daddy's construction techniques made his peers uncomfortable. Architects, engineers, and building contractors whose fees and commissions were a percentage of the cost of the buildings they worked on felt threatened by this interloper. High-cost architecture suited them. They were openly hostile and warned that Baker's buildings were precarious and unsafe. He laughed away their criticism. His architecture was in a language that most of his peers were not able to read or understand. He worked on-site, hands-on with his masons, all of them learning as they went along.

Like Mrs. Roy, Baker, too, was an upstream-swimming fish. When they met, they recognized this about each other instantly. Neither was easy for the other to get on with. Baker was elusive and hard to pin down. He never kept appointments. She, of course, was She. They grumbled about each other's intractability and eccentricity, but secretly they loved and respected each other.

He visited *motta kunnu* and was delighted by the challenges it posed. Work began immediately. Not a tree would be cut. Not a slope leveled. Not a paisa wasted. The progeny of the union between Mummy and Daddy was a sort of spirit architecture, a school campus so idiosyncratic, so beautiful, that it contributed as much, if not more, to the children's education as their formal lessons did. It grew slowly and took years to become what it is today. Some of the buildings were constructed long after Baker died. He had made the drawings but there wasn't enough money to construct them. Mrs. Roy salted them away and bided her time.

The building of the new campus began modestly. We moved out of the rented hostel-home and the Rotary Club just as soon as the first phase was complete.

The administration block had a reception space, a waiting area for parents, and a tiny office for the principal, which, at night, became a bedroom for my mother and, occasionally, perilously, for me. Open classrooms with three walls and no doors, each a different shape, each at a different level, circumscribed a central space that doubled as a sunken stage. All the children had to do was swivel around on their stools, face away from the blackboard, and they had themselves a little auditorium. The wide steps leading down from the classrooms to the stage worked as additional seating. Farther up the hill, accessible by a flight of rough stone steps cut into the hillside, were the large, airy kitchen, the children's and teachers' dining hall, a few dormitories, and a sickroom. My brother slept in the sickroom or in one of the classrooms. The money Mrs. Roy raised wasn't enough to cover the cost of roofs, not even filler-slab roofs, so for the first few years the classrooms had thatched roofs.

At the base of *motta kunnu*, down a winding road with a hairpin bend, was the garage for the school bus and an open shed, which was the nursery school until noon and in the afternoons was used for music, dance, and theater practice. In front of it was a small sports field surrounded by wild pepper vines and coppices of banana trees. The nursery shed also served as a pavilion for parents to watch their children perform on Sports Day. Sometimes things were turned around and the shed became a stage. The audience sat on chairs arranged under an awning in the sports field.

Watching Baker's buildings grow out of the earth almost like trees and plants fascinated me. I learned that design could evoke the same kind of joy in me as music, dance, and literature. Meeting Laurie Baker, listening to him, watching him pull out a little pocket notebook and sketch exactly what he was thinking—in the way that someone else might jot down a sentence from a poem—was exhilarating to the fifteen-year-old me. I wanted to draw like him, think like him, walk around construction sites like he did; I wanted to be him.

To want to study architecture was not, at the time, a simple ambition for a girl from Kottayam. But if that girl was Mrs. Roy's daughter, and if Mrs. Roy backed her, then nothing was impossible. Between her bouts of rage and increasing physical violence, Mrs. Roy told her daughter that if she put her mind to it, she could be anything she wanted to be. To her daughter those words were a life raft that tided her over pitch darkness, wild currents, and a deadly undertow. Meeting Laurie Baker made me swerve sharply away from what had always been not just an idea, but an assumption: when I grew up,

I would be a writer. Baker made me think that nothing would be more exciting than studying architecture. But truthfully, the fuel in my engine that propelled me all the way from Kottayam to Delhi was made of baser, less noble things. The usual, actually—money and sex. Money, because I realized that to survive, I had to get away from home as quickly as I could, and I had heard that once you were in Architecture School, you could start working and earning even before you graduated. And sex—sexual desire—because the day I met Laurie Baker, I also met someone else.

As it turned out, the day Mummy met Daddy was the day Baby decided she must fly away. Although it would take her a while to make the arrangements.

# Joe, Jimi, Janis, and Jesus

Our journey to Trivandrum to meet Baker for the first time was embarrassing from the outset. We drove the five or more hours south from Kottayam in the school van. There were four of us: the school driver, Mrs. Roy, me, and Kunjamma, one of the maintenance staff from the hostel-home. Her job was to manage the big bag that contained water, a flask of hot coffee, egg sandwiches, emergency medicines, the asthma inhaler, and the spare asthma inhaler. And to fan my hot (in every sense of the word) mother with a lush, round peacock-feather fan. Large as the van was, and even though I sat way away in the back, I was apprehensive about having to be in a confined space with Mrs. Roy for five hours at a stretch, and mortified because I was at that age when the frothy, overdesigned clothes that she insisted I wear when we went visiting made me feel ridiculous. My clothes—everybody's clothes—were a project for Mrs. Roy. She decided exactly what all of us, everybody around her, must wear. She chose the fabric with care, sketched out her ideas, and had them made by the local tailor for me. On the wardrobe front, I did not suffer from a lack of attention. I suffered from the opposite.

It was the mid-seventies. On a boarding-school weekend outing I had smuggled myself into Assembly Rooms, the local cinema hall in Ooty, which was the town closest to my school, to watch the film about Woodstock. We lived in a time warp. Everything—music, fashion, cinema—arrived a few years late. I heard Joe Cocker and Jimi Hendrix. And Janis Joplin. After that everything changed. I longed for bell-bottoms and headbands and beads and rock 'n' roll. Instead, I submitted to silly blouses with frills and billowing sleeves and kept my longings to myself. Anything I said those days ended in a storm of insults and anger. And asthma. And blame about being the cause of Mrs. Roy's impending death. As a consequence, I had more or less stopped talking.

Our peacock-feather circus rolled into Trivandrum late in the evening. The only thing I can remember about the relative we stayed with is that a coconut had fallen from a tree onto her daughter's head, but nothing much had happened.

Lucky.

We met Baker in his beautiful, rambling home the next morning. He called it Hamlet. I'm not sure whether he meant *Hamlet* the play or *hamlet* as in "a little village." It was our first encounter with Baker Beauty, and just that one building was more than enough to convince Mrs. Roy that he was the man she was looking for. He would have been close to sixty at the time. Tall, slightly stooped, bearded, almost bald, outfitted comfortably in bush shirt and trousers. His arms were freckled, the skin loose and clammy looking because of the humidity. His laughing eyes were oddly magnified by the thick lenses of his spectacles. He seemed kind and relaxed, full of energy. I couldn't understand his accent. It was very different from Mrs. Mathews the missionary's.

Mummy and Daddy had a long, animated conversation. They seemed enchanted with each other. I, the awkward teenager, was stubbornly uncharmed and withdrawn. It would take me a while to understand the significance of who it was that I had just met. And even longer to fall into abject hero worship. Baker suggested that we spend the day in Trivandrum looking at some of his buildings and telling him what we liked and what we didn't. He included me in the conversation and made me feel as though my opinion counted, too, which startled me. I worried that this might annoy Mrs. Roy, but it didn't. He said he would send his young assistant with us, a third-year student from the Delhi School of Architecture, who had taken a year off to apprentice with him. We could pick him up from a building site where he was currently working with Daddy's masons.

We did.

The young assistant threaded his way through the little heaps of building material on the site. I couldn't believe it. He was Jesus. He was rock 'n' roll. And he had walked on water all the way from Woodstock to Kerala just to meet me. I was nearly fifteen, he was nineteen, and for the first time in my life I understood what sexual desire was. My brain, my heart, my soul—all parked themselves in my groin. He had long, lank Jesus hair, a Jesus beard, and a lean, flat, easy-walking Jesus body. Brown Jesus, I mean, not the geographically relocated, genetically modified blond one. Apart from a black sarong, he was bare bodied and barefoot. As he came up to the van, he casually stubbed out the bidi he was smoking on the calloused heel of his foot. I died.

I wasn't sure how Mrs. Roy would react. She surprised me by greeting him warmly, as though he was just another young person. And as though he was wearing clothes. When he got in, she introduced me to him. He said hello, I said hello. Although he had walked all the way from Woodstock to meet me, I didn't want to meet him. Not like that, not in my mother's school van, not in my stupid clothes, not with her around. I disappeared. I melted into the back seat of the van. I *became* the back seat of the van.

We drove around town from Baker building to Baker building. Though Jesus wasn't a Malayali and spoke no Malayalam, he managed to communicate with workers on-site. He explained the cost-saving techniques to Mrs. Roy; he showed her how bricks were laid in what Baker called a "rat-trap bond," with an air gap in between; he demonstrated how a filler slab was cast; and he showed us a range of brick jalis. He had a calm, intelligent, gentle way of speaking. I died some more, if that was even possible. Mrs. Roy was fascinated and attentive, drinking in every detail, flashing her beautiful dimples at him. He was Daddy's proud son, showing off his father's accomplishments to Mummy. I trailed them carrying the bag with her inhaler and medical paraphernalia. I had never seen her so animated. There was no sign of asthma. Joe Cocker and Jimi Hendrix trailed me, falling about laughing. They made my life feel small and hopeless. Janis Joplin played the opening chords of "Piece of My Heart" and then gave up and went away. She just wasn't the Trivandrum type. She needed a different canvas. By late afternoon we dropped Jesus back at the site we had picked him up from. My body was exhausted by all its new feelings. We started driving home.

Once we reached the outskirts of town, Mrs. Roy turned on me.

"Congratulations. That boy must have thought you were a genius."

I didn't respond.

"You couldn't think of a single intelligent thing to say?"

The air in the van began to thicken with that familiar feeling of deepening dread. My cold moth flitted between the seats. Mrs. Roy was about to embark on a rampage. She started in a quiet, reasonable tone, which always signaled grave danger.

"Do you think it's nice for me to have people thinking that my daughter is a complete fool?"

I sincerely wanted to reply but couldn't. I had stepped through a portal and caught a glimpse of another world. I had learned a new language and couldn't use old words anymore.

*"Answer me!"*

The school-driver's head twisted around like an alarmed owl's.

I couldn't think of a single thing to say, intelligent or not. She asked the driver to pull up on the side of the road.

"Get out."

I got out. I was so used to getting out. *Get out of my house. Get out of my car. Get out of my life.* Every other day. She drove away. Still being fanned by the peacock-feather fan.

Picture me, valiant organ-child, freshly sexually awakened, completely dazed, dressed like a frothy fairy, perched pathetically on a milestone on the side of the Kottayam–Trivandrum highway. I had no plans other than to sit on that milestone for the rest of my life. Years later, when I met my father, I learned that kicking me out of the car was something of a sport for them. He told me, laughing, that the first time it happened we were driving on a jungle road from the tea estate we lived on in Nowgong to Shillong. I was just under three years old. Being annoying on long drives is obviously a talent I was born with.

It was almost dark by the time Mrs. Roy circled back in the van.

"Get in."

We drove the five hours back to Kottayam in dead silence. I couldn't tell who had won, her or me. Me, probably.

# "How's That Crazy Mother of Yours?"

Eighteen months after that, at the age of sixteen, I finished high school and applied for admission to the Delhi School of Planning and Architecture. Mrs. Roy backed me and did everything she could to help me get in. I had to go to Delhi and appear for the entrance exam. It was a chancy thing. Thirty places, thousands of applicants. There was no way of knowing whether I would get through. As a precaution, I applied for and gained admission to a women's college in Delhi as well. In those days, university education was heavily subsidized by the government. If you were fortunate enough to get in, it was not as expensive as it is today. This was true for my brother, too, who was in Madras, doing a BSc in chemistry. Mrs. Roy (our banker) had a harder time putting us through boarding school than she did paying our college fees.

I took a train to Delhi—three days and two nights (with a knife in my bag). The exam wasn't difficult. I didn't think I had done too badly. But my name wasn't on the first list of admissions. Heartbroken, I joined the women's college—my precautionary second choice. For no reason I could fathom, the principal summoned me to her office. She was puffed up like a big, flightless raptor sitting in her elaborate nest, full of trophies and memorabilia she had collected during the times she had been able to fly. She tapped her talons on her glass-topped desk, and the reflection tapped back. She told me that she had been in the job for more than ten years and could recognize trouble when she saw it. She admonished me in advance for the offenses she was sure I was going to commit and assured me that she would be watching me closely and would show no leniency because my morality and reputation—*all* the girls' morality and reputations—had been entrusted to her by our parents.

I was taken aback. Who was this person inside me that she seemed to know and whom I hadn't yet met? Whoever she was, she sounded like someone I ought to meet. I can still remember the stench of the damp, moldy carpet in the principal's office. Fortunately, two days later, after some students dropped out, the second admissions list of the School of Architecture was published and this time my name was on it. I packed my suitcase and bolted.

\*　　　\*　　　\*

The moment I walked through the shabby gates of the Delhi School of Planning and Architecture and looked around at the grungy students lolling on the balding lawn, zombie-eyed from having worked all night; at the common room, fogged up with cigarette smoke, full of broken furniture; and at the watchman with a bright gold tooth (who soon became my good friend and dope supplier), I knew that I didn't need to die if Mrs. Roy did. My lungs returned to my body and breathed only for me. The valiant organ-child seceded and became a strange country inside her own skin. I wanted to fall on my knees and kiss the filthy driveway as though it were holy ground. I didn't, of course, but it was no ordinary rite of passage.

I dropped my first name, Susanna. Starting then, I gradually, deliberately, transformed myself into somebody else.

\*　　　\*　　　\*

The hostel was an ugly concrete building close to the banks of the Yamuna. There weren't many girls in the School of Architecture at the time—maybe four or five in each class of thirty students. And hardly any in the hostel. The women's hostel was just a few rooms cordoned off from the men's hostel. An outrageous arrangement to anybody who might have been paying attention or been concerned about our prized virginity. Nobody was.

Lucky.

In the toilets the graffiti had not been painted over from the time when the women's hostel had been a part of the men's hostel. Architecture schools have interesting graffiti. The one I remember was a pretty good crayon drawing of a penis wearing a sun hat and a smile. Underneath it said HAVE A NICE DAY.

My first roommate was Hisila Yami, from Nepal, who would, along with her husband, Baburam Bhattarai, a postgraduate student in our college, go on to lead a Maoist rebellion in their country. They would spend years underground at the head of a guerrilla army before Baburam became the first Communist prime minister of Nepal and Hisila a senior cabinet minister. (And then of course, the various factions that made up the government became sworn enemies as often happens in Communist parties, and it all fell apart.) But at the time we joined college, she was, like me, a clueless sixteen-year-old trying to get her bearings in a city we knew absolutely nothing about.

The constant sense of dread that I grew up with—the cold moth on my heart—had in some ways stunted me, circumscribed me. All my energies were directed toward decrypting and surviving my immediate environment almost hourly. I lived in the immediate present. I could not look up. I had no sense of the big winds that were blowing. I had no idea that in that year (1976) India was going through its biggest political crisis since Independence.

In 1975, to deal with the massive unrest and resentment building up against her, Indira Gandhi, the prime minister, had declared a state of Emergency. Civil rights had been suspended; thousands had been jailed. The judiciary was compromised, the press was on its knees. Mrs. Gandhi's younger son, Sanjay Gandhi, and his small coterie of privileged hoodlums were promoting population control by organizing camps in which thousands of men, most of them Muslim, were forcibly sterilized. The coterie's other fixation was urban beautification. In cities across the country, slums were bulldozed and the poor driven to the outskirts. Not far from our hostel, in Turkman Gate, just outside the walled city of Old Delhi, hundreds of people protesting against the demolition of their homes were mowed down, massacred. Insulated by my private teenage trauma, I was entirely unaware of all this. It took me a year to educate myself, orient myself, by which time the Emergency was over. In 1977 Mrs. Gandhi called elections and lost. I celebrated as though I had personally led the resistance.

The first real friend I made in Architecture School was Golak. He was from Odisha; his family lived in Rourkela, where his father was a worker in the Rourkela Steel Plant. We noticed each other while we were making still-life sketches for the entrance exam. He made it somewhere close to the top of the list. I squeaked in somewhere close to the bottom. Some cruel senior students who wanted to bully him brought him to me, hoping to make fun of his lack of English. "Tell her in English what you like about her." He said haltingly, "I like her hair." My hair was ridiculous, but (sadly for the seniors) Golak and I instantly became friends and so we remain. We came from opposite ends of the emotional spectrum. He was the beloved, eldest son of a big, doting family, and I was . . . God knows. Golak spoke neither English nor Hindi. I spoke no Odia, so at first we communicated in sketches. His extraordinary, mine mediocre. We both learned Hindi together, starting by developing an elaborate vocabulary of invectives and then inventing some of our own. Golak's favorites were *Chhipkali ki bund ka pasina*, "You bead of sweat in a lizard's asshole," and *Tera teen din ke liye tatti bandh*, "You won't be able to shit for three days." That one, delivered like the curse of a sage, seemed to really upset people.

Although I had learned Hindi in high school, it was my optional third language after Malayalam. I played the fool in class, made no effort, and understood nothing. The only sentence I remembered in Hindi was from a lesson in my Class VII textbook called *Swamibhakt Kutiya*: "the devoted dog," or more accurately "the devoted bitch." It was a crude, stupid story about a loyal dog who had saved its owner's baby from a snake by getting bitten herself. The last sentence in the lesson was *Subah uthke dekha to kutiya mari padi thi*, "When he woke up in the morning, he saw the bitch was dead." It was my consistent reply to any question anybody ever asked me in Hindi. Where are you going? What class do we have today? Can I hold your hand? *Subah uthke dekha to kutiya mari padi thi.*

Golak's and my first act of friendship was to buy a cheap blanket, cut it in two, and make ourselves identical ponchos for the Delhi winter. Our second was to have our ears pierced together. We wore identical silver earrings.

Within days of joining the School of Architecture, who did I bump into? Jesus himself. Let me call him JC. He had finished his apprenticeship with Baker and rejoined school. He was in his fourth year. He was wearing a shirt this time, a fantastically ugly printed shirt, and trousers. It didn't matter; I had X-ray vision and knew what the pretty body that lay under that ugly shirt looked like. I didn't expect he would recognize me—the silent, van-seat-shaped, asthma-inhaler carrier—but he did. This time I was ready to meet him. I was *there* to meet him.

I had turned my trousers into bell-bottoms by inserting inverted V-shaped patches along the sides, below the knees, and had stolen a few of my brother's shirts and three of his short-sleeved undervests that I secretly dyed. They looked like worn-out T-shirts. The most successful color was a patchy, faded mauve. In those days T-shirts, or any ready-made clothes, weren't easy to buy. In any case I had no money. Our improvised, self-made wardrobes were much more fun than the label shopping that goes on today. I wore blue and purple cow beads—fat glass beads on a rope that cowherds strung across their cows' horns—as a choker around my throat. They had become a fad among the girls in my military boarding school. Cowherds from the nearby villages would nonchalantly graze their cattle in the meadows near the hostel, waiting for schoolgirls to buy the beads with their pocket money. They were cool and fabulous. The trade led to beaded girls in the dormitories and bare-horned cows in the meadows.

JC walked up to me smiling, with nothing of the air of a senior student addressing a fresher. I was transfixed by his ugly shirt—the ugliness was some sort of declaration. I was sure of that—and determined that one day it would be mine.

"Hello, it's nice to see you here. How's that crazy mother of yours?"

I don't remember if I replied to his question or just let it pass. He could not have known the impact it had on me. I turned the phrase over and over in my mind. *That crazy mother of yours.* Is that what she seemed like to neutral outsiders? Did all of us in Mrs. Roy's fiefdom give that impression or was it just her? How could somebody so brilliant, so efficient, so beloved by her students, be crazy? Did he mean clinically crazy? Or just eccentric?

After all these years of thinking about it, I have concluded that I grew up in a cult. A good cult, a fabulous one even, but a cult nevertheless, in which the outside world was a fuzzy entity, and in the inside world, unquestioning obedience and frequently demonstrated adoration of the Mother Guru were the basic requirements for membership. The only involuntary members, press-ganged into the ways of the cult, were my brother and I.

Perhaps Mary Roy didn't have many options. One of her school drivers said it best to me. *Mrs. Royude vattu-style maathramey nammude ee Kottayathu nadakkathollu,* "It's only this crazy-lady style of Mrs. Roy's that will work in this Kottayam of ours." What he meant was that were it not for her rage and unpredictability, she, being a woman, would never have been able to run a school like hers in a town like ours.

Maybe he was right. She needed to be the way she was. I was just collateral for a more important enterprise. I was my problem, not hers. Fair enough.

JC and I became friends. When I felt comfortable enough, I asked him casually, "What did you mean when you said, 'That crazy mother of yours'?"

He said, "Who in today's world goes around in a school van being fanned by an attendant with a peacock-feather fan?"

I had to concede that, put like that, it did sound odd. But it was nowhere near as odd as things actually were at my school-hostel-home in Kottayam.

Twenty years later, soon after *The God of Small Things* was published, I was in Durban, South Africa, for a conference of writers.

Ashwin, the most entertaining speaker of us all, offered to drop me back at my hotel after the meeting, but said he needed to stop at his parents' home for a minute. When we pulled up at their house, he asked me to stay in the car, a dangerous proposition in Durban, especially in the dark. But clearly, he considered his parents' home to be even more dangerous.

"My mother is a little unpredictable, I never know what she might say or do."

"Does she, for example, immerse herself naked in lukewarm water in a zinc tub while one secretary is clipping her toenails and the other is taking dictation for a letter to the municipality?"

He held my gaze for a second to see whether I was joking and quickly realized I wasn't.

"Come on in."

*      *      *

I asked JC whether when he first met me in the school van he thought I was a fool because I didn't say anything.

"I thought you were a beautiful girl."

I was delighted. I had never, not for half of half a second, thought of myself as beautiful. It wasn't something that preoccupied me or kept me awake at night. My cousin—Mrs. Joseph's daughter—was beautiful. Not me. I was the opposite of what Syrian Christian girls were meant to be—I was thin and dark and risky. (Risky because of my divorced mother and unknown father. Risky also because I didn't seem to properly understand or be cognizant of my social disadvantages.) For Mrs. Joseph this made me not just risky, but a liability. Her daughter who was a little older than me was ready for marriage. Now that I was in the same city as she was, Mrs. Joseph, whose husband had become a Regional Manager of Indian Airlines, worried that having me around when a prospective groom or his family came to visit might adversely affect her daughter's prospects. She asked me delicately, conspiratorially, as though we were sharing a family secret, not to visit her. Initially I obeyed, but later I began to drop in deliberately, just to annoy her, with a different boy each time. Once when one of my false front teeth fell out, I climbed over her gate in the middle of the night to hide because I didn't want to be seen toothless by my fellow students.

So, it was nice to be thought of as beautiful, even if it was the opinion of a minority of one.

Life in the hostel was anarchic and insane. We lived under a smoky sky, inside a cloud of soot that was belched out of the chimneys of the Indraprastha power station that was less than a kilometer away. During the rains when the Yamuna flooded, garbage-laden water submerged the campus. On one occasion it rose all the way up to our rooms on the first floor and ruined our drawings and the rolls of expensive Gateway paper—the tracing paper architects use—that some of us struggled to afford. We got malaria in shifts. I was exhilarated by what I was learning in class, even though none of it inspired me remotely as much as Laurie Baker did. We were being taught the kind of architecture and philosophy of design that was almost the opposite of what Baker believed in. It made me truculent and argumentative. And angry. Still, I worked extremely hard and daydreamed about being able to sleep just for a few hours. I started smoking, and not just tobacco. I witnessed my first Delhi dust storm while I was looking out at the traffic on the main road, cradled in the inverted arch of a horrible modernist, brick-and-mortar sculpture—a student's "art thesis"—one of many that littered the hostel grounds. I was completely stoned when the sky suddenly darkened and the wind rose, driving dust, bicycles, chairs, bottle caps, and rubbish high into the air and down the road. I became one of those bottle caps. I began to drift away from Kottayam and my valiant organ-life on a fast current.

A few months into my first year a granduncle of mine from Kerala, a retired engineer and a great disparager of Baker, came to visit me. I couldn't work out why, since I didn't really know him, nor he me. I understood only when he stroked my back in a grandavuncular way and said, "Not wearing a bra?" Men like him and the Kottayam Wild Boar Santa seemed to have an unerring radar for unprotected girls and women. Since I had nothing to say to him, I offered to walk him to the gate.

He looked around disapprovingly at the casually intimate couples on the bald lawn and asked, "Aren't you going out of bounds?"

"We have no bounds."

"Who's your warden?"

"We have no warden."

"What time do you have to come back at night?"

"We don't have to come back."

He was visibly shocked. "This is not a good place. You should have gone for the civil services."

"Why?"

"You would have found a better match."

A better husband, he meant. Better than the one he assumed I was going to find.

With that he hurried away to spread the news in Kottayam. *The girl's gone bad.* I felt nothing but contempt. It may have been the first time I became aware of that emotion. There was something tired about it. I had just turned seventeen.

# "You're a Millstone Around My Neck"

At the end of my first year I went home for the summer vacation. Instead of the three-day-and-two-night journey to Kottayam, I had to take a slightly shorter train ride to Bangalore and then a bus to a naturopathy health center where Mrs. Roy had admitted herself to treat her asthma and worryingly increasing weight. An overfriendly, garrulous young bank employee was squashed against me on the bus seat. His arm hairs tickled me. Within no time he told me the story of his life, the highlight of which was that a well-known movie star had been his girlfriend before she became a movie star. And now she pretended that she never knew him. We exchanged some bitter platitudes about the behavior of famous people, as though we were great experts on the subject.

Suddenly his manner changed. He began to pay me all kinds of compliments. The one that has passed the test of time was "You are so cute, just like a bonsai plant." (You know, those stunted, twisted miniature trees that people grow in flowerpots for no good reason.) He offered me various snacks that he bought whenever the bus stopped. Cucumber with salt and red chilly powder, half-ripe guavas, boiled eggs, potato chips . . . and then, as casually as one might ask for a cigarette, he asked me if I would marry him. I told him my father was a senior police officer and would only allow me to marry either a policeman or a soldier. Bankers were out. He became weepy and insistent. Maybe he was on something. I put my head against the window bars and pretended to sleep, trying not to giggle at my own joke.

Half an hour later, he suddenly jerked me out of my seat. A bus had collided with ours, just feet away from my head. It wasn't a terrible accident, just a sharp turn badly taken, one of those reckless-driving-at-slow-speed type of things. Nobody was hurt. Still, he had saved me from something bad. I was shaken and felt the least I could do was to marry him. (Being unaccustomed to kindness, I was often overgrateful.) Luckily my stop arrived quite soon; I thanked him and got off. He waved goodbye, tears streaming down his face. He was definitely on something.

My pulse hadn't settled from that experience as I made my way through the grounds of the health center—passing groups of severely overweight people who were there for treatment, either walking (recklessly at slow speed) or doing yoga—to the cottage that Mrs. Roy had booked herself into. The door was open. I had barely put down my bag when I found myself in front of a firing squad. With no idea what my crime was. Her insults bored into me like a volley of bullets. My metaphoric execution ended with "You're a millstone around my neck. I should have dumped you in an orphanage the day you were born." I'd heard that many times before. It always made me feel drowsy. Airless. I wanted to sleep for a long time. I used to dream of millstones stacked high in a ship's hold and wonder how they knew how many to take when they started on a journey. How did they calculate how many people would die on board and need to be buried at sea with millstones around their necks so that their corpses didn't float around?

I learned later that she had been put on a harsh, heartless diet of only lime juice and no food *at all* for a whole ten days. She—devotee of good food—was out of her mind with hunger. And suddenly her teenage daughter arrives. Scrawny bonsai plant. Smelling of sex and cigarette smoke, with "Ruby Tuesday" humming in her bone marrow. She probably realized in an instant that it was an impostor and not her valiant organ-child standing in the doorway.

*       *       *

For all her gangsterism, the one line that Mrs. Roy never crossed as far as I know was that of sexual probity. That part of herself, she, beautiful woman, kept bottled up. Perhaps that is what made her as volatile and as temperamental as she was. It certainly made her hostile to every whiff or rumor of sexual affection or attraction between anybody and anybody (this included roosters, dogs, birds, and other creatures) in her immediate vicinity. And when it came to me, even a whiff wasn't necessary. As I grew older, my very existence seemed to be enough to enrage her.

When I heard about her diet, I switched sides. I might have shot me, too. She calmed down in a few days and we traveled to Kottayam together by train. My body was straining to accommodate everything I was feeling—my sadness, my love for her, and most of all my pent-up anger, which I could never, ever express for fear of triggering a fatal attack of asthma. I knew that my days at home were numbered. My childhood was over. I was no longer prepared to be humiliated, particularly not in front of the students and teachers in our school-hostel-home. I was no longer prepared to understand that when she hit me and raged at me, quite often it was because she was angry at someone else who she couldn't hit or insult in the same way, so I stood in for them. I knew that. She knew that I knew that. But that unspoken arrangement wasn't acceptable to me anymore.

*       *       *

For my holiday assignment I did a study on the Kerala Marxist government's housing-for-the-landless scheme, in which tens of thousands of people were given small plots of land. G. Isaac took me to one of the colonies. He had by then, much to the consternation of the Cosmopolitans, married a young woman called Soosy, who worked in the factory. She was at least fifteen years younger than him. The whole family, including Mrs. Roy, behaved obnoxiously with her. A class war in reverse. Although everybody was quarreling with everybody, they were united in their bad behavior toward somebody who came from a less privileged background than they did. G. Isaac, now playing the part of Professor Higgins in *My Fair Lady*, flaunted his attractive young wife at Rotary Club meetings and, although he was a Marxist, in church. He put her in charge of a new branch of his factory, where pineapples were sliced and canned in sugar syrup. He then organized his mostly-women workforce into a labor union and encouraged them to go on strike against him (the management). He erected a pandal for them so they could sit in the shade over the several days of their sit-in. He offered to hand over the management of the factory to them in return for a monthly salary, seeing as he was the founder of the factory. They turned down his offer and returned to work.

Many families we visited in the housing colony sustained themselves by daily labor and bootlegging. I made drawings of their homes, a rough site plan of the colony, and earnest adolescent charts detailing all of this. I realized they were all perfectly capable of building their own homes with what little they had. What they needed was some land, some hope, an income, and a sense of security, not architects. The Marxists had done right by them.

Apart from this assignment, I knew I needed to cultivate emergency working skills—any possible skill. In the evenings I taught myself to type from a handbook, *The Quick Brown Fox Jumps over the Lazy Hedgehog*, the tapping of the typewriter keys somehow synchronizing with the backbeat of rock 'n' roll, heightening the hunger, the longing to escape everything that life in Kerala seemed to have in store for me. "A good match" (as in an arranged marriage) was nowhere on the horizon, but the idea, the very possibility of it, made me break into a cold sweat.

There was nothing I feared more than being trapped in Kottayam with Mrs. Roy. Real life was a trap. But those fabled stories about small-town folks going to the movies to escape real life and ignite their dreams didn't work out for me either. The movies were even worse than real life.

*　　　*　　　*

My moviegoing companion those days was Kurussammal, who lived in the school permanently and went home to Ooty once a year to visit her family. We usually went to Star Theatre, which, in the early days, had a canvas roof, folding wooden chairs, and a mud floor that gave it an outdoorsy, funfair feel. Children sometimes peed in the aisles. Only the very little ones. Men peed in the stinky steep lane that ran alongside the theater. Women, the few who came to watch movies, had no toilets and no steep lanes to pee in. They had to hold on till they got home. The sound quality in Star Theatre was inadvertently enhanced by the uneven surface, created by thousands of paper rockets lodged in the canvas roof. (*Baffling*, I learned later in Architecture School, was the technical word for it.) The rockets were made from the swirl of newspaper cones, each with about twenty peanuts in them, that were sold for ten paisa while the movie was playing. Making a good paper rocket and getting it to soar straight up and park its nose in the film of grease that coated the canvas ceiling was a skill I never mastered. The people who owned the theater also manufactured and serviced car batteries in the same compound, which probably accounted for the pervasiveness of the grease.

As Kottayam modernized, Star Theatre was outdone by two new theaters, Anand and Anupama.

Kurussammal only liked movies that made her cry. So those were the ones we went to see. *Rombo sangadam,* "very sad," was her highest form of praise for a film. The actors she loved were Tamil cinema's favorite couple, MGR and Jayalalitha, both of whom eventually became bizarre yet beloved chief ministers of Tamil Nadu. He first, and after he died, she—his (so the rumor went) lover, political heir, and acolyte. It seemed inconceivable to us in Kerala that an actor or actress could become chief minister of our state. We didn't have that sort of relationship with cinema. As genres, the Malayalam and Tamil films we saw were the polar opposites of each other. The Malayalam films, deeply influenced by the Left, were about hunger, famine, unemployment, landlordism, and political rage. The Tamil films (which also played in Kerala) that Kurussammal and I went to see were about kings and slaves, and Hindu gods and goddesses who cavorted with their consorts in the clouds with oversize musical instruments. Neither genre offered me any kind of solace or escape. For women, mortal or divine, they only valorized absolute submission to the python coils of tradition and convention. According to them, my bones would be broken, and when I turned to mush, I would be swallowed whole, sentenced to picking my husband's letters off the floor.

For the woman who transgressed, movies held out the prospect of terrible punishment and lifelong disgrace. In many of the Malayalam films, the heroine got raped. The assault was usually coyly reflected in the stern steel eye of the revolving ceiling fan, or in images of flowers falling from their stems, or petals dropping off their calyx, accompanied by an ambiguous, breathy, moaning soundtrack, which gave the impression that the woman might have been enjoying it.

As a young girl growing up on a diet of these films, I used to believe that all women were raped, it was just a matter of when and where. That accounted for the knife in my bag when I first arrived at the Nizamuddin railway station in Delhi.

Surrounded by these stories that used fear to control us, for women in Kottayam, particularly for her girl students, Mrs. Roy was the hope for escape. She was the burning flame of courage and defiance. She lit their path, she showed the way. Not so for me. My escape route always circled back to what I was trying to escape from.

When it came to me, Mrs. Roy taught me how to think, then raged against my thoughts. She taught me to be free and raged against my freedom. She taught me to write and resented the author I became.

*　　　*　　　*

I returned to Delhi, a second-year student. I would turn eighteen in a few months. My holiday assignment about the housing colony was received with scorn and raised eyebrows by my professors. "This, young lady, has nothing to do with what you are here to learn. You are here to study design, not social service." I had made a chart in which I had columns with peoples' incomes and occupations. I was chastised for putting "prostitution" against the name of one person under the column marked "profession." They said it was indecent and

77

wrong of me to put that down. I said it was a job, like any other; that prostitutes had clients, just as architects did. That didn't go down well.

My battles with my teachers intensified. From being Mummy's valiant organ-child, I became Daddy's. I carried Baker's pennant into every argument in our design studio. I argued about building materials, techniques, cost, aesthetics, and, most of all, politics.

I had become a city creature by then, acutely aware of what was going on around me. In all of this I was backed by JC, who was in his final year and doing his thesis on the resettlement of the former residents of Turkman Gate, whose homes had been bulldozed during the Emergency. They had been flung away to the outskirts of Delhi, where they lived in tin shacks and had no work, no way of earning their living. JC and I were wrapped around each other, and it was almost impossible to imagine a life where this had not been so. We worked hard, walked around the city, and went to movies screened for free by various embassies. We saw *Memories of Underdevelopment* at the Cuban Cultural Centre and Kurosawa's *Dersu Uzala* at a regular theater. We went for late-night shows and sat in the cheapest seats, in the front row. We looked up the nostrils of the actors in *The Reincarnation of Peter Proud*.

It was a somewhat different experience from watching movies in Star Theatre with Kurussammal. As a shout-out to moviegoing men in Kottayam, on our way back to the bus stop from the Archana Theatre in Delhi, where we went most often, I made a point of peeing on rich peoples' lawns that we had to walk past.

In class Golak and I were a team. Our best moments were in the art studio, where our assignments gleefully mimicked and reproduced—undetected and with great success—the corny fakery and posturing of our art professor. As I look back, that level of fakery was almost endearing compared to the industrial scale on which it happens now.

Golak was, and is, a brilliant painter. I just hitched a ride on his coat-tails. I was happy and breathing deep, perhaps for the first time in my life. I loved the city, the soot, the chaos, and above all the anonymity. Today Delhi is a nightmare city full of guards and surveillance cameras. There is zero chance of peeing on anybody's lawn. I am one of those (relatively) rich people now, but fortunately I do not have a lawn or a guard. My only protection is street dogs, who I love and who love me back. More than twenty million of us humans live here, polluting the air, depleting the groundwater, but still I find myself thanking the city every day because she saved me, liberated me from the prospect of a life I shudder to think about. I cannot ever forget that. Toward the end of my second year, JC and I were lovers. I got the boy. I got his body. And I got his ugly shirt.

I wrote to Mrs. Roy and told her that far from thinking I was a fool, JC was my boyfriend. Terrible mistake. I can't believe I was so stupid.

# "Doesn't She Sound Like That Person in *The Exorcist*?"

The summer holidays of 1978, after I had completed my second year, would be my last in Kerala. As the train pulled into Kottayam station, I saw that Ammal, a relatively new recruit to the roster of maintenance staff in the school, had been sent to pick me up. Immediately my mind set to decoding what that meant. Was She angry, busy, out of town? That's what living inside a cult does to you. Members must constantly read the signs, test the air, whisper and wonder what the Mother Guru's mood of the moment is, and how to position oneself.

Ammal was the older of two quarrelsome sisters who had recently joined the cult. They were both unmarried and in their thirties. Both—unusually for Kottayam—entirely illiterate. Mariamma, the younger of the two, was an exceptional cook. She worked in the school kitchen, which catered to almost a hundred people every day. Ammal's job was in HQ: the personal care and round-the-clock adoration of Mrs. Roy. Ammal fulfilled her duties with evangelical zeal. She bore my mother's tantrums by chastising herself even more than my mother did, beating her chest, slapping herself, hiding under the table or under my mother's bed, and asking God to forgive her for the coffee not being hot enough, the lime juice not being cold enough, the fish not being fresh enough. She would emerge from the office-bedroom with food dripping down her face or a tray full of smashed glass; she dodged flying teacups and mopped up pools of hot tea; she insisted it was all a manifestation of her Kochamma's—Little Mother's—love for her. She flew into a jealous rage when my mother got angry at someone else. She wanted it all for herself.

One of my earliest (fortunately unpublished) stories was about a relationship like theirs. It was called "Christmas in Ayemenem." Miss E. John Eapen was the Mrs. Roy–like mistress (with a bit of Miss Kurien mixed in) and Ammal her devoted servant. Every Christmas Miss E. John Eapen would gather the children of the village and make them perform the Nativity in her garden. The most fair-skinned girl would be chosen to play the Virgin Mary. That was the sole criterion for the casting of that part. The rest of the children would be angels with wings made of tracing paper stretched over wire frames strapped to their shoulders like backpacks, shepherds wearing checked serviettes on their heads, the Three Wise Men in dressing gowns and turbans, and a wide variety of animals in the manger. Ammal's only dream was to be cast as Mary. That of course could never be. She didn't have the complexion. When Miss E. John Eapen falls ill, Ammal looks after her with frantic devotion, feeding her lukewarm onion juice, a syrup of garlic and turmeric and all sorts of other disgusting potions. Nothing helps. Miss E. John Eapen dies. When Ammal's sister comes looking for her, she finds the house in disarray. The costume trunk lies open on the floor. Ammal is sitting on a low stool draped in the Virgin's blue veil with the name tag MARY still stapled to one corner. In her arms she holds the corpse of the chubby Miss E. John Eapen. A profane pietà.

Magic realism you might say. But no. It was pretty much the only kind of realism I knew. At the time it didn't feel magical. Now, occasionally, it does.

As soon as she spotted me on the station platform, Ammal rushed toward me. Her eyes were blurry and fat tears made their way down her cheeks. That only made me smile. She held both her arms up to heaven like a Jehovah's Witness and looked as though she might start speaking in tongues. She spoke a kind of biblical, overdramatic Malayalam. Her body vibrated; her drooping earlobes juddered under the weight of heavy gold earrings. Her voice quivered.

"As Christ is my witness, it's only because she loves you. . . . "

She began beating her chest. Really hard. I had to put down my bag and hold both her hands in mine to stop her.

"OK. Enough. Just tell me. What is it? What are our orders? Shall I lie down and die right here?"

She looked around, worried that a passing spy might have over-heard my disrespectful tone. Her eyes turned conspiratorial. She lowered her voice to a whisper to communicate the instructions.

"Kochamma doesn't want to see you. You must stay in the sick-room. You will get your food there. You are not to appear before her. She doesn't want to set eyes on you." The tears began again. "It's only because she loves you."

In my head the Beatles went *Yeah! Yeah! Yeah!*

I put my arm around Ammal's shoulders. Sergeant Pepper's Lonely Hearts Club Band, dressed in full regalia, got off the train, too, and followed us down the Kottayam railway station platform all the way to our school-hostel-home on the hill.

*　　*　　*

Each time I came home from Delhi, more buildings had come up on the new campus. Dorms, classrooms, a library. Mrs. Roy's school was all the rage. The cult, including students, teachers, and maintenance staff, was nearly three hundred strong. Parents were booking places for their children even before they were born. She had become one of the most sought-after, influential people in Kottayam town. But she didn't have a home of her own yet and still lived out of her tiny office. Everything she had built, everything she had done, she had done alone. With no capital of her own, with very little help (and a fair amount of harm) from her family.

She had begun to speak out in public about the trauma she had endured as a child and young woman. She spoke of her Imperial Entomologist father's violence toward her and her mother. She described how he would hold her by her hair and whip her with his riding crop, how he would beat her mother till she bled and turn them all out of their house during the cold Delhi winters. About how, enraged by his wife's musical accomplishment, her father had smashed her mother's violin. Mrs. Roy publicly said she married the first man who proposed to her to get away from her father. She told the story of her husband's addiction to alcohol, her decision to leave him even though her children were young, her move to Ooty and her grim life in the cottage that her dead father had owned. She kept her married name she said because choosing between a husband's name and a father's name didn't leave a woman much of a choice. She told the story of how my grandmother and G. Isaac arrived in Ooty and ordered her to leave the cottage immediately because, according to them, she, being a daughter, had no right to her father's property.

It was only after that, Mrs. Roy said, that she became aware of the Travancore Christian Succession Act, which gave daughters the right to inherit a fourth of their father's property, or five thousand rupees (a pittance), whichever was less.

By telling these stories she was cannily molding public opinion, preparing the ground for when she would petition the Supreme Court in Delhi and ask for the Travancore Christian Succession Act to be struck down as unconstitutional. It would not be only a selfless, public act. And rightly so. She would demand an equal share in her father's ancestral property in Kottayam, which was the headquarters of the Malabar Coast Products. Where my grandmother, G. Isaac, his wife, Soosy, and their two children lived in a temporary shed next to the main house, which functioned as the factory and front office. They had moved out of Miss Kurien's house in Ayemenem. They had no idea about the storm that was coming their way.

It would be a while before Mrs. Roy filed her petition.

For all her volatility, she was capable of being a patient hunter.

\*          \*          \*

As her school grew and consolidated its reputation, Mrs. Roy embarked on a campaign of radical kindness. Radical because her kindness was gruff, practical, and asked nothing in return. It was politics by other means. The best kind. When she heard of women in distress or read about terrible incidents in the papers, she walked into hospitals and courtrooms and offered women her protection. She didn't commiserate or try to console them; she offered them an option. If they weren't quick to recognize it, she walked away. If they misused it, sniveled, or solicited sympathy, she kicked them out. There was nothing of the charitable do-gooder or social worker in her. Her actions came from a sense of steely outrage. She gave scholarships to orphans and jobs to women who had been abandoned or abused by their husbands or other men. She had a way of comforting children who were traumatized by the death of a parent or grandparent, a way of insulating them from pain before the blow fully landed. The campus was buzzing with bright-eyed little humans going about their busy days. It was such a happy place. Quite often I found myself wishing I were her student and not her daughter.

It has taken me years to come to terms with the fact that I was a middle child, one of three siblings, not two. My older sibling was a boy, and my younger sibling was a school. There was never any doubt about who our mother's favorite child was. She loved, fought for, and protected her youngest child with everything she had. That kind of focused, ferocious love, regardless of what it may choose as its object, is a blessed love. The challenge for those of us who are not chosen and instead watch love pass us by is to learn from it, marvel at it, and not grow bitter and incapable of love ourselves.

\*     \*     \*

That last summer, when home stopped being home, my brother was there, too. He had just graduated from his college in Madras and was not sure what he would do next. We never spoke to each other about anything real, he and I. Especially not our feelings. We didn't need to. We understood each other perfectly. We could sit together for hours and not speak. After a week or so of my banishment to the sickroom, a chit was delivered to me. Chits were delivered to people up and down the hillside. They were feared because they usually bore bad tidings. Mine said, *Baker is coming for lunch tomorrow. You will lay the table in the teachers' dining room and make sure that you are present.* The unspoken instructions were, of course, *You will make intelligent conversation and not appear to be a complete fool.*

What would Janis Joplin have done if her mother had asked her to lay the table? She'd have probably lain on it and humped it. *Look, Ma, no hands!*

I had no clue how to lay a table. My mother had forgotten to teach me the manners and social graces of the Cosmopolitans. I had eaten at "laid" tables a few times, at Miss Kurien's home when she had guests. But that was long ago, and I hadn't paid attention. Mostly I was raised on a riverbank, and in the school-hostel dining room's steel-thali culture in which no laying was involved. The staff in the hostel kitchen helped me to locate some glass plates and side plates, and we put them out. We put out some cups for coffee, which I knew Mrs. Roy liked to drink. That was about it. Everybody sensed that I was in serious trouble. The air was quaking.

Baker arrived in his genial, cheerful way, with no idea what he was walking into. I can't remember a single thing that was said. In my memory of that meal, except for the clinking of the crockery and cutlery, the soundtrack is switched off. It was the last time I met him before I graduated, but I gained nothing from that occasion because my ears were humming, and my stomach muscles were rigid in preparation for the coming assault. Once Baker left, it began.

It started with the coffee cups—which turned out to have been teacups—being smashed.

"In all these years you haven't managed to learn the difference between teacups and coffee cups?"

The insults washed over me like a tide. Apart from the usual ones, the additional theme of course was "whore" and "prostitute." It went on forever, while everybody watched. That was the thing. Everybody watched. We had no home. No privacy. She would calm down and then get incensed and start screaming again, in waves. Eventually she left the dining room and began to walk down the stone steps cut into the hillside to her office-bedroom, screaming all the way so the whole school could hear. Even the fish in the fish tank looked alarmed. I imagined everything in the school had come to a standstill—teachers immobilized chalk in hand, children with open books, athletes mid-sprint, toys mid-squeak. That a woman in our part of the world could wield such power, all those years ago, was something. I was aware of that even back then, in the middle of that storm. Once she quietened down, everybody went back to whatever they had been doing. I sat on the steps exhausted and oddly relieved. My brother appeared from nowhere and sat next to me. The silence sat between us like a third person. A well-loved friend.

Suddenly, without looking at me, he said, "Doesn't she sound like that person in *The Exorcist*?"

I couldn't help laughing. It was the first time either of us had admitted to ourselves or each other what we were going through.

"I don't know when I'll ever see you, but I'll never come home again."

"What will you do? How will you manage?"

"I don't know. Work. Whatever. I'll find a way. But I'm never coming back."

For the rest of the summer break, like millions of others in troubled homes, I listened to the Beatles' "She's Leaving Home" on a loop. I was ten years too late, a couple of continents removed, and completely alone. Even the very poor had families, communities. I had nobody. There were no kind relatives. There was no commune to join. No Haight-Ashbury. I knew of no other young women like myself who were on the loose. And Mrs. Roy was nothing like the clueless parents in that Beatles song.

I was luckier than Dido at least, the last member of the cult known to have been up-front about her boyfriend. She had arrived as a puppy when we were still in the hostel-home next to the Rotary Club. When she was full-grown and stood on her hind legs with her paws on my shoulders, she was as tall as I was. We would dance together. She would let me bite her. Her stomach was the safest place in the world for me to park my face. She slept on my bed and took up most of the space. When I was sent away to boarding school, I missed her more than anyone else. When I returned home for my holidays, she wasn't there. She hadn't killed herself for love, like Dido, Queen of Carthage. Mrs. Roy had had her shot. Because she mated with an unknown street dog. It was a kind of honor killing. She was buried at the back of the house. Dido was three, I was thirteen.

There was no question of my reacting or asking questions. Because the only response would have been an attack of asthma and perhaps a trip to hospital, which would be my fault. For some reason Dido's empty kennel, which was as big as a little room, moved with us to the new campus and stood there empty. During those last few weeks at home, I wanted to live in it. I didn't, of course. I would have risked being shot, too.

At the end of the holidays, I trained my mind as best I could to shed every vestige of the valiant organ-child. After I returned to Delhi, I wrote and told her that I loved her but wouldn't be coming home again and that I would no longer need money from her. Her responses were so insulting that I stopped reading them.

# In Which Jesus Marries
# a Japanese Parcel

Back in Architecture School, I had to move out of the hostel. Since the school fees were subsidized by the state, they were manageable even without Mrs. Roy's help, but I could no longer afford the hostel and mess fees. JC had graduated and had a low-paying job in the Delhi Development Authority. I worked as a badly exploited junior draftsman in architects' offices outside school hours, and as a jack-of-all-trades at the trade fairs that were held at Pragati Maidan, the vast exhibition ground not far from our college. Golak and I, outfitted in our identical blanket ponchos, skipped class and camped out in the fairground for days, offering ourselves as skilled daily labor—painters, calligraphers, model and mural makers. We would be commissioned by various pavilions to make all sorts of hideous art. Plywood peacocks, papier-mâché elephants, artificial trees. Our contractors were always behind schedule, so as the panic of the press-opening day of the trade fair approached, like cheap blackmailers we would raise our fees steeply.

JC and I desperately needed a place to live. Until we found one, we squatted.

Our design studios and classrooms were in a separate block, a five-story building, half a kilometer away from the hostel. There was nobody there at night except for a watchman. (Not my gold-toothed friend, another one.) JC and I lived on the fourth floor in a storeroom attached to one of the main studios where spare drawing boards and drafting tables were stacked. I was a fugitive all over again. After the last classes finished, we had the whole building to ourselves until the next morning. I used the men's toilet on our floor. Next to the row of urinals someone had scrawled PLEASE DON'T THROW YOUR CIGARETTE BUTTS INTO THE URINALS BECAUSE THEY GET SOGGY AND HARD TO LIGHT.

We knew that squatting in a storeroom couldn't be a permanent arrangement. Our Architecture School canteen manager, who was a friend, had a hut that was sprinting distance from college. He offered it to us for a nominal rent. It was in a tiny shanty colony that had grown organically along the outer stone walls of the ruins of a fourteenth-century fortress called Feroz Shah Kotla—one of the ancient walled cities of Delhi. It had community toilets and open drains into which children practiced aiming their shit. Our hut had a tin roof and a low doorway which JC had to literally bend over double to get through. Outside the walls, but within the grounds of the fortress, there was a rose-less rose garden and a restaurant called Rosebud, where bar dancers performed nightly cabarets.

To move into a shanty colony in Feroz Shah Kotla as an unmarried couple would have invited serious trouble. Especially for me. So, JC and I decided to get married. I was eighteen. We went to the Tis Hazari court and queued up with other cross-faith and cross-caste runaways, drifters, and vagabonds—those who had fallen out of the pan of the great Indian arranged-marriage transactions—hoping to fill in forms and register our marriage. After waiting for hours in the queue we eventually got bored, or ran out of bidis, and left. One of us, I can't remember whether it was JC or me, had the idea of staging a wedding ceremony and taking photographs of it to show anybody who questioned the nature of our relationship.

We needed to find a suitable temple and a suitably profane priest for the ceremony. We agreed that our priest could only be our beloved long-haired Roman friend, Carlo Buldrini. Carlo was an architect, too. He had come to Delhi in 1971 as an adult student to do a post-graduate course in urban planning and had never left. He had more or less given up architecture. He was half journalist, half monk, and a superb photographer. He wrote for *Lotta Continua*, "the struggle continues," a far-left Italian paper. During the 1968 student uprising in Europe, he belonged to a group of anarchists who were known as Gli Uccelli, "the birds," who were rumored to have visited a famous Italian writer and shat on his Persian carpets. Alberto Moravia, I think it was. Carlo had a way of neither confirming nor denying this story. By the time I met him he was more Buddhist than communist. His irreverence had become so entrenched that it came across as dead serious. I think it is he who settled and organized the basic building blocks of my personality. At the time he was thirty-six years old and would say, "*Senti*, Arundhatina, I am thirrrty-six. I am an old man. It is your turn now. You must do something wonderful." It's no different from the way in which, when I call him in Rome these days, he says, "*Senti*, Arundhatina, I am an old man now, I am eighty years old. You must do something. I don't want to die watching our beloved India being ruled by fascists."

Carlo lived in a small room above a garage in Nizamuddin East, near the railway station. That was our temple and marriage hall. We settled for nothing but the best. Carlo was our high priest; Golak and another friend, Eugene, were our witnesses. We choreographed an esoteric ritual that appeared to hold great symbolic meaning, although it didn't. I wore a V-necked caftan the color and texture of sackcloth with what looked like Japanese calligraphy on it. JC wore a white kurta and looked delectable. To an unsuspecting observer it would have appeared as though Christ were marrying a Japanese parcel.

Armed with the photographs Carlo took of our "wedding," we moved into our boiling hut in Feroz Shah Kotla. It wasn't just JC and me. Golak the witness virtually moved in, too. We spent our days together and he went back to his hostel room at night. JC and I slept on an old student's thesis—a discarded urban-design model base that we had purloined (smuggled out at night by bribing the watchman) from the storeroom we used to live in. It was a utopian proposal for a riverfront development project in which the swampy, malaria-ridden banks of the garbage-choked Yamuna had been made to look like something in Amsterdam or Copenhagen. To be able to put a mattress on it, we knocked off the little model trees, peeled away the cork-sheet contours, and stripped the model down to its wooden base. In our tin-roofed oven we smoked a lot, listened to music, and poured buckets of water on our mattress to keep ourselves from melting. I wore secondhand clothes—mostly inappropriate Western garments that were shipped in as relief for refugees or cyclone victims, clothes that even they had probably rejected and that had consequently ended up in flea markets near the Jama Masjid in Old Delhi. With a little imagination, it was possible to make the clothes look interesting. Between class assignments, JC's office job, and my moneymaking endeavors to remain afloat, we worked all the time and virtually never slept. (In today's world of private universities with exorbitant fees, even with JC's help I would never have been able to put myself through college.) In a year and a half we moved out of Feroz Shah Kotla into a one-room *barsati* on the second floor in Krishna Nagar. This time we had a toilet to ourselves at the other end of our small terrace.

In December 1980 I was a few months away from submitting my thesis when Carlo gave me a gift: a set of large square-format color negatives of the Beatles animated film *Yellow Submarine*. I was overwhelmed. He said it was a baton in life's relay, and that his run was done. (Because he was a verry old man now, Arundhatina.) I took them home and put them away carefully. The next day John Lennon was assassinated. I felt personally responsible. I had dropped the baton. Inside me everything turned to rubble. I was too distraught to betray any signs of distress.

To finish my thesis in time, I started taking Dexedrine. Speed. It helped me stay awake and work. I went without sleep for days together. Golak, who had by then run amok, had failed twice and was two years junior to me. He helped me with my drawings, of which there were very few. My thesis was, for the most part, a written one: "Post-Colonial Urban Development in Delhi: How the City Came to Be What It Is, and What It Does to Those Who Live in It." It hadn't been easy to persuade my professors to allow me to do this instead of a straightforward architectural design project—a hospital, or a multistory office complex or a cinema hall. My thesis was about "the City" and "the Non-City"—about "noncitizens" who live in the cracks of the city, who are packed into the crevices between urban institutions and city plans. Not for them the formal housing schemes, the neighborhood markets, the land-use laws. Nothing for them. Not even the sewerage system, which they shit on *top* of. As a concession to the format of how an architecture thesis was supposed to be, I presented it on twenty-three large sheets the size of architectural drawings. But they were really like giant galleys of a handwritten book (in architectural calligraphy) with drawings, graphs, maps, and photographs.

The work required immense concentration because a single mistake meant I had to redo the whole sheet.

We had an old record player assembled from spare parts, whose only party trick was that its needle would automatically go back and play the same record from the start unless we changed it. We were so busy, and so bombed, that we didn't change it for days on end. In the final run-up to my thesis submission, the Rolling Stones album *Gimme Shelter* played over and over for days. An earworm from "Love in Vain" lodged itself in my Dexedrine-saturated brain. It wouldn't go away. At my mock jury, which was practice for our real jury, in response to a question about Delhi's new land-use plan, I inadvertently sang it out loud:

*Whoa, the blue light was my baby*
*And the red light was my mind*

Fortunately, my professors understood that something was wrong. They did not take offense and kindly sent me home to sleep. A few days later, at the real jury, I managed to conduct myself with a little more dignity. One jury member did, however, notice a graphic of half of a tiny yellow submarine at the bottom edge of the last sheet of my set of drawings and asked me what it was. I told him it was me, sailing away.

\*       \*       \*

I graduated as a qualified architect at the age of twenty-one. That was just a number. In truth I was far older than others my age. I had become a strange person, of a somewhat vagrant disposition. I hadn't had the parental guardrails that my classmates did. I hadn't been inside a home or met people's parents or used a phone or eaten at a "laid" table with a family for years. My unceasing sense of apprehension and the instinct to survive from day to day, moment to moment, were still intact. Perhaps my old friend, the cold, furry moth on my heart, saved me from drifting into a life of addiction to drugs or alcohol or crime, which would have been the most natural thing to happen to someone like me. But anxiety and apprehension still constricted me, narrowed me, and prevented me from taking a longer view of things, which I ought to have been doing at that stage of my life. I was a small person with spikes. And a degree in architecture. It had been three years since I had met or communicated with Mrs. Roy. I thought of her often, but mostly with relief that I had escaped. I worried about her, but I knew that I did not yet have what it took to withstand her, to survive.

# Cake Walkin' Baby

After we graduated, most or at any rate many of my classmates moved to Europe or the United States to do their postgraduation. JC had, for the love of me, worked for two full years in a job he hated, supporting me and waiting for me to graduate. It is a debt I will never be able to repay. He was keen to move to Goa, where his family was from, although they didn't live there. In those days Goa was not the second-home and holiday destination for the elite from Delhi and Bombay that it is now. The towns were still Goan, but the beaches had been taken over by European and American hippies. The Russian drug mafia was beginning to find its foothold. The beaches were known according to which drug was most prevalent. LSD, heroin, datura (a poisonous, psychoactive flowering plant). On Christmas and New Year's Eve, Goans, many of whom were Christian, wore suits and Western dresses for their parties, and the hippies wore what they thought were "Indian" clothes—harem pants, mirror-work waistcoats, peacock feathers, and beads. They passed each other on the streets on their way to wherever they were going.

JC and I rented a one-room shack on a beach called Candolim. Our landlords were two brothers and their sister, Alice. All three of them had the same dim eyes and cobwebby hair. (We're all headed there.) She was seventy-eight. Her brothers were both in their eighties. They were extremely poor; their only source of income was the few hundred rupees we paid them as rent. As for us, we had rapidly evaporating small savings from our work in Delhi, but no source of income whatsoever. Alice and her brothers told us they had just returned from Burma, where they had a confectionary store and bakery. By "just" they meant 1948. They taught us how to bake a cake on a charcoal fire using sand instead of an oven. We went into a fifty-fifty partnership in the cake business. It made us barely enough for rent and food. JC and I would buy the ingredients, help them mix the batter and bake the cake. Every evening, we would walk the two and a half kilometers along the beach to Calangute, where we set up a little table and sold pieces of cake to the hippies and stoneheads who gathered there.

The more I got to know the hippies, the more I began to dislike dealing with them. Behind their dreamy, flower-power affectations, I saw, in so many of them, small-heartedness, petty calculation, and overt racism. They had little or no respect for the place in which or the people among whom they were playing out their stopgap fantasies before they went back to their regular lives. In my rush to judgment, I didn't stop to wonder whether I was guilty of doing the same thing. When they said they loved cows or drew on the peace pipe saying *Boom Shankar Bumbolay* or greeted each other with a namaste, it made my teeth curl. Something about living among them, something about the shallow violence of tourists in a tourist paradise, offended me. I became desperate to return to Delhi. JC was reluctant. For him Goa was home, I understood that.

Things got a little complicated for me when his mother came to visit us. We stayed with her in an empty flat that belonged to one of

JC's relatives. Maybe his brother. She was a pretty, vivacious woman who adored and idolized her son. Some lazy Sunday afternoons she would lie between us, and when JC was asleep, she would say, "Isn't he the most beautiful boy?"

I agreed with her. He was. But given the kind of mother I was used to, JC's mother's behavior disoriented and bewildered me. Through no fault of his, as he slept, she domesticated him, took the rock 'n' roll out of him, turned him into a normal Indian man with a normal Indian mother who was obsessed with her son. I gradually lost the Jesus-bodied man I had watched from my mother's school-van window and swooned over as he stubbed out his bidi on his cracked heel. It was unfair of me, but thanks to Mrs. Roy, those were feelings I didn't fully understand and could do nothing about. I was disconcerted by conventional, loving families, by their version of normality. They seemed to belong to a kind of alternative reality, sealed off from mine. I didn't envy them, I didn't long to be a part of them.

I grew restless and unhappy. Once again for me, the safest place became the most dangerous. Once again, I made it so. Eventually I decided I would return to Delhi alone, if only for a few months. JC sensed, quite rightly, that the few months would last forever. He was heartbroken. I was, too. But I couldn't see myself living in Goa for the rest of my life. The trauma was hard for both of us to bear, particularly because my behavior was inexplicable even to myself.

In the days we were tearing apart, like a single organism being savagely ripped in two, an acquaintance of JC's, a qualified psychiatrist and devout Catholic, told me that he thought I was mentally unbalanced, that I needed professional help, and that he could help me. I agreed with him about my mental balance. Our therapy started (and ended) with a long walk on the beach. It was drizzling, the sea was gray and unfriendly. He told me I was wrong to think of leaving JC and should reconsider my decision. When his attempts at persuasion and gentle emotional blackmail failed, he turned unpleasant.

"I know what women like you need. A good tight slap every now and then. You want a man to behave like a man."

The wind picked up and the sea got rougher. I considered giving him a good tight slap and making a run for it. There was nobody on the beach and he didn't look capable of catching me. He continued with his exegesis based on what he thought was a profound understanding of my character.

"The thing about women like you is that you will do anything to get what you want. You'll even sell your body."

I assured him he was spot-on, except that I didn't think I would get very much for the sale. I turned and ran as fast as I could, for as long as I could, in the opposite direction, on shining wet sand left behind by the tide that was quickly pulling out. The overcast, cloudy sky was reflected in it. I ran not out of fear, but to put some distance between him and me. When I thought I was far away enough, I waded into the sea and climbed onto a tall rock. I sat there for hours. I watched lightning drop onto the horizon. I watched a red cow walk deep into the water without wetting her horns. I got drenched in the warm rain and cursed myself for what I was about to do. It was inexcusable and probably suicidal. Mentally unbalanced. Yes. I was about to leave a man I loved, a man who loved me, cared for me, supported me. For *what*? *Why*? What would I do? What was wrong with me? What would become of me?

I had no idea.

I felt like that red cow. What was driving her? What was driving me? Would we grow wings? Would we sink or swim? I knew for sure that I'd get my horns wet. And I knew I was breaking the last link between Mrs. Roy and me. JC was the only one among my friends who had met her, even if ephemerally, and had some idea of who she was and where I came from. I loved them both. Her, with a sort of deep anxiety because I knew that to go back to her at this point would be to die. And him with a hazy, helpless sense of guilt. I wondered when I would stop running.

I sold a ring, the only piece of jewelry I owned, to a man at a fruit-juice stall. He gave me a few hundred rupees and a banana shake. Enough for my passage to Delhi.

On the lower deck of the steamer between Goa and Bombay, my clothes quickly became lined with a shiny layer of bedbugs. I found myself inside a swirl of my former cake customers. I could see their antennae perk up as soon as they realized that I was alone. When it became clear to them that I only had a vague, fuzzy plan for my immediate future, I was inundated with business proposals. Would I go with X to Varanasi, buy silk saris, convert them into shirts, and export them to Canada? Would I go with Y to Kashmir and carry a kilo of hashish for him to Goa? I looked innocent enough to be a good drug mule, he said. I promised them all that I would consider their offers and get back to them.

In Bombay I spent a night at a dirt cheap hotel frequented mostly by poor Arabs and European hippies. While I was checking in, a man—a hotel guest—in a white dishdasha lay across the reception counter. It sounds ridiculous, but it's true. We had to conduct the formalities over his generous body. All night people banged on my door. I stopped breathing. I prayed that the bolts would hold. I cursed myself for being immature and foolhardy. I decided I would take the first bus back to Goa and beg JC to forgive me. But when the sun rose, my resolve returned. I checked out of the hotel and spent the next night on the station platform. Finally, some friendly, protective Malayali waiters at the railway canteen managed to get me a ticket on a slow train to Delhi.

On the train my panic surged and subsided as I swung between capitulation and courage. I mulled over the several business proposals I had received on the steamer, including the semi-criminal and outright criminal ones, even to the point of going for a second meeting with some folks after we reached Delhi. Fortunately, nothing came of any of it. It was not any great strength of character or steely artistic ambition that saved me from prison or serious harm. It was just happenstance, and a series of small impulsive decisions, taken on the fly.

I think I had a cool seraph watching over me. Especially each time I was at a crossroads and had to make a decision. My education, the class I came from, and, above all, the fact that I spoke English protected me and gave me options that millions of others did not have. Those were gifts bestowed on me by Mrs. Roy. At no point, no matter how untenable my circumstance, did I ever forget that.

# In the Shade of Hazrat Nizamuddin Auliya

In Delhi I burned my bedbug-infested clothes and found a temporary job at the National Institute of Urban Affairs, which was headed by my former thesis adviser. He knew my work and did not judge me by my appearance, which was in those days somewhat dog-eared, emaciated, and severely sunburned. I was deputed to help with their in-house magazine—*Urban India*. (In my brief time there I guest-edited an issue for which I contributed a piece of fiction—some sort of urban surrealism.) I rented a room on the roof, a second-floor storeroom, right next to the dargah of the beloved fourteenth-century Sufi saint Hazrat Nizamuddin Auliya. Buried near his tomb were his spiritual disciple the scholar-poet Amīr Khusro, and Delhi's most iconic Urdu poet, Mirza Ghalib.

Even then, before the epoch of the Saffron Flag and the Hindu Nation, before Muslims were demonized, ghettoized, and turned into second-class citizens, the dargah was not different from the way it is now. Thousands of devotees visited every day. The worldly squalor around it seemed to be inversely proportionate to the ethereal, luminous minds of the men who were buried there. The narrow lanes, their gutters brimming with offal and refuse, were packed tight with small eating-joints serving kebabs and biryani, and shops selling amulets, satin chaders, and tiny replicas of the dargah. Rats the size of cats with stiff, bristly fur made off with food and pilgrims' smelly shoes. Beggars, some with missing limbs and the most spectacular injuries and illnesses, which they put on display like shopkeepers exhibiting their wares, lined the lanes.

On Thursdays the best Qawwali singers would perform late into the night. If the night was quiet and a breeze was blowing my way, I could hear them faintly from my terrace—which my landlord used as a junkyard—while I perched on the parapet wall, smoking. My old friend Bahadur, the gold-toothed watchman in the School of Architecture, supplied me with the marijuana. He lived in a solitary shack in the deserted Muslim graveyard not far from the school. When I visited, he would dig up a bottle of cheap alcohol that he kept buried in a hole in the ground (his pantry) and offer me a drink.

My room had a red cement floor that reminded me of Kerala. The window was boarded up because most of the windowpanes were broken. I slept on a *charpai*—a string cot. My other possessions were an earthen *matka* to store drinking water and a cardboard carton for my clothes. The only thing I lacked was money. I thought about money all the time, almost to the exclusion of everything else. To be absolutely alone in the world, with almost no money, made me rigid with anxiety. But the idea of returning home to Mrs. Roy was not something I even considered. I could clearly see what would happen to me if I did. My annihilation played before my eyes like a movie.

Whichever way I sliced it, I couldn't manage on my salary. I would borrow two hundred rupees from my friend and high priest Carlo in the last week of every month and return it the day I got paid. He lived close by, and we'd spend many of our evenings together. Briefly we crossed the line into a different sort of relationship. But we both realized quickly that it wasn't the true nature of our friendship. (Because I was twenty-two and he was a "verry old man, Arundhatina.")

A little less than half of my extremely meager salary went toward my rent, which was seven hundred rupees a month. To get to work I'd hire a bicycle for one rupee an hour. It oughtn't to have been an ordeal. Millions of working men in the city cycled long distances. For a woman though, it was different. It involved being chased down, hooted at, ogled. My only other option was to submit to being molested twice a day in a crowded city bus. That, on top of everything else, used to make my mind shut down. I didn't have the bandwidth to accommodate Delhi's male commuters who thought of women passengers as snacks they could help themselves to whenever they felt like it. The indignity made me oscillate between self-pity and violent fantasies of vengeance. There were days when I would get off a bus mid-journey and walk, hating myself for the tears of shame and rage I could not control. Millions of women put up with this every day.

On my cycle it would take me about half an hour to get to the office. I had visions of JC's pretty mother pulling up in a car next to me at a traffic light and blowing my head off for what I had done to her beautiful boy. Some days, the registrar in the National Institute of Urban Affairs, who actively disliked me, would overtake me in his office jeep, flash me a triumphant smile, and mark me absent if I reached work even a few minutes late. That meant a day's salary docked. He probably woke up much later than I did, was served a hot breakfast by his obedient wife, and was then driven to the office to play out his vindictive little scheme.

In these tiny, incremental ways, despite all the gifts of social advantage that Mrs. Roy had bestowed on me, I learned that there's no such thing as a level playing field. I took revenge on the registrar by making nasty cartoons of him—he had a cartoon-friendly mustache—and leaving them around the office for people to find.

Since I didn't have a kitchen or an obedient wife to give me breakfast, I'd have my morning tea at a roadside stall with the beggars and vagabonds who worked the lanes around the dargah. When they were off duty, most of them were completely different human beings from the pitiful people they pretended to be during their working hours. After a lot of gentle probing on their part and sly half answers to their questions on mine, they had concluded that I was a drug-cartel moll. Like Carlo on the subject of shitting on Alberto Moravia's carpet, I neither confirmed nor denied their queries, because I felt that if people thought I had gang affiliation, it might give me a little protection. Every evening when I turned my bicycle into the dargah from the main road, my breakfast partners would greet me laughing, *Aaj bhi bach gayi?* "So, you made it safely through the day?" As though they expected me to have a terrible accident and join their ranks. Since I was all I had, I paid attention to my security and tried not to do anything too stupid, but I felt safer with them than I did with some of the men in my office.

One of them, a highly decorated former inspector general of police who had landed himself a postretirement job at the institute, would occasionally arrive at my home late at night and bang on the door at the bottom of the staircase that led up to my room from the backstreet. (What was known as the "service entrance.") He had obviously got my address from his friend the registrar. As a police officer he must have known from experience that if matters came to a head and it became his word against mine, I, disreputable lone woman with bad manners and no family, wouldn't stand a chance. From my perch on my parapet wall high above the street, I would look down at him—one more in the Kottayam Santa, back-rubbing engineer granduncle series—as he desperately, soundlessly, implored me to open the door. Protected by the power of marijuana, I was neither scared nor angry, just supremely indifferent. He looked like an ugly tattoo that had suddenly become animated. The next day, just to mess with his head, I'd see him in the office and greet him sunnily as though the previous night simply hadn't happened. My recklessness took the edge off my anxiety.

Despite all this, I was far happier around the dargah of Hazrat Nizamuddin Auliya than in the hippie paradise in Goa.

For Mrs. Roy and my brother, I had vanished into thin air. They had no way of knowing how to contact me or where I was—in truth, during those days *I* barely knew where I was or how to contact myself.

And then, with no warning, everything changed.

# "What's So Funny?"

In the National Institute of Urban Affairs, I shared office space with a woman who was my boss—a notional boss more than a real one. She was a fair bit older than me (which was still very young—in her thirties), and always nicely dressed. A boisterous, exuberant presence, with an infectious, snorting laugh. Unlike the rest of us she wasn't an architect, engineer, or urban planner. She didn't come in every day and didn't seem to have any specific duties. She was a close friend of my thesis adviser, the head of the institute, so the registrar had no power over her. (He resented that. I liked that.)

One morning her husband came by to drop something off for her. I noticed him, but only fleetingly. He looked like Eric Clapton wearing John Lennon's glasses. He was only there for a few minutes.

The next day my boss didn't come in to work. In the afternoon she sent a message asking me to deliver some files to her home, which was a five-minute cycle ride away from our office.

I arrived at the tall green iron gates of an imposing white house covered with creepers in a part of town that was called the Diplomatic Enclave. I had been instructed to take the files to the apartment on the second floor. As I walked up a quaint spiral staircase enveloped in honeysuckle, through the huge picture windows on the ground floor I could see what I later learned was a bridge party. Old ladies with water-waved jet-black hair in chiffon saris and diamonds, and cigar-smoking men in tweed coats, were playing cards in a large carpeted room with velvet-upholstered settees and elaborate hanging lights. A bearer was serving a pink drink and sandwiches arranged on a silver tray. A scene from another world, another era. I must still have been chuckling as I crossed the terrace full of potted plants and rang the front doorbell. My boss's husband opened the door. He had a lovely toothy smile and a ridiculously pretty young child in his arms. Two sausage dogs, one black, one tan, each only a little bigger than my Dido's head, came out barking. They looked like a family in an advertisement.

"Hello, come in. What's so funny?"

"Nothing . . . just that you have the most peculiar landlords."

I had assumed that tenants didn't mind their landlords being laughed at.

He grinned. "Oh, they're my parents. They're having a bridge party."

He didn't seem annoyed. And I wasn't sorry for what I had said.

I handed over the files and accepted the offer of tea. It was a tiny three-room apartment, exquisitely appointed. The first real "home" I had been invited into in years. There was a lot of low wood-and-rope furniture. A rendition of a Rajasthani folk epic painted on canvas was stretched across the entire length of one wall. The floor was covered with a woven-jute—or perhaps it was pineapple fiber—carpet. Bright cushions with ethnic prints were carelessly strewn around. A picture of perfect domesticity. I felt as if I were looking at them through a viewfinder—a faraway world that I could neither feel nor touch even though I was physically present in it. I had the distinct sense that I was being "looked at," too, assessed in some way. I was there for no more than twenty minutes before I set off on my ride back to Nizamuddin and my *Aaj bhi bach gayi?* friends waiting for me in our very different kind of drawing room.

When I think back to that moment in the tasteful apartment, I see it first as a picture frame without me in it. The moment I walk into it, it begins to pixelate and disperse with the foreknowledge of what was to come. I did not cause the picture to dissipate, but perhaps something about my presence made it impossible for its artifice to endure. How could I have imagined then that the house would become my home, the man would be my man, love of my life, the dogs (and their descendants) would be my dogs, and that the young child in her father's arms and her older sister would become mine to love and help raise? The only thing that I should perhaps have been able to predict but didn't is that just when everything became dependable and secure, when the children were grown-up and love was a way of life, the stars in our sky, all our constellations big and small, public and private, would move and realign, and I would—yet again—run. Once again, the safest place would become the most dangerous. Because I would make it so. Because I am my mother's daughter. Because I could not do otherwise.

The morning after my file-delivery mission my beautifully dressed notional boss came to the office smiling broadly.

"My husband is in love with you."

She sounded quite pleased. I had no idea what she meant. She told me that her husband had a project he wanted to talk to me about and asked me to drop by at their house once more.

This time he was alone. I learned his name was Pradip. He had written a screenplay that had won the first prize in the National Film

Development Corporation's screenwriting competition. The NFDC had sanctioned a budget for him to make the film. It was a shoestring budget, so the cast could only be paid a token fee. The casting was almost complete except for the main female lead. When he saw me in his wife's office, he said, he knew at once that he had found her. Saila was her name. I laughed. I told him I didn't know the first thing about acting and that my Hindi was rotten. He said it didn't matter because Saila didn't have any speaking lines. That made my secret eyebrows shoot up in my head. A lead female character with no lines? Ah well. I behaved myself and didn't react. Thanks to Mrs. Roy and her asthma, I held a double doctorate in Not Reacting.

He had the most beautiful hands and a lovely way of speaking. I had never met anyone like him. There was something irreverent and brilliant about him. I especially loved the way he was with his dogs.

He gave me the screenplay and asked me to take it home and think about it. He said the story was loosely based on a novel set in colonial Nigeria called *Mister Johnson* by Joyce Cary and that I was on no account to read it because he didn't want me to be influenced by it. His movie was going to be called *Massey Sahib*. It was about an Indian Christian clerk in a British Collector's office in a small colonial outpost in Central India. Saila was from a local tribe. She was Massey's recalcitrant wife, upon whom he practiced his dreams of becoming a respectable white man with a respectable white wife. The story as he told it was funny, touching, and eventually tragic.

Fanon would probably have flinched. But it wasn't any of my business.

That evening, I met Carlo and told him casually that I had met a man who asked me to act in his movie.

"And what did you say?"

"Nothing. But I'm going to say no. Obviously."

"Why 'obviously'?"

"Come on, Carlo, how can I be in a movie? It's not what I want to do."

Carlo took me down. I had never seen him like that. He was almost angry. He accused me of being boring, closed, dogmatic, unimaginative, and unadventurous.

"You may not want to act, but don't you want to learn how movies are made? How scripts are written? How sets are designed? How they're lit and shot? Who gets a chance like this?"

"But I'll have to give up my job and they're not paying anything."

"You'll find another job. Do it."

So, I agreed. I borrowed money from Carlo and bought *Mister Johnson*. It was a vivid, skillfully written book, but I didn't like it. I felt it was a colonialist's view of a bumbling, idiotic, endearing black minion who wanted, more than anything else, to be white. It must have made white folks feel so warm and cuddly to imagine that everybody loved them, wanted to serve them and be like them.

Fanon would definitely have flinched.

The screenplay was better, but I was not entirely comfortable with it either. Perhaps it was just my young, crude, somewhat oppositional mind at work. Who was I anyway? Some sort of orphan upstart with a degree in architecture from a local college. Pradip, I learned, had been to Oxford and was a Balliol man like G. Isaac. And a lecturer in modern Indian history before he gave up his job to make documentary films. So, in deference to my new nonspeaking part, I kept my opinion to myself. Being inscrutable was fun. (Not long ago a stranger walked up to me—a male stranger to be clear—and said, "You know, of all the things you've done *Massey Sahib* was the best because you didn't say a word.")

Pradip said he would pick me up from Nizamuddin to introduce me to the rest of the cast and crew. He didn't really need to pick me up. Understandably he wanted to know a little more than what his wife had told him about the person he planned to cast in his film—which wasn't much. All they knew was that I was an architect married to a fellow architect and that I lived in West Nizamuddin. Pradip told me later that he expected a younger version of himself and his wife, in a slightly less nice house in a certainly less nice neighborhood. I won't ever forget our conversation as we climbed the narrow, walled-in stairs up to my storeroom.

"Is your husband in?"

"My husband?"

"Aren't you married?"

I thought back to the ceremony that had taken place in Carlo's home, not far from where we were, in which Christ had married a Japanese parcel. It wasn't a legal marriage, so obviously it wasn't a legal divorce. What could I say about it?

"Oh . . . yes . . . actually no . . . I'm not sure. No. Not really."

He was behind me so I couldn't see his expression.

"Where are you from?"

"Who me? I'm . . . well . . . I'm here now."

The more our world fractures into dagger-shaped shards, the more we club each other to death with our genes, our gods, our flags, our languages, the color of our skin, the purity of our roots, our histories both true and false—the more my answer to that question remains the same. *I'm here now.* It isn't a slogan or a solution to anything. Just the personal feelings of an off-grid drifter.

"What I mean is, where's home? What does your father do?"

"My father? I have no idea. What about yours?"

"He's retired from the Foreign Service. He was an ambassador."

Heck. I longed to get over the preliminaries and talk about something—anything—else. Stalin's gulag, Le Corbusier's ugly architecture, the mating rituals of parakeets. Anything but the story of my life so far. Once we got to the storeroom, there was nothing for us to do but go down again. There was no chair to sit on, no bookshelf to browse (*Mister Johnson* was hidden away), no paintings to look at, no tea to offer. Fat mosquitoes, tanked-up on my blood, whizzed through the air as though it were their private helipad. I was awkward and not sure what to do. But he just acted as if my room were the most normal thing in the world. I liked him for that. We stood around for a moment and then left.

My introduction to the cast and crew was like a scene out of *The Jungle Book*. I felt like a new wolf cub being introduced to the pack at Council Rock. My job was to remain very still (and express no opinions) while I was considered for membership. It took place in the flat of Barry John, the well-known British actor and director, a legend in Delhi's theater crowd. He was going to play the British collector, Massey's boss. Present at the pack meeting were only men— the cameraman, the sound recordist, the lead actor who was to play Massey (he was later replaced by an exceptional actor called Raghubir Yadav), and a young assistant director. There was a quiet, unspoken excitement in the room. I could tell they were all in complete awe of Pradip, so there were no vetoes. I was welcomed and granted membership. Some of us wolves became friends for life.

In those early years, most of my friends were men. Very straight men. Which is not the case now. It probably has to do with the fact that, at the time, girls my age were either still living with their parents or married and not living the vagrant life. And the off-grid others were living in the shadows. Today it's almost the opposite—the straight men are enfolded in home and marriage. Women who have had enough of that are breaking free. And the off-grid others are slowly but surely coming out. For people like me of the vagrant mentality, it's an excellent time for friendship. Friendship is the raft I sail on. Friendship is the pennant I fly.

One of the young wolves at Council Rock was Pradip's chief assistant director, Sanjay K, aged a ripe old twenty-three. He was very tall, gangly, zealously efficient, obsessively organized. If Pradip became one pole of the axis around which my life revolved, Sanjay became the other.

Our first encounter was as hilarious as my first meeting with Pradip, but in a very different way. I have no idea why I felt free to behave badly with Sanjay. Maybe because we were roughly the same age. I thought he was a rich boy because he had his own scooter. One night after a rehearsal, which for me only meant standing around and hitting my chalk marks, he invited me home for dinner.

"No thanks."

We were in the back lane at the base of the staircase to my storeroom. (Where the horny tattoo—the decorated police officer—would arrive at night.)

"Why are you so rude and why are you so sure?"

"Because I don't want to come to your neat little home and meet your neat little parents and have them neatly disapprove of me."

I knew nothing about his home or his parents. He had done nothing to deserve this response. It was just the wreckage of Mrs. Roy's parenting speaking. I ought to have been made to apologize and wash my mouth out with soap or something. It got worse.

"Why do you think I live with my parents?"

"Well, look at you—with neat clothes ironed by your neat mama and your neat side hair-parting and your neat little scooter."

"The scooter is borrowed. As for the rest, I hate to break it to you, but I'm this anal all by myself. I don't live with my parents."

I sat on my doorstep and laughed. Then I got back on his scooter, and we went to his room for dinner. Just rice and something. It was a single room on a second-floor terrace in Jangpura B. Much nicer than mine. He even had a fridge. And a gas cooker. Everything was neatly folded and in its place. He was a tall, neat angel. In my head I called him Neat.

It's been forty years since then. Now he's one of India's best known documentary filmmakers, a responsible husband, adoring father, and grandfather—which ought to send me running in the opposite direction—but our dinner hasn't ended yet. He was the first person in my life with whom I had been openly and deliberately insufferable. His reaction to my nonsense laid the foundations for a relationship with no artifice. Fortunately, we never made the mistake of introducing me to his parents (who would most certainly have disapproved), and even more fortunately I never put myself into that safest place, which would have turned into the most dangerous. So, our forty-year-old dinner goes on.

# They're Gonna Put Me in the Movies

*Massey Sahib* was shot in and around a small, forested hill station called Pachmarhi in Central India. The shoot was scheduled for the winter of 1982. I went into it motherless, fatherless, brotherless, jobless, homeless. Reckless.

On my last day at work the former inspector general of police came up to me and whispered, "So you have decided to discard me like a used sanitary towel?" I wanted to give him a medal for bravery. For protecting the vulnerable as a good policeman should.

When I told my friends at the Nizamuddin dargah that I was going to act in a movie, they were genuinely puzzled. *Par tumhare jaise to bazaar mein bhi mil jayega.* "But girls like you are available a dime a dozen. What's so special about you?" They didn't mean to be insulting. In that drawing room of ours, social etiquette was a little—well, different. What puzzled them most was the color of my skin. My not-whiteness. I was in every way the opposite of what their idea of a movie actress should be: tall, fair skinned, glossy haired, doe-eyed. Like the actresses in Hindi movies. I said goodbye and shook the hands of those who had hands to shake. And I was gone.

To tide me over what would be a post-shoot job crisis, I had, with Carlo's help, applied for and won a modest six-month scholarship to study the restoration of monuments and historical urban centers in Italy. I'd have to fly out as soon as I finished my shooting schedule. At the time nothing was further from my mind than restoring monuments and historical urban centers. But the idea of six months of scholarship money that I could save if I lived frugally was the main attraction. I hoped it would buy me enough time to look for another job when I got back.

*      *      *

Carlo was right. The shoot turned my life around. Not just because I had a ringside view of how a film is made, how a script is written, broken down into shots, and rewritten on set as actors rehearse, but also because I had fallen helplessly and dangerously in love. For Pradip it started just as a fling with his little starlet. Easy for him. Train wreck for her.

I was dazzled by him. To me he was the man who knew everything. He was a historian, a botanist, a zoologist. He had made documentary films about insects and birds. He knew the Beatles backward. He had made a film about the Manganiars—desert musicians in Rajasthan. He was a swimmer and a tennis player. He had reared a baby spotted owlet. He could recite Ted Hughes's "The Thought-Fox":

> *Till, with a sudden sharp hot stink of fox*
> *It enters the dark hole of the head.*
> *The window is starless still; the clock ticks,*
> *The page is printed.*

That wasn't all. Technology didn't faze him. He took beautiful photographs. On set he knew exactly what he wanted from the cameraman, the light men, and the sound recordist. He gave them precise instructions. He was ten years older than me. In his company I was flattened by what I thought of as my ordinariness.

He told me quite frankly that both he and his wife were in relationships with other people, but they had no intention of leaving each other. I acted as though I were in relationships with at least ten other men, and he was just another notch on my gun. Lies of course. A twenty-two-year-old's pathetic defense mechanism.

During the shoot I shared my room with an older actress. She reminded me of JC's mother. One day she said to me, by way of advice:

"All these men are running behind you now, but don't let that turn your head. You must be careful, you're not the kind of girl they'll ever take home and introduce to their parents."

She spoke in an undertone, even though nobody else was in the room.

I acted surprised. "Why? What's wrong with me?" I was being nasty. I wanted her to say whatever was on her mind out loud. I wanted her idiot words to flap in the air like ugly clothes on a washing line.

"You know what I mean. . . . " She dropped her voice even further, in that tone of sisterly solidarity in which one woman tells another that her bra strap or butt crack is showing.

We worked night and day, in the cold, in the rain, in the fog. My training in the School of Architecture helped me survive those most intense, sleepless weeks. It was wonderful and unbearable. The film shoot was the talk of Pachmarhi, the hill-station we were shooting in. Small crowds gathered to watch, waiting for some fabulous-looking actors to show up, but they never did. The least interesting and most traumatic part for me was the acting. I felt miscast and I hated my costume. I was uncomfortable and awkward. I contributed nothing to the part.

Then the unthinkable happened. I missed my period. I couldn't believe it. This was only meant to happen to other girls, not me. I was headed for Roman Catholic Italy, where an abortion would not be possible. I told Pradip, but I knew there was nothing he could do to help without jeopardizing the film shoot, this opportunity of a lifetime. I wouldn't have let him do that. I was out of my mind, desperate. I did not for one second think about keeping the baby. The idea of motherhood alarmed me more than almost anything else. I waited for a break in my shooting schedule and returned to Delhi. I went straight to Daryaganj, outside the walled city of Old Delhi, not far from the School of Architecture, where I remembered noticing some clinics. The doctor in the one I chose agreed to do the abortion, but said she couldn't give me general anesthesia unless I had somebody with me to sign a form. The clinic looked clean and professional. Thanks to the government's broad-mindedness on this issue at least, it was completely legal. I told her to do it without anesthesia. She advised me against it and asked me to bring either the man, or my mother. She said I looked like a girl from a good family. I told her that it wasn't true, it just looked that way. (I don't know why she thought that, because I looked like a wreck. Maybe it was my English.) I had my eye on my watch. I had to catch the evening train back. I submitted to a stern lecture about morality and responsibility. I filed it away in my Bad Girl file along with the women's college principal's predictions about my questionable moral character and the Goa psychiatrist's observations about my failings. Finally, my desperation prevailed on her.

It was horrible. But it was done.

I made it to the station in time. To get to Pachmarhi I needed to take an overnight train to Hoshangabad, change trains to a town called Pipariya and then catch a bus from there to Pachmarhi. It was late evening by the time I got to the Pipariya bus stop. I had to wait for a few hours for the next bus to Pachmarhi. Sitting alone there at that hour, I was seen as someone—an immoral someone—who was asking for trouble. Sure enough, I caught bad trouble. It was New Year's Eve.

A few young men at the bus stop recognized me as the "heroine" of the film that was being shot in Pachmarhi. Word flew around, and in no time a leering crowd of men gathered in a ring around me. I knew it wasn't me that excited them so much as the idea of me—a young woman associated with the movies. They kept up a running commentary and the ring closed in. One man brought his face close to mine and combed his oily hair as though he was looking in a mirror. I made my face expressionless, my body immobile. As though I wasn't really there. I knew that the slightest reaction from me would give them an easy pass to do whatever they wanted. The man at the ticket counter tried to diffuse the tension by inviting me into the tin booth that was his office. The men then crowded around, their faces pressed up against the iron grill. I could just see mouths and eyes. And hear their sick remarks and hyena laughs. By the time the bus came, my nerve ends were shredded into micro-vermicelli. The bus driver was a good soul and gave me a seat next to him, right up in front, and we began our journey up the winding hill road, through the beautiful, forested Satpura range.

We were driving through a particularly dark, lonely stretch when a police jeep overtook us and stopped the bus. Four policemen boarded with an air of brisk self-importance, as though they were on a mission.

"Where's the girl from Delhi? That actress?"

I wasn't hard to spot. They said they had information that there was a plan to kidnap me. They asked me to get off the bus and go with them. I refused. I told them there wasn't a soul in the world that knew I was on that bus, so there couldn't possibly be a plan. As soon as the words were out of my mouth, I realized it wasn't the wisest thing to say. It quickly turned into a standoff between me and the police. Most of the passengers and the bus driver took my side. The compromise was that they made me sign a hilariously worded letter saying that I had been warned by the Pipariya police about my possible kidnapping and was proceeding at my own risk. Finally, with a policeman seated on either side of me for my "protection," our journey continued. Some hours before dawn I was delivered directly to the film unit, like a dangerous package, a defused letter bomb. The policemen saluted and left. The film crew was mystified.

I like to think that those policemen didn't have anything terrible on their minds. They just wanted a little excitement, a local thriller of their own in which they played a starring role that ran parallel to *Massey Sahib*. But who can say?

I wasn't easily shaken, but all of it together—the anesthesia-less abortion, the bus-stop mobbing, the fake kidnapping drama, the police escort—was a little too much even for me. I gave Pradip a sketchy account of what had happened, but he was drowning in a logistical crisis unfolding on the set. I told Sanjay, too. He sat with me on the steps of the bungalow we were staying in for the few hours until the sun rose, as I cried my eyes out. He didn't try to comfort me, and that was a great help. From then to now he has been the cave that shelters me when I have nowhere else to go. I shelter him, too.

By midmorning I was back on set.

The shoot continued for ten more days and then suddenly it was all over and time for me to leave. My last scene was shot in a beautiful meadow of golden grass. I had to run through the grass holding a little baby—a supreme irony given my recent undertakings. We had to pad my prominent collarbones to protect the baby's head from banging against them. The grass was sharp and pokey. It slashed at my skin and sari. On the whole, what was asked of me was pretty impossible. That scene did not make it to the final cut of the film.

It was dawn when Pradip called a wrap. I was sitting under a tree, quite far away from everybody else, when I heard a sort of strange bellowing—halfway between a moo and a roar. I walked toward it. And froze.

A buffalo had fallen into a shallow pit and wasn't able to get out. As my eyes adjusted to the light, I saw a dhole—a wild dog—exactly the same color as the grass, spring out of the pit. Local people called them *son kutta*, "golden dog." A golden dog in the golden grass in the golden light. Then I saw another and another and another. It took a while for my eyes to pick them out, one by one. A whole pack of them were arranged in a ring, perfectly camouflaged. They stood absolutely still and dead quiet, with their ears pricked, looking straight at me. Somehow, I wasn't scared. I was sorry for the buffalo but knew I was watching the law of the jungle at work. I could hear Mrs. Roy's voice in my head, reading me Kipling.

> *Now Chil the Kite brings home the night*
> *That Mang the Bat sets free—*
> *The herds are shut in byre and hut,*
> *For loosed till dawn are we*
> *This is the hour of pride and power,*
> *Talon and tush and claw.*
> *Oh, hear the call!—Good hunting all*
> *That keep the Jungle Law!*

I backed away slowly. In my uncomfortable costume and my padded collarbones.

I left Pachmarhi. But my heart remained behind, tangled up in the lights and reflectors, the power cables and the pokey grass.

# "Have You Ever Considered Becoming a Writer?"

Straight from the madness of a film shoot in the jungles of Central India, I landed at the Leonardo da Vinci Fiumicino Airport in Rome. Alone, and unpregnant.

Lucky.

The only familiar thing I could see was a small cardboard sign for Saila, a brand of cheap Italian mints in an airport stall. It was the name of my character in *Massey Sahib*. I stole the cardboard sign. I still have it.

From Rome I had to go to Napoli for a one-month Italian-language course and then to Firenze for the actual course on the restoration of monuments and historical urban centers.

Those months in Carlo's country passed in a blur of heartache and longing to return. Every cell in my body wanted to be back in Pachmarhi with Pradip, Sanjay, and the film crew. Or back in Delhi with Carlo. And Golak. I don't think I attended more than three or four classes. I wandered the streets all day, an unenlightened fool, impervious to the charms and splendor of Italy. Considering I was a student of architecture, this was almost criminal behavior. But I learned some basic Italian (following the same techniques as Golak's and my Hindi learning), and drank a lot of cheap wine. I sat alone in an absolutely empty movie theater and watched a film of a Paul McCartney concert.

I longed for news from India. It was 1983. In my halting Italian, I read about the massacre of thousands of Muslims in Nellie, Assam, by a local tribe, egged on by Assamese and mainstream Hindu nationalists. I read about how Phoolan Devi—the legendary female bandit of the Chambal valley—had surrendered before a crowd of thousands and been put into prison. The newspapers carried spectacular photographs of her handing over her rifle, wearing khaki fatigues and a red bandanna. (Almost exactly ten years later she would be released from jail and our paths would cross in a most unexpected way.) I saw Richard Attenborough's *Gandhi* dubbed into Italian and laughed my head off at my friend Barry John—who was still shooting with Pradip in Pachmarhi—playing a policeman. He arrests Gandhi in Italian: *Mi dispiace informarla, Signor Gandhi, ma lei è in arresto.* I visited the bank diligently every month to collect and stash away my scholarship money.

I observed and experienced the fine art of Italian courtship. I developed a thesis about why (notwithstanding Urdu poetry and movie songs) most Indian men are so bad at it—their parents deliver them a woman of the right caste and class on a platter, with a dowry thrown in. They don't need to do a thing except snatch and grab.

At night, every single night, I'd write a letter to Pradip. These were not love letters. They were just descriptions of my daily life. They had only one purpose. I wanted that brilliant man to write back and say, *Have you ever considered becoming a writer?* That is exactly what he did.

\*　　　\*　　　\*

As a child, it's all I ever thought I'd be. Nothing made me forget the world like reading did. Nothing made me think about the world like reading did. Nothing else filled me up. Nothing else emptied me out. Sentences and paragraphs would drift through my head like clouds. Kipling, Shakespeare, the opening passage of *Lolita*, G. Isaac's sentences purloined from Joyce's *Ulysses*—"Belluomo rises from the bed of his wife's lover's wife, the kerchiefed house-wife is astir"—streaked like comets across my reading sky. I waited for "crude sunlight on her lemon streets" (which never came) and mornings that would qualify as "rosy-fingered dawn" (which did). I shuddered at the thought of Leopold Bloom slipping a kidney wrapped in paper into his pocket and taking it home for his wife's faintly urine-scented breakfast. It wasn't all high-minded literature. Lines of purple prose would trip off my tongue in purply moments: "The moon was a ghostly galleon tossed upon cloudy seas. . . . " (Thanks to G. Isaac and Mrs. Roy, my early literary education was dominated by white, male writers.)

One of the foundational practices in Mrs. Roy's school was what she called "free writing." Much before she started her school—from the time I could hold a pencil—she encouraged me to write what was on my mind. She preserved the notebook in which I wrote my first sentence. It was about Miss Mitten the Australian missionary who was my teacher in Ooty when I was five years old. She was teaching us arithmetic and gave us a sum that involved counting up to more than ten. When she wasn't looking, I took off my socks, counted on my toes, then put the socks on again. I was a stealthy child because I lived under conditions in which I never knew what would come at me and when. I needed to be prepared at all times

125

for anything. Like Estha (one of the twins in *The God of Small Things*), I knew that

(a.) Anything Can Happen to Anyone
(b.) It's Best to Be Prepared

And that it's best never to show your hand or, for that matter, your feet. Or the chicken pox on your stomach.

Miss Mitten demanded to know how I had got the sum right. Something about her manner made me feel I had done something very wrong and that counting on toes was unchristian and a sin. The more I insisted that I had done it in "my head," the angrier she became. She told me I was wicked and that she could see Satan in my eyes. When I went home that day, my mother told me to write about what happened at school. (Five was a little young to be able to write, but I was precocious because I had sat in while Mrs. Roy was teaching my brother.) I wrote, *I hate Miss Mitten. Whenever I see her I see rags. I think her gnickers are torn.* I don't know why Mrs. Roy preserved it because clearly these sentences did not make any sense and did not herald the birth of a writer.

All through school I did consistently badly in English language and literature. I never understood the rules. Mrs. Roy would slash through my little essays and compositions, mark me three out of ten, and write comments like *Horrible. Nonsense.* She was right—they were complete and utter rubbish. Even then I knew that the language I wrote in was not mine. By *mine* I don't mean mother tongue, and by *language* I don't mean English, Hindi, or Malayalam, I mean a *writer's* language. Language that I used, not language that used me. A language in which I could describe my multilingual world to myself. I knew even then that that language was outside me, not inside me. I knew it would not come to me on its own. I needed to hunt it down like prey. Disembowel it, eat it. And when I did, I knew that language, *my* language, would ease the way blood flowed through my body. It was out there somewhere, a live language-animal, a striped and spotted thing, grazing, waiting for me the predator. That was the law of my jungle. It wasn't a nonviolent, vegetarian dream.

But once I started running, when all I could ever think about was day-to-day survival, my hunt for language stopped. It needed time, and practice. I needed to train, just like a painter or dancer or swimmer might—except that my ambition was more basic. It had to do with regulating my body temperature and the way the blood flowed in my veins. It had to do with keeping my sanity, my equanimity, with finding a way to talk to myself.

To train, I needed shelter. Not physical, but emotional—somewhere to sit down, even for a little while. I didn't have that. I had never had that.

Once I started running, once I joined Architecture School, I thought that a writer was the last thing I could ever be. I gave up.

And then, years later came that letter. *Have you ever considered becoming a writer?* I knew that I hadn't found the grazing language-animal. But the bloodhound in me caught the faint, faraway scent of it on the breeze.

\*     \*     \*

The Alitalia flight from Rome back to Delhi was almost empty. I had a high fever. Once again, I had no idea what to do or where to go when I landed. There were no business proposals on board this time around. But I had most of my scholarship money saved up and wasn't as desperate as I had been on the Goa–Bombay steamer. The

Italian steward and stewardess on the flight, who had nothing much to do since there were hardly any passengers, came and chatted to me. When I told them about the fix I was in, they told me they were married to each other, so if I needed somewhere to go for the night, they had a spare hotel room. That came as a huge relief. I think my fever dropped almost immediately.

Fortunately I didn't need their hotel room. Pradip was at the airport to meet me with strange news. His wife had moved out. He wasn't sure whether she would come back. He seemed a little disoriented. He said that he and his children had moved in with his parents temporarily, so I could stay in his apartment for the night. When we got there, I understood why he had moved downstairs. The apartment was stripped bare. No carpets, no paintings, no cushions, no curtains, and not a stick of furniture. There was a mattress on the floor and a bottle of drinking water. That made me feel completely at home. He settled me in and dropped down to his parents' home through a trapdoor that must previously have been hidden under the carpeting. I liked that. It looked like a magic trick. One of the dogs, Kuthujee, a soulful brown dachshund, decided he would spend the night with me along with his life companion who never left his side—a gnawed, moth-eaten red Frisbee. I felt more honored than I had in long time. It was my first night with a dog in my bed since Dido.

The next day I arrived with my suitcase and my stash of saved-up scholarship money at Sanjay's place, where I stayed for a few days until I found a new room. I had bought him a whiskey glass from Firenze. Just one, because it was all I could afford. Sanjay knew about my increasingly serious relationship with Pradip of course. It hurt him. But between us we had a truth-telling pact. Though we were very nearly the same age I told him I was far too old for him. The age difference between us was roughly one hundred years. Neat & Tidy could not make up for Fatherless Motherless Homeless Jobless Reckless. He on the other hand believed he was one hundred years my senior. We agreed to disagree. He still has that whiskey glass.

*       *       *

My new home was yet another second-floor room on the roof, this time in a posh area called Malcha Marg, walking distance from Pradip's home. The rent was only slightly higher than what I'd paid in Nizamuddin because the room, although not a storeroom like my previous one, was fit only for a temporary camper. It had an attached toilet, a window, a small, battered dressing table, and a proper wooden bed. No kitchen. Sanjay donated me one of his prized possessions—a shatterproof-glass jeep windshield, which I propped up on a couple of bricks. On it I put a crude coil heater, a plate, a glass, and a pan in which I could boil rice and dal. My kitchen counter. There was nobody to have breakfast with in that colony, and no bicycle-hire place. I invested some of my precious scholarship money in a big black bicycle. A step up because I owned it, a step down because it was really ugly. My new landlords wouldn't let me park it downstairs. They said it made them look cheap. So, I chained it to the fence of the small park outside. It looked cheap there, too, but since the cheapness wasn't attached to a particular address, nobody objected.

There were monkeys in that park. A troop of rhesus macaques that wandered in from the Ridge—a stretch of city forest just across the road. In the Ridge there were blue bulls and wild pigs (real ones, not the Kottayam Santa variety), and jackals who would howl all night. A young female monkey spent a night under my bed clutching a dead puppy—her surrogate baby—while I sat on the terrace and left all the doors open so that she didn't feel threatened. She went away early in the morning.

As the months went by, my relationship with Pradip grew more intense as did my money problems. I did a few illustration projects, including for a children's book that never got published. None of it earned me much of an income. My stash of saved-up scholarship money was quickly dwindling. I was reluctant to go back to work in an architectural firm. That to me signified defeat, retreat. Pradip would spend weeks away in Bombay editing *Massey Sahib*. He had bad run-ins with a vindictive producer at the National Film Development Corporation, who seemed to be doing everything he could to delay completion of the film.

For the first time in my life in Delhi, I didn't have people, city sounds, hustle-bustle around me. I felt alone and isolated in that posh colony. I lost my shine, my strut; I began to shrink and spiral into despair. I was caught in that classic trap—a very young woman involved with an older, married man. But I loved that married man with all my heart.

\*     \*     \*

Then came 1984. Delhi's nightmare year. On the morning of the last day of October, Indira Gandhi, who had made a political come-back after the Emergency and was prime minister once again, was shot down in her garden by her Sikh bodyguards. Her assassination was revenge for Operation Blue Star, the military strike she had ordered against armed militants bunkered up in the Golden Temple, the holiest of holy Sikh shrines in Amritsar, Punjab. The temple was badly damaged during the operation and many militants were killed. Among them Jarnail Singh Bhindranwale—leader of the Sikh separatist movement—who Mrs. Gandhi had once cultivated as a political ally.

My rooms in Malcha Marg and Pradip's parents' home were both a five-minute drive from Indira Gandhi's house. We felt as though if we had listened carefully, we'd have heard the shots. Her body was rushed to the All India Institute of Medical Sciences. The city went into shock. The minute she was declared dead, carnage was unleashed. Organized gangs of Congress Party goons and right-wing Hindu nationalists slaughtered thousands of Sikhs in Delhi—tailors, shop-keepers, taxi drivers—"necklacing" them with burning tires South Africa–style or beating them to death while the police stood by and watched. Standing on a hillock in the Ridge Forest, we could see columns of smoke spiraling into the sky as our snarling city bared its fangs. Mrs. Gandhi's older son, Rajiv Gandhi, dismissed the massacre callously: "When a big tree falls, the ground shakes." He would soon be elected prime minister with a huge majority in Parliament. That victory went a long way toward convincing politicians and political parties that murdering minorities helped them to win elections. In the years to come we would watch it happen over and over.

I was so numbed by my own despair that I felt I was watching it all from some other lonely, faraway planet. I didn't realize that I—as I often did—had locked away my rage and disgust in a sealed chamber of my brain. I would unseal it much later, when I became a properly functioning human.

If I were to permit myself some retrospective insight, I'd say the numbness also came from helplessness. From witnessing horror and being unable to do anything. From not having a language to describe it, even to myself.

Shaken by the massacre, I began to spend more and more time with Pradip, even staying over in his apartment on most nights. But

I still kept my rented room in Malcha Marg. I was terrified of being dependent on anyone, even him. I did not want another "banker" to replace the one I had run from. Not that Pradip had much money. But food, and a roof over his head were not things he had ever had to worry about. To me, that signified wealth.

# Mama Bear, Papa Bear

Seven years had gone by since I'd last seen Mrs. Roy.

The strangest thing is that I cannot remember how she and I came to be in contact with each other again. It could be that I wrote to her and told her about *Massey Sahib* and my trip to Italy. I really don't know. It's a hole in my memory. But soon after the 1984 carnage, I found myself on a railway platform in Nizamuddin Station, waiting for the train that would bring her to Delhi.

She got off the train with her secretary and an inhaler-bag-bearing attendant. (No peacock-feather fan fortunately.) She didn't recognize me standing there on the station platform and walked right past. I didn't realize how much I had changed. She looked the same. I went up to her and hugged her. I felt her stiffen. She did not like physical affection. In all the photographs of me and her, I'm the one who is kissing her. If she, by any chance, has an arm around me, her fingers are raised awkwardly, to minimize contact.

She was in Delhi to see her lawyers about her petition in the Supreme Court against the Travancore Christian Succession Act. I was not ready to meet her. I had no money. I was literally living on air. I had no idea what I was doing with my life. And something about my complicated situation with Pradip had sapped my spirit. I had lost the reckless insouciance of my student days. My defenses were down. I felt that if I told her anything about my situation, she would crush me with her contempt.

We took a taxi to the Young Women's Christian Association (YWCA) where she had booked a room. Looking out of the window, I felt we were so small, so *nothing* in Delhi. I didn't mind about myself because I *was* nothing. But I minded that nobody knew what an amazing woman Mrs. Roy was. Nobody knew about her beautiful school and its Laurie Baker campus. Nobody knew what it had taken for her to build it.

She had a spacious room at the YWCA. I helped her unpack and settle in. It was strange and tense between us. It didn't take more than an hour for things to deteriorate into something that resembled old times. As always, I didn't react, but I excused myself and left as quickly as I could. The next morning, she came to my room in Malcha Marg. She walked up two floors, which wasn't easy for her. Standing at my door, she said, "I thought I'd never see you again." She had brought me my old typewriter, the one I had learned to type on. That further broke my already-broken heart. This was the power she had always had over me. She could break my heart and mend it, too. With a snap of her fingers. I wanted to kiss her and tell her how much I loved her. But I didn't. I just said, "Thank you." I meant *Thank you for knowing that your daughter has a writer's heart.*

The rest of her trip passed without any explosions. She didn't mention my brother at all and instinct told me not to ask about him. I went with her to some of her meetings. The one I remember most clearly is when an older Syrian Christian woman, I think she was a doctor or the wife of a doctor, said, "Why are you trying to destroy our beautiful community? What will we do with these rights you want us to have?" I don't think either Mrs. Roy or I made any attempt to hide our feelings.

After we walked out of the door, I had to resist the urge to storm back in and sweep all the cute mementos off her coffee table and say, "Excuse me, ma'am, do you have any idea who you just met? If you think she's just fighting for equal inheritance, you're wrong. She's actually fighting for the right not to be a perfect mother, for the right not to be a nice, obedient woman, and most of all for the right not to be a fucking bore like you."

Before Mrs. Roy left Delhi she bought me a little fridge. I considered selling it, but decided against that. I used it as a cupboard to keep my books and clothes in.

Now that she had an address for me, she began writing to me. The nastiness started up again. To avoid being emotionally mangled, I appointed Sanjay my designated letter reader. I asked him to tell me if there was anything important that I needed to know. Just the facts. No adjectives. He would perform this task with delight, smiling to himself. After he read a letter and gave me the gist, just to annoy me he'd say, "Hey, you've got to admit—she really writes well."

I was almost his equal now. I had a fridge, but no scooter yet.

I also had a mother, but no father yet. That was about to change.

*     *     *

A few months after my reunion with Mrs. Roy, my brother found me. In an old magazine. Although *Massey Sahib* was still tied up in NFDC red tape, the press had been writing about the forthcoming film for a while. *India Today*, a major weekly magazine, had published a black-and-white photograph of me (taken by Carlo) on its back page with a short text that made me sound as though I badly needed a brain. It mentioned that the film had been produced by the NFDC. My brother contacted them, and they gave him Pradip's number. He called Pradip and told him that he was in Delhi. He left a number for me to call. It had been seven years since I last saw or spoke to him.

I felt I needed to be in a safe, familiar space when I made the call. I cycled all the way to Nizamuddin. I passed through the dargah, said hello to those of my old friends who were still there, then went to the noisy sweetshop behind the gas station where Carlo and I would occasionally have tea, and from where I used to make any phone calls I needed to. (Carlo didn't live there anymore. He had a new job teaching Italian at the cultural center and had moved to a better address.) I dialed the number. It turned out to be a hotel. I could see myself reflected in the smudged glass of the sweetshop counter. From the way the receptionist spoke I guessed it was a hotel like the one in Bombay where I had stayed on my way back from Goa. A hippie-trail hotel. I gave him my brother's name, and in moments he came on the line.

"LKC! Where are you?"

"In Delhi. In a hotel near the station. It's quite dirty. I've left home. I couldn't stay there anymore."

"You can stay with me. Why don't you?"

"I'll tell you when I see you. Hey, your accent has changed."

"What d'you mean? Changed how?"

"I don't know. Changed. Here, someone wants to speak to you. Guess."

"Baba?"

Baba. Our father. Our mother's husband. The Nothing Man. I hadn't seen him since I was three.

"How did you know?"

It's almost unbelievable. But I knew. I could hear it in the excitement in my brother's voice. I had always sensed that he believed that if it isn't Mummy, it has to be Daddy. Somebody must surely love us. I had no such illusions.

"I don't know. I guessed. LKC? I don't want to speak to him on the phone."

"Why?"

"I don't know . . . but please, please, please not on the phone. . . ."

Another voice came on. "Hello! Why're you shouting? You know who this is?"

"Yes."

"Who?"

"Baba."

"Correct. You remember me at all?"

"No."

"D'you still use bad language?"

"What d'you mean?"

"You don't remember? You used to swear on your sister's whatsit. The workers on the tea estate taught you. Forgotten? *Teri behen ka lauda,* you used to say. Hello? Here speak to your brother."

I had no idea what this person on the phone, this complete stranger, was talking about. My brother and I agreed to meet the next morning. He said he would pick me up because he wanted to see where I lived.

*     *     *

The noise in my head was louder than the chatter in the sweetshop and the roar of traffic on the main road. I cycled back to my room in a daze. I spent that whole night awake, sitting at my rickety dressing table staring at myself in the dim mirror, as though that would somehow help me to envision what the man I was going to meet the next day would look like. Would he look like an older version of the photograph of him and my brother and me in the gray album? In that photo he was handsome, slim, sporty looking, in an open-collared white shirt and glasses. My brother sits astride his shoulders, resting his chin on his father's head, looking pleased and secure. (I've never seen that expression on his face again.) I'm less than a year old, hanging over my father's forearm like an angry toy, clutching his wristwatch as if it were the only thing I trusted. It's the only photograph we had of us and him.

I own that gray album now. There isn't a single photograph of all four of us together. And only one of us as young children with our mother. That one is a tiny print, two inches square. We're standing outside the Entomologist's cottage in Ooty. All of us look ill and grim. My mother looks as though she isn't really there. My brother looks as though he doesn't want to be there. I'm on the extreme right. One arm is stretched across both of them as though I'm protecting them from something. My expression frightens me. No child should look like that.

I had always believed that our parents' separation affected my brother much more than it did me. It's only now, when we are in our sixties, that we seem to have reversed roles. He is an expansive, exuberant seafood tycoon, and I have gone quiet on the inside, a little haunted by things that happened so long ago. As children, every night when we had to say our prayers out loud, his prayer was aways "Please bless Mama and please don't let her get asthma. Please don't let Pothachen [the landlord of our rented Kottayam hostel-home] bother her. Please bless Baba and don't let him drink. Amen." I prayed for our mother and her asthma, and against our creepy landlord, but I never prayed for Baba. As I grew older, I grew more and more obnoxious and gratuitous about how I would refer to him. Sometimes as the Photograph. Sometimes as the Sperm. I'd say I was the product of parthenogenesis. That I was immaculately conceived and was the evil twin (with Satan in her eyes) of the blessed one, who was born smiling with a halo. And that my mother's name was Mary, too. It was the scornful armor I wore to protect myself in our fathercentric world. On one occasion, when I was asked to put my father's name down in some government form, I put my mother's name down instead. The man at the counter said that was not acceptable because "this is India, my dear." I told him I was a bastard and didn't know who my father was. Finally, in exasperation, he filled it in himself. He wrote *Shri Mary Roy.* "Mr." Mary Roy. I accepted that compromise. Because this was India, my dear.

It had taken just that one phone call for all my facile glibness to fall away. My first worry was that meeting my father would amount to betraying my mother. As I stared at myself in the mirror, trying to conjure him, I dredged up all the intelligence I had gathered from Mrs. Roy's stray remarks about her husband over the years. There wasn't much. He came from a well-known family in Calcutta who had migrated from what is now Bangladesh. His father (my grandfather) had been in the Royal Artillery in Britain in the First World War. After the war he returned to India and became a champion amateur boxer. (I always found that interesting. Of my two grandfathers, one was an entomologist and the other was a soldier-boxer. And it was the entomologist who turned out to be the violent one.) In time, the champion boxer started drinking and drank the family into penury. Baba was the second youngest of three brothers and two sisters. His pet name was Micky because of his Mickey Mouse ears. (I have them, too.) He loved his father and would introduce himself as "Micky Roy the Boxer's Boy." (Now when I think about it, that must have been the early influence, still fresh in his mind, that made my brother box the air around me in our Ooty days and call himself Cassius Clay.)

What exasperated her most about Micky, my mother said, was that he had no respect for the truth. He told harmless lies, for the hell of it. Because he enjoyed lying. It wasn't hard for her to catch him out, and when she did, he'd just giggle. She made us look up the word *inane* in the dictionary because it described his giggle perfectly:

lacking sense, significance, or ideas
empty; void

The second-most exasperating thing, she said, was the terrible business of his sitting around doing nothing. *Nothing.* No reading, no talking, no thinking. How did she know for sure that he wasn't thinking? I once asked her tentatively. She *knew.* She had never known him to think, she said. He just sat. Sometimes he shivered his leg so much the whole sofa they were sitting on would shake. Sometimes he blew spit-bubbles. For hours on end. These were things that needed to be corrected before the age of sixteen, according to her. After that it was too late. She put the problem down to both his parents having been too drunk to bother with him. Whenever my brother was lazy, or sitting hunched over, or shivering his leg, she would tell him she knew where he got that from. (As a child, to imagine my father, I blew spit-bubbles, too, but never in front of her.) Anything that wasn't good about us, according to her, we got from our father. It didn't seem to occur to her that blaming our genes left us doubting ourselves in terrifying ways. As though one-half of us were a garbage bin into which any kind of litter could be thrown. The main reason she left him, she said, wasn't the lying and the laziness, it was the drinking.

\*　　　\*　　　\*

I was dressed and ready when my brother arrived. He looked the same as before. Thin and flat, like a boy. Only his mustache hairs were harder. We didn't have one of those great dramatic reunions. We weren't like that. When we were small, he would stand on his head on my bum. Once you've done that, you don't need to talk and say hello and be demonstrative or explain things. My joy at seeing him after so many years was overtaken by my anxiety about meeting Micky Roy.

My brother sat on my bed and looked around my room. He liked my jeep-windshield kitchen. He thought it was an excellent idea. He burrowed in my handbag and examined each thing. He wanted to see my other clothes so he could present me to our father looking my best. He was shining.

"Don't you have something blue to match your jeans? Oh, wow, you've had your ears pierced! You *still* have these shoes?"

He had kept the auto-rickshaw waiting, so we hurried downstairs.

Over the rattle of the rickshaw, he had to shout to be heard.

"You'll really like him. He's really nice. Always joking."

I had planned in advance to feel nothing.

"You know it's impossible to imagine them married. They're so different. He's very popular."

"Popular with whom?"

"With people in Calcutta."

Popular with the people of Calcutta. I turned to look at my brother to see if he really believed what he was saying. But he was looking out, smiling at the buses, the cyclists, the paraplegics on their improvised square skateboards begging at the lights, the traffic fumes, and the hot Delhi dust.

"And he's bloody generous. He's the kind of chap who if he has five rupees says 'You take two, I'll keep three.'"

"How did you find him?"

"I went to Calcutta. I found him."

Our rickshaw had turned into the chaos of Paharganj near the New Delhi Railway Station. LKC had to shout even louder.

"He's hoping to get this job. He's been through a bit of a bad patch."

I learned later that the bad patch included living on the streets and a short spell at Mother Teresa's home for the dying destitute.

"He's come to Delhi for an interview. For a job. So have I actually. Maybe we can all stay together."

*And what about Her?* I wanted to say but didn't.

"Does he look nice? I mean is he nice-looking? Like in the photograph?"

"He's very relaxed."

I don't know why I had this shallow anxiety about his looks. Maybe I had a premonition.

What happened next is seared into my memory forever, although I might not have remembered it word for word, song for song, oil stain for oil stain, if I hadn't written it down. I wrote it on the typewriter Mrs. Roy gave me. Free writing. Like Mrs. Roy taught me. Free writing without flinching. It's easier for me to write about politics, or to write fiction, than to write what I am about to write. There's no glory in this. Nor—relatively speaking—any great tragedy. I wonder why I need to make this very private moment public. I think it's because there is a sweet, vanquished, impish tenderness about it that is precious. It's an ode to harmless roguery. Although calling it harmless may be an affront to those who try so hard to be responsible parents. Perhaps I use that word because I survived it without great harm to myself.

Lucky.

The hotel was exactly as I imagined it would be. Most of the guests were hippies in limp clothes on their way to and from Goa or Manali. Dope sellers were openly selling hashish and heroin in the corridor, which was infused with the sharp ammonia stench of stale urine. There were metal trays with old food and slanting towers of stained teacups outside most of the rooms. Room seventeen was on the ground floor. It was built around a double bed. You could just about sidestep your way and slide along the wall to the bathroom. Nothing could have prepared me for what I encountered.

My first sighting of my father.

He was lying on his stomach with his knees bent, his feet waving at the ceiling. The ash from his cigarette had fallen onto the bed. When he saw me, he flicked his cigarette to the floor and rubbed the ash into the sheets. Then he stood up on the bed and held his hand out for me to shake. To get to him I needed to climb onto the bed. I kicked off my shoes and climbed on. We shook hands. My brother, beaming, climbed on, too. We stood like that for a while, bouncing gently to keep our balance on the soft, spongy mattress.

The Yalta Conference. Stalin, Roosevelt, and Churchill.

Micky Roy was as frail as a small bird, lame and hunched over. One eye was milky and opaque with an unattended-to cataract. His right earlobe was missing. His skin looked scorched. His bone-thin legs came down together to his knees, then splayed apart and ended in two socked feet that sank into the dirty sheets. Through the space between his calves, I could see a triangle of hotel wall, peeling plaster, hair-oil stains. I could tell that he was severely malnourished, like people in UN pamphlets. My brother and he looked at me and laughed. Micky called my brother Kapil Dev—the legendary captain of the Indian cricket team that had for the first time ever won the World Cup. He was right. There was a slight resemblance.

"So, Kapil Dev!" he said, and slapped my brother on his back. He wasn't sure what to say to me, so he slapped me on my back, too, and grinned.

"I believe you heard I was dead?"

"No."

My brother stepped in. "I was the one that heard you were dead. Not her. She doesn't know about it. I haven't seen her for some time." He turned to me. "You know he almost died? He used to be a real boozer."

Another hearty slap on the back for Kapil Dev. And a short abstract of the story for me.

After he lost his job on the tea estate in Assam, he had moved in with one of his brothers in Calcutta. Things were chugging along nicely until he started on the local liquor. The Orange Stuff and the Yellow Stuff. Then his brother's wife threw him out. His other brother wouldn't have him, so he stayed with friends, a week at a time. He had lots of friends.

"See, I told you . . . he's really popular."

Everybody decided that giving him money would do him more harm than good. So, they gave him food instead. Only his planter friends from the tea estates understood and sympathized with his situation. When they came to Calcutta on business visits, they gave him free sample packets of tea that he could sell. This way he made enough money to buy himself a bottle and a half of local liquor a day. Later, when he recovered, they told him at the hospital that the liquor he had been drinking contained large quantities of varnish.

Micky laughed.

"But it was so damn cheap. Just five chips and fifty paisa a bottle. For seven seventy-five I could get well and truly sozzled. Imagine."

*Chips.* I had forgotten that turn of phrase.

He skipped the Mother Teresa part.

He said he had completely recovered from the varnish. He would be borrowing his son's gold chain for his interview. In his mind he had the job already.

"How d'you find me looking?" he wanted to know from me.

"Oh, fine. Really good."

"You should have seen me two months ago." He giggled. I understood what my mother meant about inane.

"You would never have believed I was your father. You look so much more like me than your mother. Doesn't she, Kapil Dev? Same nose. Same eyes . . . sorry eye (Giggle). I say, Orundhuti, do you hit the bottle?"

He pronounced my name the Bengali way.

"Me? No."

"Oh, go on. Tell the truth. All good Roys hit the bottle. Whaddyou say, Kapil Dev?" (Giggle. Slap.)

I felt a slight stirring of unease. I knew what he was talking about. I was a good Roy. The sleeping hound of addiction was alive and well in me. It leaped up at a moment's notice. One cigarette a day went to two and then to forty in a week. And, yes, I knew about the Orange Stuff and the Yellow Stuff, too. (It's what I drank with Bahadur the watchman in the graveyard.) But I had kept the hound on a tight leash. I had seen enough wreckage among the drugged-out hippies in Goa to know that my life depended on hanging on to that leash and never forgetting about the hound for one single second, even when it was pretending to be asleep.

"Anyway, one piece of advice. Don't go for the local stuff. The Orange Stuff and the Yellow Stuff. You don't remember me at all? Our house in Nowgong? Kapil Dev remembers a little. You remember the time I burnt your hand with a cigarette by mistake and you said *chutiya* [asshole] and I gave you such a walloping? Forgotten? And the time when we were driving through the jungle to the club? At night? You were bawling about something, and I stopped the car and said one more choo out of you and you can go home? And you just opened the car door and walked off, mite that you were?"

I made a note of that one area of harmony and compatibility between Mr. and Mrs. Roy—kicking their daughter out of cars in jungles and strange cities.

"But the funniest was when your mother thrashed you. Kapil Dev, d'you know what your sister did? She went to your mother one day and said, 'Mama, I love the smell of men.' Can you imagine? Not even three years old. D'you know what smell she was talking about? Booze. All the planters who came and played with her were boozed. So, Orundhuti, don't tell me you don't knock it back. At three you showed all the signs. . . . Why're you sitting there looking so *muggrah*? You used to be so much more interesting before. When I knew you, you wouldn't stop talking. Come on. Tell us some news. So, you don't booze. D'you still like the smell of men? D'you have a boyfriend? Why don't you bring him here so I can break his teeth?"

*Muggrah,* I learned, meant "grumpy." Or something between serious and grumpy. New word. I wondered what I should call him, because Baba was the Photograph. This was someone else. Micky, maybe.

"If I go out with you, everybody will say who's this old bugger with that beautiful young girl, and I'll say, 'She's my daughter, dammit. Mind your mouth.'"

For a moment I felt alarmed at the idea of being seen anywhere with him. Then I felt ashamed of being ashamed. After my initial disbelief at his appearance, I thought about how much worse I'd have felt if he was some smarmy, rich, cigar-smoking CEO.

"Kapil Dev, move! I want to sit next to her for some time. I've had enough of you for the time being." Slap. Giggle. He rubbed some more cigarette ash into the sheets. And patted the space next to him.

"So, Orundhuti, let's hear your exploits."

While he waited to hear about my exploits, he started to shiver his leg. I looked at it fascinated. My brother was delighted. He felt vindicated. He had tracked the leg-shivering gene to its source.

Micky responded with a naughty grin.

"Looking at my leg? Your mother used to get so angry. I still haven't understood why. What's wrong with shaking your leg if you feel like it? Lots of people do it. It's not a sin. There are so many things about her that I just never understood. Like when I—"

My brother sensed loyalty trouble. On my part, not his. He quickly changed the subject.

"Tell her about your ear, Baba. About when your old man died." He turned to me. "P. L. Roy, the Father of Indian Boxing. The newspaper clipping is in the photograph album. Remember?"

Of course I did: VETERAN SPORTSMAN P. L. ROY DEAD.

"You tell her." Micky was suddenly shy. As though he were about to come in for high praise.

My brother began to laugh helplessly even before he started to tell the story. "P. L. Roy, his father—our grandfather—was ill and in hospital. Baba was supposed to be nursing him. Instead, they had a booze-up and the old man just popped off. Imagine."

*Popped off.* I had forgotten about that turn of phrase, too.

Father and son went into peals of laughter.

"Anyway, the funeral was full of boxers and army and air force guys from all over the place. Baba landed up drunk and saluted the corpse and started to sing some stupid song."

"What song?"

Micky sang:

> *Why did you join the army?*
> *Why did you join the PAC*
> *You must've been bloody well barmy*

My brother returned to the story. "There was a big bust-up and one of the boxers bit off part of his ear."

That was one mystery solved. The mystery of the missing earlobe. "The Missing Earlobe & the Marvelous Funeral." A short story by Orundhuti Roy.

The whole bed was shivering. The phone rang. My brother picked it up.

"It's Pishi. Shall I tell her to come in?"

*Pishi*—"aunt" in Bengali—was Micky's older sister. She lived in Delhi. She had come to take him to his interview.

"Ohmygod. OK. Dust the counterpane. I'm not supposed to smoke. OK, tell her to come. No, tell her to wait downstairs. I have to go to the bathroom first. Before I go . . . can you lend me some money? How much have you got here? Fine, I'll take it for now. Kapil Dev, I've already taken some from your wallet. Don't tell Pishi, OK? And next time, Orundhuti, can you get me a torch? I badly need a torch. OK, now I'm going to the bathroom."

When he came out, he had a damp stain near his crotch that was spreading fast. My brother wasn't subtle about pointing it out.

"Hey, you're pissing in your pants."

Micky looked at his crotch and giggled. Then he lay on the bed and put his legs in the air as though that would make the patch go back to where it came from.

"It'll dry."

As he left, a frail hunchback on toothpick legs, he turned and made a pair of binoculars with his hands and peered at me.

"Ta-ta then. Bye-O. Don't be good."

We sat on the hotel bed with its ash-smeared sheets, my brother and I, a pair of chumps. Utterly charmed, and relieved of all our money.

*     *     *

Incredibly, Micky got the job he interviewed for and moved to Katni, in Madhya Pradesh, to manage a grape farm. My cousin told me later that he was a genius planter and had green fingers. Micky and I would meet again, but not for some years.

My brother returned to Kerala. Before leaving, he filled in the blanks about his life for me. Soon after he graduated, he found a job on a remote tea estate in Wayanad, in the exquisite, misty, violent north of Kerala, where landlords were beheaded, where wild elephants roam free, where there is a whole dictionary of words for different kinds of rain, and people are said to measure the distance home by counting bolts of lightning. Like his father, my brother became an assistant manager, whose job was labor management. He described the ferocious rivalry between the various labor unions that were affiliated with various mainstream political parties and their splinter groups and their splinter-splinter groups. People killed each other in broad daylight, he said. He had seen the dead bodies of workers he knew well, with thirty and forty stab wounds on them. He was only twenty-two or twenty-three then and had already developed severe ulcers from the stress. Mrs. Roy, worried, would visit him regularly, driving eight and nine hours from Kottayam to his estate.

"She was so sweet," he said wonderingly. "She would bring food, and bedsheets and curtains. She did up my house. Like a normal mother. I couldn't believe it."

My innocent, guileless, trusting brother, who longed to be loved by a parent, allowed himself to be taken in. Once he was snared in the Mummy trap and his defenses were down, the new, motherly Mrs. Roy persuaded him to give up his job and return to Kottayam and help her with the school. He could not have made a bigger mistake. Once she had him under her control, the old Mrs. Roy came roaring back.

"The more she screamed at me, the more I froze. I couldn't get myself to do anything. So, everything she said about me became true. I became the useless, lazy bastard she accused me of being. I knew that. But I couldn't help it. I kept making everything worse."

It ended with her turning him out of her house. (He had to describe her house to me because I hadn't seen it.)

"It's good you left before you got thrown out, too."

He then committed the cardinal sin of joining the Malabar Coast Products. The enemy camp. By then my grandmother and G. Isaac were aware of Mrs. Roy's petition against the Travancore Christian Succession Act. The epic family feud—G. Isaac versus Mary Roy, pickle factory versus school—had begun. For the little town of Kottayam, this was high entertainment by a pair of eccentrics who had never been considered a part of Kottayam society. Sadly for LKC, things weren't going well in the pickle business. He told me that G. Isaac's wife, Soosy, felt, understandably, that he (my brother) was a threat to the prospects of her own children. As for G. Isaac—we knew from his long-ago visit to us in Ooty and the wild fights we witnessed when we lived together in Ayemenem that he was capable of exactly the same kind of cruelty as his sister. (They were both the progeny of the Imperial Entomologist after all.) My brother was humiliated and forced out of the pickle factory, too.

After that he struck out on his own, working in a travel agency, earning barely enough to make ends meet. That was the situation he was in when I saw him in Delhi. We had both, more or less, hit rock bottom. Emotionally as well as financially.

When LKC returned to Kottayam after our meeting with Micky, things changed dramatically for him. He infuriated Mrs. Roy further by marrying a young woman who worked at her school. Mrs. Roy sacked her, refused to go to their wedding, and refused to see their baby daughter, who was born on the same day as she was. When their daughter was about a year old, my brother got a job in Madras in a seafood company. He moved there with his little family. Loved and valued by his employers, he worked his way up over the years to become the man he is now. The man who, years later (together with me and G. Isaac's children), would bail out and financially support G. Isaac and his wife when they went bankrupt.

# The Exquisite Art of Failure

Micky and Mary Roy. Thinking about them as a couple makes me laugh. I cannot imagine them being married for even five minutes, let alone five years. Which God, which stars, in which heaven made that happen? He, defeated in every possible way. She, successful, admired, and loved—adored—in every possible way. His spirit so light and rascally. Hers so heavy, so unhappy. But often, in her own way, extremely naughty, too. Their paths must have crossed while she was angrily rolling her rock uphill and he was cheerfully hurtling downhill with his. Were they the way they were only because they were inherently different personalities? Were their temperaments so clear-cut, so deeply defined, that life's circumstances—failure, success, loss, love, children, addiction, and ill-health—could not alter them? Had Micky been a woman, would the world have made place for such buoyancy, such mischief, such beguiling irresponsibility? In the end, who was successful and who was not? Who can say? What was defeat and what was triumph?

\*　　　　\*　　　　\*

I was initiated into contemplating the many aspects and meanings of failure at an early age. The agent provocateur of this high-minded enterprise was none other than the grandest failure of them all— G. Isaac. Rhodes scholar turned pickle baron. It would have been my sixth or seventh birthday. We were still living in Ayemenem. There may or may not have been a cake. I don't remember. I do remember that everybody gave me lots of the usual advice about studying hard and doing well in life. Not G. Isaac. Instead, he took me to his room, his annex, which had a separate entrance of its own. As children we were rarely admitted into that hallowed space. Being taken there was a gift in itself. It looked like a bombed-out air base for broken airplanes. He was obsessed with aero-modeling. Almost every week a new kit would arrive in the post. Balsawood airplanes that had crash-landed when he tried to fly them littered the floor. (Clearly, he was frittering away the profits from the pickle factory.) He dangled a cheap bauble in front of me, a chain with a sparkly locket.

"Do you want this?"

"Yes!" My greedy, acquisitive little heart soared.

"I'll give it to you if you fail."

My six-year-old self was stumped. I remember feeling as though I had bumped into something. Something that made me stop. He made failure sound fascinating, even worth striving for. It really made me think. From then onward I began to view failure with great interest. I realized that the people I liked best, including G. Isaac himself, were considered failures. People who thought of themselves as successful and prosperous suddenly seemed like such an embarrassment, the way they strutted around and stole the light.

Meeting Micky took me back to that incident. But that birthday moment in G. Isaac's broken-airplane base was still a kindergarten class. Not long after I met Micky, G. Isaac gave me an adult master class in the exquisite art of failure.

*       *       *

I had begun to make short trips to Kottayam, a few days at a time, leaving each time just before (if I was lucky) or just after the sky fell on my head. It would have been 1986. I was twenty-six years old. My mother had won her case. The Supreme Court of India had struck down the Travancore Christian Succession Act, giving Christian women in Kerala equal rights in their father's property. Mary Roy had become a national feminist icon and G. Isaac their whipping boy. In Kerala the reaction to the judgment was muted. The Church made its displeasure known. There were still years of legal wrangling to go through before G. Isaac would physically and unceremoniously be removed from his house by the police, and the Malabar Coast Products would cease to exist. But there was no doubt that was the direction in which things were headed.

A well-known journalist from Delhi arrived in Kottayam to make a documentary about the Mary Roy case. His name was Rashid Talib. (This was in the time before Muslims began to be pushed out of public life in India. Out of politics, out of business, out of journalism, out of housing colonies and Hindu neighborhoods.) Talib wanted to interview both Mrs. Roy and G. Isaac. I happened to be at the school when he arrived.

Talib was a sophisticated, urbane person. He gave off the slightly superior air of a big-city man who had come to patronize a pair of quarrelsome small-town hicks. He had no idea what he was flying into. His interview with Mrs. Roy took place in her beautiful unplastered brick Laurie Baker home.

The first time I saw it I was floored by the simple genius of its design. It was a ring—actually a single spiral on two levels—built around a split-level circular courtyard with a tree in the middle. More than a house, it was like a deep veranda with a few enclosures sectioned off that could be used as rooms. It was almost transparent in its radical openness. It seemed to have been designed to house only a solitary, militant pilgrim soul. When it rained, it was as though you were inside the rain—you could feel it, smell it, without getting wet. Still, it looked like a real home, with books and rugs and curtains. Even a dining table. When I first saw it, the fact that she had finally made herself a home that was so complete, so *her*, and that it had no place for me, hit me with something like a physical force. My mother's home didn't include me at all. But it included Ammal, Mariamma, and Kurussammal—they were all still there. It also included her students, who would come up in batches for treats, or to chat to her. She was complete without me, and I was incomplete without her. I was wrecked. Perhaps I had no right to be.

Once Talib had set up his shot, Mrs. Roy arrived for the interview like an empress. She was dressed in a flamboyant caftan, huge beads around her neck, and a massive crimson sticker bindi that I think she wore just to provoke the Christian community. I hated sticker bindis. She was followed, as always, by a frightened minion carrying her asthma inhaler, as though it were a crown, or a scepter of some sort. She took her seat in front of the camera. For no reason that I could fathom, she decided to answer Rashid Talib's questions as though she were teaching English diction to a group of Malayali children in kindergarten.

*RejOice in the Lo-Ord Or-orlways*
*And again I say rejOice*

She spoke slowly, enunciating every word carefully, exaggerating her vowels and *z*'s, which Malayalis usually softened into *s*'s. Nothing that her interviewer could say to put her at her ease made her change the way she spoke. The interview was as good as useless. Or so I thought.

Talib's next port of call was the disputed ancestral property near the State Transport bus stop in Kottayam town, the centerpiece of the court case. He wanted to interview the Defendant, G. Isaac, CEO of the Malabar Coast Products. I went along.

The CEO was busy when we arrived, so Talib and his cameraman occupied themselves shooting cutaways of the doomed pickle factory at work. They filmed blue-aproned women stirring huge vats of salted mango and lime, packing curry powder, sticking labels. He filmed the "sleeping partner" of the company, my blind grandmother, wearing dark glasses, sitting in the front room playing Bach on her violin, the melody climbing into the vinegar-smelling air. Talib decided that the best place for the interview with the Defendant would be under the shade of a frangipani tree in the tiny pebbled front yard. In Malayalam we called it a *mittam*.

A chair was brought out. I sat in for the CEO so that Talib could finalize his frame. In a while G. Isaac came out of the dingy thatch-roofed shed he lived in, smiling, blinking at the sunlight as though he had been incarcerated in a dungeon for several years and was pleased to have been released. He had put on even more weight and was as round as his sister. He wore a white bush shirt and *mundu* (sarong) that looked precarious and liable to come undone at any moment. If I remember right, he had just transitioned from Marxism to Gandhism. He greeted Rashid Talib with good cheer.

"Tell me, sir, what can I do for you?"

Talib invited him to sit down, and after a few adjustments with the positioning of the chair—a bit to the right, to the left, slightly forward please—the interview began.

"Mr. Isaac, as a leader of the Syrian Christian community here in Kerala, could you tell us your views on the striking down of the Travancore Christian Succession Act?"

G. Isaac peered shortsightedly into the camera and thought for a while as though it were the first time he had heard of the Succession Act and the judgment. Then, still deep in thought, he picked at some ugly black scabs on his elbows. He had always enjoyed being disgusting. The camera rolled on. I could sense the interviewer's growing impatience. Finally, the Defendant began to speak, slowly, deliberately, outlining his thesis on the tiniest of tiny minorities in India, the highly educated, extremely privileged Syrian Christians of Kerala.

"You know, Mr. Talib, we Syrian Christians are a very diverse community. We have the Syrian Protestants—the Mar Thomites, the CSI, that's the Church of South India—we have the Syrian Catholics, the Jacobites, we have the Knanayas, the Canaanites, and then more recently there are the born-agains, the Church of God, the Pentecostals, who you might have come across, preaching in tongues at every street corner. We all have separate churches, we don't intermarry, we rarely agree with each other about anything. But if you question people closely, you will find that there *is* one thing they all unanimously agree about."

He paused theatrically. Rashid Talib, anticipating the high point of his film, the Red Line of disagreement between brother and sister, between women and the Church, between law and tradition—the pivot on which his documentary would turn—grew very still.

"And that is that Mr. Isaac is *not* a leader of the community."

G. Isaac began to shake with silent laughter at his own joke.

Rashid Talib had his camera switched off. I don't think that documentary ever got made.

But I had learned the lesson of a lifetime: how to make friends with defeat. My metaphoric room was full of broken planes, too. G. Isaac showed me that making friends with defeat is the very opposite of accepting it. For that alone, I forgave him his past cruelty toward us and loved him till the day he died.

# Flying Rhinos and the Banyan Tree

Around then, the remote possibility of my becoming a writer began to coalesce into something like hopeful reality. It began with rhinos. Two filmmakers who worked for a British wildlife-film production company came to see Pradip. Ashish and his partner, Joanna, had just made a documentary about the pheasant-tailed jacana, a waterbird so beautifully engineered that it could walk on floating leaves. They were in the midst of shooting another film, about the relocation of five wild rhinos who were to be flown from Kaziranga National Park in Assam and then driven in trucks to the Dudhwa National Park in Uttar Pradesh, where rhinos once roamed but had been poached into oblivion. Poachers killed them for their horns, which were ground down and used as an aphrodisiac in China.

The Indian government wanted to try to raise a new population of rhinos, a new gene pool, in the Terai grasslands of eastern Uttar Pradesh. The rhinos would fly from Bagdogra Airport to Delhi in a gigantic Russian Antonov-An 124 cargo plane. Ashish would fly with them. He wanted Pradip to film the aircraft landing in Delhi and the rhinos being unloaded. I went along to take notes for the commentary

159

to accompany the images. Ashish asked if we would travel with the rhino convoy on the ten-to-twelve-hour drive from Delhi to Dudhwa. We were more than delighted.

We tailed the convoy of trucks, each one carrying a crated greater one-horned rhinoceros through the dusty towns and villages of Uttar Pradesh. We stopped by rivers and streams to water them and feed them. And to feed the fantasies of the villagers who gathered to peep at the prehistoric creatures through gaps in the wooden slats of the crates. When we reached Dudhwa, the rhinos were released into wooden stockades, where they were held for some weeks before being set free in the open grasslands, prime rhino habitat. We returned to shoot that, too.

Pradip edited the film. I wrote the commentary. I decided to write it in the hectic, urgent spirit of a cricket commentary, with some unlikely cricketers as protagonists. The film was called *How the Rhinoceros Returned*. Ashish and Joanna had a tiny budget and couldn't afford to pay us anything more than the costs we had incurred, but it was the most fun I had had in a long time.

Things had begun to look up by then. *Massey Sahib* was ready and had been invited to the Venice Film Festival, where it won an award. Pradip now had an award-winning feature film on his CV. The timing couldn't have been better for us. Doordarshan—state television—was opening up. It had begun to broadcast films and television serials sponsored by private companies. Friends of Pradip's set up a production company and asked him to direct a period drama series set against the backdrop of the Freedom movement.

By now, Pradip and I thought of ourselves as a team. We began work immediately. It took us a while to outline the story. We started in 1921 with Gandhi's first Non-Cooperation Movement and ended in 1947 with the departure of the British, the creation of Pakistan, and the horror of Partition, in which a million people lost their lives and millions more became refugees. It was an ambitious project. We would have to scout for and shoot in multiple locations and construct massive sets. Work had to begin on several fronts simultaneously. The production company was aware that I had had a big part in outlining the story and creating the characters. They asked if I would take on the responsibility of writing all twenty-six episodes. They had one condition. Pradip would be credited as the scriptwriter. Not me. Their reason for this bizarre request was that I was completely unknown (also very young, very woman), and my name would add no weight to the project when they went looking for sponsorship. We desperately needed the work. But I refused. The project floundered for a while. No work got done. Eventually they signed me up as the scriptwriter with full, formal credit. We hired a small team of researchers to make sure every historical detail was accurate. Raghubir Yadav, the actor from *Massey Sahib*, and Alok Rai, a writer and professor of literature, worked on the dialogues in Hindi and regional dialects, Awadhi in particular.

Even though I still had my room in Malcha Marg, Pradip and I were spending all our time together. His parents allowed me to write in their basement, surrounded by their old trunks interlaced with cobwebs. My writing desk was a wooden drawing board set on the stand of an antique sewing machine with a foot pedal. For months I worked there, pedaling as I wrote, like the hidden-away family lunatic in a Victorian novel. I wrote with a pencil, on pale green paper. There were no computers then, and typing was too tedious because we were constantly changing and correcting things. Kuthujee the dachshund was my cowriter and constant companion. When he farted, which was often, I had to surface for air.

I knew I still wasn't really writing, only practicing. Learning. But I had found a vast canvas to practice on.

The series was called *Bargad*, "banyan tree." It followed the lives of four college friends through the years. Most of it was set in and around Allahabad and Lucknow. As each episode rose like smoke out of the basement, the design department started scouting for locations and securing permissions. Casting began. We had an elaborate costume and props department. It was a gigantic production. The pressure was exhilarating.

\*　　　\*　　　\*

By then I had become friends with Pradip's bridge-playing parents.

There had been a terrible tragedy in the family. Pradip's wife, my former boss, who had been living with her father, suddenly died. She had a bad fall and hemorrhaged internally. She died in her sleep.

The thing that I had dreaded more than anything else as a child—the death of my mother—had actually happened to Pradip's children. My nightmare had come true, not for me, for them. An irrational part of me felt vaguely responsible. The children were too young to comprehend the tragedy immediately, but it would scar them in ways that only a parent's death can. Fortunately, their circumstances were very different from what mine had been. They were surrounded by love and attention. Their grandparents became their doting, hands-on parents. I had grown extremely close to them and did everything I could to try to soften the blow. Having spent most of my life taking care of the younger students in Mrs. Roy's school, I was easy around children. But I was keenly aware that my experience of motherhood (Mrs. Royhood) did not make me ideal mother material. The girls and I forged a unique relationship of our own. Once we got really close, they asked if I was their new mama. To me that word conjured fear and apprehension. Punishment, asthma, hospital. Anger. I did not want to be associated with it.

I told them that they already had a mama even though she had gone away to another room, and that they should always love her. I explained that I was their father's girlfriend and that I loved them just as much as their mother had. We decided to find another, special name for me that only they could use. We settled on Noonie. It was a word from a folk song in *Massey Sahib*. One afternoon, soon after that policy decision and naming ceremony, I heard a great clanging of cutlery and crockery at the improvised dining table they ate at when they came home from school. It was a raucous orchestra, with both of them banging their spoons on their steel plates and yelling, "Noonie's Babi's girlfren! Noonie's Babi's girlfren!" Babi was what they called their father. In their minds we became a single unit—NoonieBabi. In our own minds, Pradip's and mine, we were already that.

Pradip's mother was an eccentric, good-looking woman, with porcelain-white skin, which she had passed on (with a pale brown tint) to her daughters and granddaughters. She spoke no Hindi and her English accent was so British that it made me laugh. The only Indian thing about her was that she wore saris. We came from different planets and got on together as aliens might. She was entirely preoccupied with her grand house, her little garden, her parties, clothes, beauty, and skin color. For her, people with brown and black skin were "servant class" and did not belong to her universe. I told her (truthfully) that when I was in Italy, I was often mistaken for being African. Ethiopian actually. A tiny bonsai Ethiopian. She'd say, "Yes, darling, but you have a beautiful neck." I rarely got upset with her because I couldn't take her seriously. Pradip had a testy relationship with his mother, which I found reassuring. They clashed often because she wanted him to be a civil servant like his father and taunted him for not earning a regular salary. In her own way, which was different from Mrs. Roy the Banker's way, she extracted her pound of flesh from him.

When she began to suspect that I might become more than just a transient presence in her family's lives, she took me aside for a serious conversation. She wanted me to promise never to have a baby. I had no intention of having one, nor of making any promises to her. I knew she was worried about my turning into an evil stepmother with an eye on her property. I thought that was fair enough. She knew nothing about me. Why should she trust me? But then she went a step further and asked me if I would consider applying for a government job.

"Why?"

"Because you'll have a steady salary and you can pay for the children and get medical insurance. It'll leave Pradip free to find himself. He's an artist, you know."

Indian mothers and their obsession with their sons. They'll blindside you. Come at you from every angle. Even if they criticize their sons, quarrel with them, they cannot see beyond them.

Except for my mother with her son.

*         *         *

On one of Mrs. Roy's trips to Delhi, I introduced her to Pradip's parents. She was polite but wary. There was no common ground between them. None whatsoever.

"It's all very well," she said to me later, "but you must always have your own income and a home of your own. This is their house, not yours. It never will be."

It was a wise but pretty destructive thing to say. I recognized her familiar bitterness and antipathy toward any kind of love between a man and a woman. The reason for which Dido got a bullet in her skull. I didn't need my mother's advice because my life with her (*Get out of my house! Get out of my car!*) had already taught me to live like a bird on a wire. And to prepare to prepare to be prepared.

Government jobs, medical insurance, owning houses—these were the last things on my mind.

I was on an altogether different kind of hunt.

\*       \*       \*

The *Bargad* shoot began. We had some well-known actors and a British makeup crew who specialized in prosthetics. We needed their expertise because in the story the main characters aged more than twenty years. Assisting them was none other than Golak, who had finally graduated from Architecture School and become an accomplished painter who refused to take himself seriously.

Most of our locations were in Uttar Pradesh, known in the days of the British Raj as the United Provinces. We shot in Allahabad, Lucknow, and in the countryside. We worked for months on a grinding schedule. We constructed and dressed massive sets—markets, streets, colleges, classrooms, in the style of that period. For some of the big Gandhian satyagraha scenes we had a cast of thousands.

Several months into the shoot, camped out in Allahabad, wholly immersed in our make-believe world, the money ran out. The production company we were working for more or less collapsed. The shoot stopped. It was like being shot in the knees while we were running the final lap of a marathon.

We had to return to Delhi. We did everything we could to revive it but failed. *Bargad* died a painful, long-drawn-out death. We almost died with it. We were owed money. We hadn't been paid in months. There was no chance that we ever would be. The landlady of the house where our props and costumes were stored was furious that she was no longer being paid rent. We heard that she had broken the locks on the doors and emptied the flat. She sold all our carefully created, curated—and in many cases borrowed with solemn promises of return—props and costumes, and they found their way to stalls in the secondhand market in Jama Masjid, my old haunt, where, during my vagrant, runaway days I'd bought my clothes. We rushed there and found everything—sherwanis, shawls, jodhpurs, riding boots, police uniforms, caps, hats, shoes, belts, leather saddles, old rickshaws, furniture, antique silver tea sets, valuable old crockery, ivory-handled razors, everything you need to evoke a bygone era—being hawked on the streets. Mountains of our most precious things on sale for a song. Our 1920s costumes were being flogged as cutting-edge fashion. The characters' names and scene numbers were still stitched onto the insides. It was all over. We were broke and devastated. So broke that we couldn't afford to sit down and take a breath. We didn't breathe for months. Pradip and I were fused together by sorrow. It was more intense than love.

*     *     *

A producer who knew about *Bargad* and had been watching its demise from the sidelines called me to his home. He was one of the many people who had tried to intervene, to buy the rights and help us continue with the production. He was well aware of our money crisis. He offered to employ me for what was basically a monthly pittance. "You write what you want," he said. "But everything that you write will be mine."

I replied with a pretty turn of phrase that I had learned from the villagers in Pachmarhi during the *Massey Sahib* shoot. A clever form of self-insult. (My Hindi was improving in reverse proportion to the decline of my Malayalam, which I had not spoken for years.)

*Mere maathe pe chutiya likha hai kya?* "Does it say 'asshole' on my forehead?"

He was amused and unperturbed. "You see yourself as someone special. You may or may not be. But let me give you this in writing— you will never have money. You will always need somebody like me to keep the wolf from your door."

He didn't know I'd been hanging out with those wolves since I was seventeen. But, yes, they were closing in. We needed to do something. And fast.

# In Which Annie Gives It Those Ones

Doordarshan had a new chief, a bureaucrat who was shaking up the old order. He had begun to finance small, low-budget feature films by young directors that were broadcast on the prime-time slot on Sunday night. Those films did not have the glamour and buzz of big-screen cinema, but since Doordarshan was the only television channel in the country back then, a film screened on it was guaranteed a captive audience of millions. We sought an appointment with the new chief. It lasted only a few minutes. All he said was "Bring me a script. If it's good, we'll fund it."

We played around with a few ideas, and then I asked Pradip if he would trust me to write something without overdiscussing it. He agreed.

I retreated to my room in Malcha Marg with its jeep-windshield kitchen. I emerged in three weeks.

My script was about life in the School of Architecture—the wacky anarchy of that campus, the stoned, bombed-out students and the dialect of English that we spoke—an inventive mix of Hindi and English. It was set in 1974.

We called it *In Which Annie Gives It Those Ones*. In Delhi University slang, *giving it those ones* meant "doing one's usual shit."

If *Bargad* was a solemn procession, full of pageantry and spectacle, *Annie* was the court jester, cartwheeling behind it. Annie was home for me. Finally I was swimming in familiar waters. Learning my strokes.

Annie, the protagonist, was a man—Anand Grover, Annie to his friends. He was a big, shambling fellow, repeating his fifth year for the fourth time because of the run-in he had had with the head of the department, Y. D. Billimoria, an acerbic, entertainingly rancorous Parsi gentleman who the students called Yamdoot, "messenger of the god of death."

There were no heroes in the script. Everybody was a screwball of some sort. Some overt, some covert.

Pradip was excited, but we both agreed that expecting Doordarshan to fund something as eccentric and idiosyncratic as this was unrealistic. To be safe, when we went to present the script, we took along some outlines for other more sober ideas, none of which I was enthusiastic about. We turned out to be wrong. The new chief loved *Annie*. He allocated us a tiny budget, probably a fraction of the cost of just the title sequence of a mainstream Hindi film. It was enough for us. It was exactly what those scruffy characters in the script deserved. A big budget would have ruined them. We were up and running.

As we prepared for the shoot, Pradip's apartment became our actors' workshop as well as production office. It no longer even remotely resembled the elegant apartment it had been when I first saw it. Even the dogs and children were less well-behaved than they had been and added to the mayhem. We nailed together pieces of board and plywood to make shelves and furniture; I let our two little girls loose on it with paints and paintbrushes. *Our* girls. Yes. That happened naturally, like the weather. Maybe as a reaction to

Mrs. Roy's physical coldness with me, my relationship with them was physical—we behaved more like dogs than humans. I allowed them to assault me, lick me, bite me. Sometimes we lay together in bed, a mess of entangled limbs, the room in a crescendo of screams and laughter. They would drop through the trapdoor whenever they wanted, moving freely between their grandparents' bridge-and-high-tea culture downstairs and the anarchy upstairs.

Almost without thinking about it, I gave up my room in Malcha Marg, my fear of being financially dependent, and all the other crazy caveats in my mind.

Golak rented the room I had vacated. He was, perilously, the head of hair and makeup. He inherited my fridge, but Sanjay's jeep windshield moved with me. Instead of being a kitchen, it became a low coffee table set on four fake Rubik's Cubes. Sanjay was married by now and a full-time documentary filmmaker. We met rarely, but it didn't change the nature of our friendship. Carlo had a proper, well-paid job in the Italian Cultural Center. I missed him. When I told him that I had moved in with Pradip, he laughed.

"Arundhatina, tell him to be careful."

"Why?"

"Because with you there is a risk of a man losing his sanity. He may end up walking naked up and down the railway platform with his underwear on his head. Ask me. I know."

I was a little mystified. It was not the impression I had of myself.

We shot the film in the School of Architecture over the summer vacation. Annie was played by Arjun Raina, who had worked with us on *Bargad* and had become a close friend. I had him in mind when I wrote the part. All the other parts were played by new young actors except for Yamdoot, the head of the department, who was played by Roshan Seth, famous for his role as Nehru in Richard Attenborough's

*Gandhi*. I played a student called Radha. (I fulfilled a long-standing cheap fantasy by putting her in a red sari and a felt hat in the scene where she defends her thesis before a jury.)

Pradip visualized and shot *Annie* in exactly the casual, ragged way I had imagined it. I cannot remember any arguments or disagreements between us. We were like musicians in a band, jamming to the same song. Everything went smoothly except that Golak, who had met a girl and late in his life discovered the joys of sex, arrived on set every day with a new hickey and an absent-minded air. He absentmindedly gave Annie a radical haircut, which meant we had to reshoot some scenes, find a wig for others, and adjust the lighting and camera frame in ways so that the new, post-sex haircut faded into shadow.

*     *     *

We had our first private screening at Max Mueller Bhavan—the German cultural center in Delhi. Students jammed into the hall and crowded onto the floor. I was squashed among them in the dark. Within a few minutes the audience began to yell, roar with laughter, and wolf-whistle through the film. They recognized themselves, their language, their clothes, their jokes, their silliness, and were delighted to have been deemed worthy of cinema. I was dazed. Thrilled.

Word got out somehow—even in that pre-cell-phone era—and before the screening ended, hundreds of other students had arrived at the gate demanding to see the film. Whoever was in charge at Max Mueller Bhavan that day sportingly allowed us to screen the film a second time.

*Annie* was selected for the Panorama section in the International Film Festival. At the official screening in Delhi, Derek Malcolm, film critic for *The Guardian*, who was unimpressed, turned to me and said, "You'll have to change the title, because 'giving it those ones' doesn't really mean anything in English.'" We decided to put that on our publicity flyer:

> "You'll have to change the title because 'giving it those ones' doesn't really mean anything in English."
> —*Derek Malcolm, waking up suddenly during the film*

> "Well, obviously, Mr. Malcolm, in England you don't speak English anymore."
> —*Arundhati Roy, later, wishing she had thought of it earlier*

It was never meant to be anything more than fun, fringe cinema. But when it finally showed on Doordarshan, it got an audience of millions, which would otherwise have been impossible for a film like *Annie*. Nobody could have been more shocked than Pradip and me when it won two National Awards, one of which was for Best Screenplay and the other, my favorite award of all time, "Best Film in Languages Other Than Those Specified in Schedule VIII of the Indian Constitution." A very *Annie* award.

The National Awards ceremony was a serious and glamorous occasion. Actors, actresses, directors, and technicians from the world of Bombay mainstream cinema were there, dressed up in their delectable formals. The awards were given by the President of India, a respectable, elderly, South Indian gentleman called R. Venkataraman. When I went up to get mine, one of the bureaucrats on the stage was furious at the way I was dressed (my everyday wear) and said, "From next year onwards there will be a dress code."

I said that would be fine by me, since I wouldn't be there next year. The press, crowded into the orchestra pit, mistakenly thought that the exchange had been between the president and me. They mobbed me as I stepped off the stage and asked what the president had said.

I told them that he had whispered into my ear, "Stay cool, babe!"

I noticed that the citation for my screenplay award read, "For depicting the agony of students." For a minute I thought there had been some mistake and that I had walked away with someone else's award, because agony does not make even a guest appearance in *Annie*. It wasn't a mistake, of course, just a safe citation, because, in what was at the time known as New Cinema, agony was the default theme. And rightfully so. Some wonderful, deeply political films were being made about the state of the country, violence against women, and the feudalism that we couldn't seem to shake off. But *Annie* was nothing like them. I was still nowhere close to confident enough about my skills as a writer to take on those big themes.

\*       \*       \*

The National Award was sweet revenge. Nobody would ever again suggest that I write things and give the credit to someone else. Nobody would refer to me as Pradip's assistant, secretary, or helper. Those days were over. Except for some folks in Kerala.

The media in Kerala picked up the news of Mrs. Roy's disappeared daughter who had won a big award. A journalist from a Malayalam magazine came to Delhi to see me. He seemed to have researched my life and knew all about what Micky Roy the Boxer's Boy might have called my "exploits." He asked me about growing up in Kerala among conservative Syrian Christians. I told him that my strategy had been to do exactly what I wanted to do and then let everybody know about it so that the fun went out of gossip. He asked me about my "marriage" to JC.

"How did he allow you to leave?"

I asked him if he would mind rephrasing his question. He could ask me whether JC had broken my heart, or whether I had broken his, but *allow* was not the best word to use with me.

They put a picture of me on the cover of the magazine wearing a hat with a beautiful brass hatpin. Under the photograph it said something like "Please don't ever use that word *allow* with me."

Kerala could be cool that way. Sometimes.

And sometimes not.

By speaking publicly about my life and my relationship with Pradip, I suppose I was instinctively—as Mrs. Roy once did—preparing the ground for something. I'm not sure what. Freedom, perhaps.

It was hard on her. As my mother, and as the head of a school in Kottayam, Mrs. Roy had to deal with a reality that was completely different from mine in Delhi. What I did, the way I lived, the things I said, would have affected her. But I had my own battles to fight. I couldn't tailor my life to the morality and the mores of a community that had never accepted me. Even if it had, I like to think I would have behaved in exactly the same way. Oddly, that might have been harder.

When I next met Mrs. Roy, she presented me with a curated list of barbs and insults from relatives that she had had to endure on my behalf. I had lived away for so long and with so little contact with the larger family that she had to explain who they were and what exactly the relationship was between us and the insult brigade.

X said, "Anyway, no Syrian Christian boy from a good family would marry her."

Y said, "Face it, Mary, she's just that man's mistress."

Z used the word *keep*—"At the end of the day, she's just his keep."

Charming.

# Blasphemy

Mrs. Roy wanted to stage *Jesus Christ Superstar*—the rock opera by Andrew Lloyd Webber and Tim Rice—in her school. She invited the young theater actor who played a character called Mankind in *Annie*—an irreverent, slightly cruel student who kills and eats the pet chickens Annie rears in his hostel room—to do a workshop with the students and direct the show. It's impossible to exaggerate how liberating that opera was to those of us who had grown up in that stifling, pious Christian atmosphere. I was a teenager when I first heard it. I knew every song.

The students had been rehearsing for more than two months when *Superstar* was caught up in a political storm. I wasn't in Kottayam and heard the story later from Mrs. Roy.

She said the new district collector of Kottayam—God in a small town—had written her a letter more or less ordering her to admit two students into her school. She did not reply herself, but the school office informed him that his candidates were welcome to take the entrance test like everybody else. They did, but did not do well and were not admitted.

The furious, thwarted collector suddenly realized he had certain godly duties. He banned the performance of *Jesus Christ Superstar* in Kottayam, saying it would lead to a law-and-order problem because it was blasphemous and offensive to "Christian sentiment." He accused Mrs. Roy of being a person "who elevates her contempt for humanity and sells it to the public in so-called art-form" and of "the perpetuation of hatred in innocent minds." He made it sound as though she had written the opera herself.

The play was only hours away from opening, the children were already in costume, the whole school was vibrating with excitement, when adult wickedness throttled it.

The students were devastated. All of them, even the junior school babies, had parts in the opera. They had already shot a video in which the school campus itself was the stage. Mrs. Roy's wardrobe had been plundered for costumes. The Pharisees wore her more extravagant caftans, the Apostles her more modest ones. The crowds followed Jesus around, winding their way through their Laurie Baker classrooms, waving palm fronds and singing, "Hey, JC! JC! Won't you fight for me?" Tiny lisping actors who played bit parts—the Jerusalem press for example—rolled out from under coconut trees and harangued Jesus all the way down the hairpin bend to the nursery shed:

> *Tell me, Christ, how you feel tonight*
> *Do you plan to put up a fight?*
> *Do you feel that you've had the breaks?*
> *What would you say were your big mistakes?*

The students who played Jesus, Judas, Herod, and Mary Magdalene were remarkable singers. The orchestra and choir were outstanding. They were all sandbagged by a malicious bureaucrat's petty ego.

\*　　　\*　　　\*

The district collector knew exactly what kind of sea he was swimming in. The year was 1990. The beginning of decades of politics driven by hokey outrage and contrived grievance. The world was in flux. The Berlin Wall had fallen. The Soviet Union would soon cease to exist. Not just India, but the whole of the Asian subcontinent had been in turmoil for a while. It was a time when "religious sentiment" was the wind in everybody's sails.

The U.S.-backed mujahideen were ruling Afghanistan. Pakistan had been radicalized by General Zia and the CIA, Kashmir's struggle for self-determination had turned into an overtly Islamist armed conflict. "Secular" India had lost its moorings. Two years earlier, in deference to "Muslim sentiment," the Congress government had banned Salman Rushdie's novel *The Satanic Verses* and reversed a progressive Supreme Court judgment that gave divorced Muslim women the right to alimony. Then, in deference to "Hindu sentiment," it had ordered the opening of the locks on the Babri Masjid, a disputed sixteenth-century mosque that Hindus claimed had been built over the birthplace of Lord Ram. By 1990, just when the Kottayam collector was trying to stir up his risible little "Christian sentiment" storm in Kottayam, Lal Krishna Advani, mandarin of the far-right Hindu nationalist Bharatiya Janata Party (BJP), was leading a frenzied procession across the country, demanding that the Babri Masjid be demolished and a Hindu temple built in its place. He called it a Rath Yatra, "chariot pilgrimage." His chariot was an air-conditioned Toyota minitruck with the symbol of his party, a rickety plywood lotus, tacked onto the front. There was nothing rickety or tacky about the wild delirium, the riots, the retaliatory bomb attacks and the thousands of dead that the Rath Yatra left in its wake.

To bolster his case against *Jesus Christ Superstar*, the district collector got some Syrian Christian bishops and priests to back him. Three thousand people signed a petition against the play. It said that Mary Magdalene's song "I Don't Know How to Love Him" implied a sexual relationship between her and Jesus. There were marches and threats and all the hysteria that spirals out of control in contrived situations such as these. There were calls to "shackle the wild elephant" (Mrs. Roy) and threats that if she persisted with the performance, blood would flow. Underpinning the fabricated rage of this particular set of people was also their latent wrath about the striking down of the Travancore Christian Succession Act and their amorphous hostility toward a woman who would not take orders.

Mrs. Roy refused to back down and went to court. How, she asked, could a play performed within the grounds of the school, a play that had been rehearsed for months with no complaints from anyone, a play that had been performed to Christian audiences all over the world, suddenly become blasphemous and a law-and-order problem in Kottayam? Who was the collector to decide what was and wasn't blasphemous? She had a videotape to prove that nobody had been upset while the dress rehearsal of the play was performed. There had been no complaints from parents, no unrest in the town.

A posse of policemen raided the school campus to confiscate the video cassette—evidence that could prove the collector, who only had the right to ban something if he anticipated a law-and-order problem, was talking nonsense. A friendly person in the collector's office gave Mrs. Roy prior warning about the raid, so the tape was spirited out of the school for safekeeping. Mrs. Roy got herself anticipatory bail. She framed the bail order and hung it up on her office wall. While the police searched her house and school, she sat at her table and had her nails clipped. The tape they found and triumphantly confiscated turned out to be blank.

Nevertheless, the collector won the day. The play could not be performed. The students were inconsolable. It took years for the case to make its way to the Supreme Court. Once again, the court did the right thing by her. Once again, Mrs. Roy got a judgment in her favor. *Jesus Christ Superstar* was finally staged in the school by a new generation of students.

There was no law-and-order problem.

Sad though it was, Kottayam's collector-induced religious tantrum had a happier ending than the macro versions of it that were convulsing India. The occult, bloodthirsty spirit uncorked by Advani and his Rath Yatra could not be returned to its bottle. It would go on to change India beyond recognition.

That Kottayam collector, even though he was Christian, resigned from the civil service and joined the BJP. He seemed to find no insult to Christian sentiment in the church burning, missionary murdering, and Jesus-statue smashing by vigilantes on the Hindu far right, who were allowed to operate with complete impunity once the BJP displaced the Congress and came to power.

I often think of sending him a copy of Giorgio Bassani's *The Garden of the Finzi-Continis*. So that he can read about what happened to a family of elite Jews in the town of Ferrara in Italy who thought their deliverance lay in joining the Nazi Party.

# "You Are Not Showing India in a Proper Light"

I could not be in Kottayam while my mother faced down the collector and his band of religious bigots because Pradip and I were in pre-production for our next film. *Electric Moon* was funded by Channel Four, the British television company.

The film was about the passing of an era, the death of an old elite and the rise of a new one. A somewhat (though not entirely) spurious Indian royal family, two brothers and a sister, all elderly, run a jungle lodge—the Machan—on the edge of a national park, selling clichés to white tourists who have come to India in search of tigers, temples, maharajas, and a protected ringside view of exotic oriental squalor. The oldest of the siblings, Raja Ran Bikram Singh—Bubbles—is marketed to the guests as a gruff naturalist, ace tracker, wild man, prince. He's a hit with the lady tourists.

The park, pillaged by poachers and wood smugglers, has more or less run out of animals, so a part of the Machan's service involves carefully placed mechanical animals for tourists to view, and playing recordings of animal and bird calls during their guests' elephant safaris, which make the park appear to be teeming with unseen wildlife.

Fortified by their blue blood and British accents, the hotelier family are accustomed to breaking rules, getting their way, and treating the national park as though it were their personal backyard. Their whole enterprise runs aground when a new park director is appointed. He is a middle-class, Hindi-speaking bureaucrat, clever, corrupt (in cahoots with the wood mafia), ruthless, and hostile to the family's brazen sense of entitlement. He ties them up in red tape, withholds permission for their guests to enter the national park, and gradually makes it impossible for the Machan to function.

*Electric Moon* is a somewhat cruel satire. I wrote it with my head, not my heart. I did not love it as I loved *Annie*. There was nothing lovable about it. Not a single truly likable character. Nobody soliciting the affections of the audience. A mistake, perhaps.

Since it qualified as a "foreign production," we had to get the script approved by several government departments before being given permission to start filming. Each bureaucrat insisted on us dropping a piece of dialogue, or even a whole scene, because it "does not show India in a proper light." I had heard the phrase so often during the run-up to the shoot that it made me want to bark or chirrup or bray or moo.

The bureaucrats would bring the hammer down on the silliest, most lighthearted things. For example, they objected to a scene in which a somewhat irreverent French tourist dips his samosa in bright green coriander chutney, smiles at the other guest at the table, and says, in French-accented English, "You know, in Eendia, every day my shit is a different color."

That was just one of several objections.

We agreed to the cuts and then, assuming that nobody would cross-check, shot most of them. We were banking on our utter irrelevance.

To shoot *Electric Moon*, we returned to Pachmarhi, where we shot *Massey Sahib*. It was my job to design the jungle lodge and Golak's to supervise the construction.

The delays began early. Trucks transporting our building material were held up in Bhopal for days because L. K. Advani's Rath Yatra was passing through, and the city had virtually been sealed. To watch that carnival of unconcealed hatred snake through the streets was to be put on notice. It was clear that the Rath Yatra was a long, lit fuse. The detonation would come two years later, on December 6, 1992, when a violent mob of Hindu vigilantes fell upon the Babri Masjid and literally hammered it into dust.

How was I to explain to querulous British and American crew members that my trucks were held up and the shooting schedule delayed due to the onset of fascism?

The shoot itself, which lasted several weeks, was among the most unpleasant experiences of my life. The kindest explanation for what happened is that it was a clash of work cultures. The unkindest is that it was barefaced racism. Our camera crew as well as our sound and makeup crews were from the UK. We had actors from the United States, the UK, and France. Unlike in the case of the rash of Raj films and series that had been made over the last few years—*Gandhi, A Passage to India, The Jewel in the Crown, The Far Pavilions*—where the directors, producers, and senior crew members were white, and the more junior people were Indian, in *Electric Moon* it was the other way around. We were the bosses. That didn't go down well. Granted, it wasn't an easy shoot. Given our remote location, logistics were a nightmare. We were ambushed with new problems almost every hour. We did not have the budget—the luxury hotel rooms, great catering, or frequent off days—to lubricate the bone-on-bone clashes that erupted with sickening regularity. Eventually, civilization broke down in the jungle. The savage spirit of the script spilled off the pages and came to haunt us on the sets. The white crew turned into the truculent jungle-lodge guests, unhappy with the service they were receiving. We became the irreverent staff, doing what we had to, but mocking them behind their backs. Somehow, we held it together and finished filming.

This time, unlike in *Annie,* there was a difference between how Pradip visualized the film and how I imagined it. His approach, with the actors as well as the staging, was gentle, realistic, poker-faced. He softened the savagery and the occasional vulgarity of the script. I thought it ought to be enhanced, lifted half an inch off the floor. I wanted it to have a slightly surreal, merciless, metallic quality.

*Electric Moon* opened in art-house cinemas in London and New York to some good reviews. A piece in *The Guardian* compared Pradip and me to Powell and Pressburger, the famous writer-director-producer team. We staged mock battles in which we both insisted we were Powell. Or Pressburger. We were so good that some of our friends actually fell for it and tried to pacify us.

Despite the reviews the film did not do well at all and was gone from the theaters within days. In India, apart from a few private screenings, it was not shown anywhere. Mrs. Roy never saw it. As G. Isaac's niece, trained in the art of failure, I was not devastated by what could only be described as a box-office flop. Our commissioning editor at Channel Four was happy with the film though and willing to fund another.

But the *Electric Moon* experience had unsettled me. To try to understand why the shoot had gone so wrong, I began to write an account of it. For myself. Pradip and I had bought our first computer. My furry cowriter Kuthujee had died just before the shoot, and his grumpy, longtime lady friend, Bowjee, had died during the shoot in Pachmarhi. We had two new puppies, Kuttappen Patti and Chhutkoo Mal, but they were too young to be cowriters. They had attention spans of under three seconds. So this time I wrote alone, with no dog assist.

It was a long essay that I called "In a Proper Light."

A printed copy was lying on our jeep-windshield coffee table when the editor of *Sunday*, a well-known weekly magazine, came visiting. We didn't know him. He had dropped by to pick up a friend of ours, to take her out to lunch. Our home was still in chaos, like a hostel, with people sleeping or working on every available surface. As I think back, given my hostel-home upbringing in Kottayam, that's probably the only way I knew how to live. I had turned a posh address into a squat.

While the editor waited for my friend to get ready, he began to read "In a Proper Light." When he finished, he looked up and asked, "Who's written this?"

I put my hand up, like a student in a classroom, not sure what to expect. He asked if he could publish it. He promised not to cut or edit it without my consent. And so, as casually as that, my first piece of prose was published. (In a real, not in-house, magazine.) It was 1992. I was thirty-two years old.

The editor was delighted with the reception the essay received. He called to say he would consider publishing anything that I wrote.

# The Band Breaks Up

The girls were in a boarding school in Dehradun, a few hours' drive from Delhi. The school was chosen by their grandmother, who was a Swiss finishing school all of her own. We didn't have much say in the choice because Pradip's parents were paying the fees (there was no way we could afford to) as well as taking care of the girls when we were away on shoots. The dual authority regime with its dual value system—elite Foreign Service downstairs, vagrant wanderer upstairs—might have been a little confusing for them. Although I loved them dearly, I always deferred to Pradip's mother when it came to the girls because I did not feel I had the right to do otherwise. I was just a leaf that had blown in through the window on a chance breeze. So, there were no confrontations between her and me.

Pradip and I would drive up to Dehradun in his parents' car to visit the girls, although less often than we should have, because of our film schedules. Our parenting was flawed and less responsible than it ought to have been. (In my defense, I only had Micky and Mary as role models.) The last two hours of the drive to Dehradun took us through a national park. I have a vivid memory of one of those journeys. It was a clear, beautiful night. We passed a buffalo cart with a lantern tied behind it for a taillight. The driver of the cart was lying on his back, singing to the stars, confident that his buffalo would take him home. I remember feeling jealous of him. I remember thinking that no matter how long and hard we fought, in India no woman of any religion, class, caste, or creed would ever feel safe enough to sing to the stars on a lonely highway while her buffalo took her home.

*     *     *

After the experience of shooting *Electric Moon*, I was reluctant to work on another film. I longed to work alone. To be in complete control of my writing. I did not want to confer with producers and actors, not even with my beloved lover-director. I needed to cut out the noise and for once in my life stop running. I was tired of collaborative thinking. I wanted to think alone. I wanted to know what I thought about when I thought alone. That desire came from nowhere, and it was desperate. Like hunger. Like sleep. Like sex. The explanation for this could be a crude one. My writer's fee from Channel Four was paid to me in pounds. It translated into a lot of money in rupees. I had bought myself time. For once in my life, I could sit down. And I did.

Everything I had run away from came running back to me. Ayemenem and all its creatures crowded into my brain. The Cosmopolitans lined up for an identification parade. Mrs. Roy loomed over them all. The friends with whom I had fished and played on the banks of the river reappeared and challenged me to swim with them. The Meenachil, my slow green river with all her undercurrents, metaphoric as well as literal, appeared and said, "Can you tell me what the fish are thinking? Or explain what the moon is doing floating around at night when she really should be in the sky? Can you describe the sound of the boatmen's oars?" And I said, "Yes. Without a doubt, I can. I can see you so clearly, I can feel you so near me, it's as though I never went away." My cold moth asked if she could be in the book. I told her she most certainly could.

Like a seed that had been lying in a drawer for years and had suddenly landed in fertile soil, I felt the first stirrings of germination. There was nothing gentle about it. Within the constricted confines of my seed casing, I could feel a gale-force wind rising.

I knew then that I had hunted down my language-animal. I had disemboweled it and drunk its inky blood. I knew that if I could describe my river, if I could describe the rain, if I could describe feeling in a way that you could see it, smell it, touch it, then I would consider myself a writer. My first Act of Literature would be a private pact between me and the Meenachil River. I wanted to try to write the opposite of a screenplay. A stubbornly visual but unfilmable book. Even if such a thing did not exist, I wanted to try.

Before I did that, I had to tell Pradip. He and I were a band. How could I suddenly say that I didn't want to play anymore? But I had to. Because I *couldn't* play anymore. Those Ayemenem folks wouldn't let me. I didn't have a choice. When I told him, he was upset, almost angry. Naturally. He persuaded me that we needed to do at least one more film before I stepped off the cliff. For practical reasons (money) if nothing else. He was right. If our films were fringe of fringe, it followed that a book, a novel, would be virtually undetectable, non-existent. It wouldn't even be downshifting, we would be in free fall.

Half-heartedly I wrote the outline for another screenplay and sent it to Channel Four. I cannot even remember what it was about. They commissioned it and paid me a small advance. Ironically it was called seed money. Once the script was ready and we had a budget, they would commit to funding the film. But every time I sat down to write, I found myself writing something else, and not what I had been paid to write. It was hopeless.

*       *       *

During that confusing time, Pradip's father fell ill. He was initially diagnosed with tuberculosis, but it turned out to be leukemia. He was in his early eighties. Pradip dropped everything to look after him. Toward the end we took turns to stay overnight with him at the hospital. Two nights before he died, Pradip's father called me to his bedside.

"I want to see your names written in the stars."

I don't know why he said that. It was so unlike him. He was such a quiet, dignified man. I was overcome. I kissed his cold forehead and went back to my attendant's bed. I knew his time was near. The girls were twelve and sixteen years old. He was the one who had coddled and insulated them from the trauma of their mother's death. They were more attached to him than anyone else. For them it would be like the death of another parent.

Two days later Pradip's father passed peacefully. Pradip's mother, who was a few years older than her husband, came apart. As their wedding anniversary, which fell on New Year's Eve, approached, she went into a deep depression. She couldn't stop crying. That day had been celebrated in her home for more than fifty years. (On my calendar it was marked as the day of the abortion without anesthesia, the Pipariya bus-stop mobbing, and the fake police-kidnap drama.) We thought it would cheer Pradip's mother up if we offered to get married on New Year's Eve and continue the tradition. It was a spur-of-the-moment decision. Shortsighted on my part. Why risk ruining a beautiful relationship with marriage? But we did.

This time it wasn't a Japanese-parcel / Jesus Christ affair. We had a proper, legally registered marriage. Mrs. Roy came. So did my brother and his wife, along with their sparkling three-year-old daughter. LKC had moved from Madras and was vice president of a Kochi-based seafood company. He and Mrs. Roy had arrived at a truce. His wife, whom Mrs. Roy had dismissed when she married LKC, had returned to working in the school. Ironically, her name was Mary, too. So, Lalith Roy was sandwiched between Mary Roy Sr. and Mary Roy Jr. If that wasn't enough, his daughter, born on the same day as my mother, was called Maria Roy. I could see that he was doing everything in his power to be the father he never had. His eyes, when they were on Maria, lit up with joy and wonder.

At the wedding, Mrs. Roy was extremely nice to the girls, but in private she was critical of me. She thought that I was bringing them up badly. She said they were spoiled and willful and would not find good husbands. It was my responsibility, she said, to find them good husbands. My jaw dropped, bounced on the floor, climbed through the window, and went somersaulting down the street.

Nobody took our wedding seriously. Not the bride and groom. Not our girls. Not the guests.

We had a small party downstairs in Pradip's mother's home. She cheered up a little. Sanjay was away on a shoot but wrote Pradip a letter in Hindi, making himself out to be the father of the bride. *Pradipji sambhalke rakhna isko. Bade mushkil se paal pos ke bada kiya maine.* . . . "Look after her, Pradip. I've brought her up with great difficulty. . . ."

Utter sweetness.

In the pages that follow it might be confusing for readers who are searching for conventional declarations of love, coupledom, marriage, divorce, separation, and love affairs to understand how I lived (live) my life. I often don't understand it myself. I have stopped trying. The truth is that from the time I met Sanjay and Pradip, I have loved them both. In very different ways. We have hurt one another terribly and made up again. We have protected one another, backed one another, worked with one another. We have been one another's siblings, parents, children, friends, refuge—depending on who needs what and when. We're tangled up and nothing can untangle us.

# "The Great Indian Rape Trick"

I was writing the Thing I Was Not Supposed to Be Writing, the thing I pretended not to be writing, when we were invited to a screening of what was being billed as a sensational new film.

*Bandit Queen*, based on the life of the legendary bandit Phoolan Devi, was a Channel Four production. The commissioning editor and the producer had both worked with us on *Electric Moon* and were our friends. I was a little apprehensive about watching the film because of the disturbing commentary around it. Though she had not explicitly said so herself, the myth around Phoolan Devi was that she had been gang-raped by privileged-caste men from a rival gang and she had taken revenge by shooting twenty-two of them. The idea of watching a film centered around rape worried me.

Phoolan Devi had recently been released from prison. Before she surrendered in 1983 (the surrender I had read about when I was in Italy), nobody outside the Chambal ravines had ever seen her or even knew what she looked like. She had a price on her head, and the police had hunted for her, unsuccessfully, for years. She was an elusive myth. A mystery. And now, in 1994, after serving a ten-year sentence, she was a movie. Someone else's idea of herself. The real woman, who was still young, didn't seem to matter much to anyone.

One of India's best-known writers, who considered himself an authority on women and sex, publicly said that he had fantasized about her sexually and was greatly disappointed when he finally set eyes on her after she surrendered, because she was, as he put it, so ugly. I fantasized about barging into his house with a mirror and asking him to take a look at himself.

In an interview, the director of *Bandit Queen* described how he had locked himself in a room and imagined himself being raped. Rape, he informed us, was not just the subjugation of the body but also the subjugation of the soul. It was pretty clear what the film's focus was going to be. At the screening I was invited to, he introduced the film saying, "I had a choice between truth and beauty, and I chose truth because truth is pure." I realized that I was in the presence of unalloyed genius. Sure enough, the film opened with a no-caveats claim: "This is a true story."

Over two hours it lingered vicariously on scenes of Phoolan Devi being explicitly and serially raped in various ways by various men until we almost forget who Phoolan Devi really was. It managed to turn India's most famous bandit into history's most famous victim of rape.

I wasn't surprised to see that Phoolan Devi had not been invited to the screening. I asked why and was told (confidentially) that she was too troublesome. She was living in a rented apartment only a few minutes' walk from the auditorium we had all been invited to, in her absence, to watch her being raped and re-raped and re-re-raped, while the men who made the film presented themselves as India's leading feminists.

I returned home after the screening so furious I could not sit still. The taproot of my anger reached all the way back to Kurussammal's and my Star Theatre movie-watching days in Kottayam.

The next morning's papers carried statements by Phoolan Devi in which she vociferously objected to the film and said she felt she was being raped all over again. She could easily have done the opposite—turned into a pet and drunk in the adulation. But she didn't. The Beautiful People who loved the film denounced the real Phoolan and accused her of blackmailing the filmmakers. "We mustn't forget," they whispered to one another, "she's a dacoit [bandit] after all. She's only doing it for money." Looming over everything, unspoken, was of course the fact that she was Dalit. Untouchable. Subhuman. Good for art and theory. Bad in reality. How dare she have an opinion about her own life?

I decided to go to see Phoolan Devi. I recognized something of Mrs. Roy in myself that day.

She was camped out like a dacoit, living the ravine life in an airy South Delhi apartment, paid for, I think, by a French publisher who had signed her up for a "my life as told to" type of autobiography. Hangers-on and sullen-looking men were everywhere. She was the boss of them all. Small, slight, mercurial, quick to smile, but hot-tempered, alert, and suspicious of everybody, including her old mother and new husband. She had a food taster to make sure she wasn't being poisoned. The only life she had known was in the Chambal ravines and then in prison. She was completely illiterate and was suddenly having to deal with ravines of a different kind, and different kinds of dacoits, too. People as well as the press were feeding off her and disrespecting her simultaneously. What impressed me most about her was her self-assurance. She was not intimidated by anybody, not playing for sympathy. She listened with her eyes and functioned entirely on instinct. When I spoke to her about the film, she unleashed a broadside of fabulous invective. (I wished Golak had been there to listen and learn.) She was incensed by reports of the cheering and clapping at screenings during the rape scenes. Who wouldn't be? I was, too.

But I was equally disgusted by the pretend compassion of another class of people.

It was then that it became clear to me that no one should have the right to restage the rape of a living woman without her consent. I also realized that it wasn't only the explicit and endless rapes in the film that she was concerned about. She was out on parole. She was still facing trial for the murder of twenty-two privileged-caste Thakur men who were said to have gang-raped her. The film in its wisdom (since "truth is pure") had valorized her as an avenging angel of death, an icon of Rape 'n' Retribution, and had clearly pronounced her guilty. I felt that it enhanced the danger to her life, legally as well as otherwise.

I knew that if I wrote what I wanted to write, it would be the end of our next film with Channel Four. But I found it impossible to keep quiet. "The Great Indian Rape Trick," Parts I & II, were published in *Sunday*. The second essay ended with these words:

> *Bandit Queen* the film seriously jeopardizes Phoolan Devi's life. It passes judgments that ought to be passed in Courts of Law. Not in Cinema Halls. The threads that connect Truth to Half-Truths to Lies could very quickly tighten into a noose around Phoolan Devi's neck. Or put a bullet through her head. Or a knife in her back.
>
> While We-the-Audience peep saucer-eyed out of our little lives. Not remotely aware of the fact that our superficial sympathy, our ignorance of the facts and our intellectual sloth could grease her way to the gallows.
>
> We makes me sick.

With that, obviously, I made myself a whole lot of enemies.

Phoolan Devi went to court to try to stop the film. She was represented by Indira Jaising, the lawyer who represented Mrs. Roy in the

Supreme Court in her case against the Travancore Christian Succession Act. The court took its time, as courts in India do. Meanwhile the film had begun showing to packed houses, which made Phoolan Devi's case somewhat futile. Except for the hope that a judgment in her favor would set a legal precedent for other women. But Phoolan Devi wasn't exactly into social service. She eventually agreed to an out-of-court settlement, which immediately subjected her to more contempt and hostility. (*See? It was always about extortion.*) Few in those days were willing to concede that the point of the whole debate—legal, ethical, moral—was consent. *Her* consent. It was not about free speech. It was not about her character. It was not about whether she was or was not an upright, moral woman in the eyes of society. It was not about whether explicit depictions of rape were right or wrong. It was about consent.

Two years after *Bandit Queen* was released, Phoolan Devi joined a political party and became a member of Parliament. Five years after that, in 2001 she was shot dead outside her home in Delhi. It would be irresponsible to blame the film for her death. But it would be dishonest to pretend that it did not enhance the threat to her life in a society that has a long memory for retribution and caste honor.

The "Rape Trick" essays did indeed mark the end of Pradip's and my relationship with our commissioning editor at Channel Four. He reacted like a master whose servant had suddenly jumped up and bitten him. (Which, in a way, was true.) He denounced me publicly with a barrage of invective that made me laugh. He said I wrote like an "incontinent drunk trying to piss in a small pot." It didn't strike him that it wasn't a problem that women tend to have, even if they're drunk.

I had to submit the script he had commissioned me to write or return the advance I had been paid. I wrote it up as a comedy based on the *Bandit Queen* debate. I wish I still had a copy. One of the characters was an ex-nun who wore a polka-dot habit and ran a sewing center for raped Christian women. She was the prototype for the character who would come to be called Baby Kochamma in *The God of Small Things*. I myself appeared in the script as a bitter, twisted feminist of the kind my ex-friend the commissioning editor had made me out to be. He was in it, too, as part of the Holy Feminist Trinity, who were all men. There was also a minor character who had reveries of a motorcyclist who did a circus act inside her spit bubble.

Pradip broke down the script and made a detailed, poker-faced budget for it. Nun's habit, sewing machines, motorcycle-in-spit bubble, twisted feminist's costumes . . . all of it. We submitted the script and budget to Channel Four and received a formal rejection saying that the script made no sense and the characters were not properly drawn—"There is no rationale at all for why the characters do what we do."

I will never know whether that was a typo, a deliberate error, or a Freudian slip.

At this point, the Kottayam collector's comment characterizing Mrs. Roy as a person "who elevates her contempt for humanity and sells it to the public in so-called art-form" applied more to me than to my mother.

# The God of Small Things

The important thing was that we received a check as full and final payment for the script. It bought me some more time. I was now free to work on the Thing I Was Not Supposed to Be Writing.

The more I wrote, the more it puzzled me. It behaved as though it had a volition of its own. There was a rhythm to it, a sort of backbeat, a formal architecture, that I could sense, but for a long time couldn't put my finger on. I had to trust it. Sometimes it felt as though it were writing itself, and that I just happened to be around.

I was puzzled because I realized that I wasn't writing it from beginning to end. I felt as though I were sculpting smoke. Generating it, then organizing and disciplining it.

*The God of Small Things* first came to me as an image: two young children, Rahel and Estha, a pair of twins, their faces pressed up against the window of a sky-blue Plymouth with the sun in its tail fins, advertising pickles on its roof. Rahel wears her hair on top of her head like a little fountain. She has a toy watch with the time painted onto it. It's always ten to two. Estha combs his hair into an Elvis Presley puff and wears beige and pointy shoes. They are stuck at a railway level crossing on the road to Kochi. Swarming around them is a communist workers' procession in which they spot Velutha, a man they know and love.

I had been writing for more than a year. The twins had been stuck at that level crossing for a very long time. I had fallen to wondering when it would open and let the Plymouth through and how old I'd be by then.

It was a strange time for Pradip and me. I was single-mindedly constructing and furnishing my secret world. Pradip was a little lost, a little brokenhearted about his father, and unsure of what to do with himself.

It could have been displaced sorrow (which men are good at), but as the girls grew older, Pradip became impatient and bad-tempered with them. Since I had no experience of father-daughter relationships, I had no idea what to make of this. Perhaps because of my memories of Mrs. Roy, the shouting ripped through me. (Although Pradip was nowhere close to her level.) I often found myself caught in the middle, trying to insulate the girls even if I thought they were wrong and he was right. When they wanted something, they would come to me rather than go to him. I was increasingly pushed into playing the part of the stereotypical, moderate mother figure protecting children from their angry father. I didn't want to be Mrs. Roy, but this made me uncomfortable, too. Sometimes I felt I had commandeered more than my fair share of Pradip's love, and that it would be better if I lived separately. But I realized that would only cause more pain, not less. I knew that under all the thorns and wounding laceration, there was, between all of us, real love.

Pradip decided to use his *Electric Moon* money to buy a small piece of land on the edge of the forest, right next to a little village outside Pachmarhi (where we had shot both *Massey Sahib* and *Electric Moon*), and build a house. I was a little angular about that. I wondered how the sudden arrival of city folks who had decided to live in their midst would affect the villagers. Also, I was uncomfortable about second homes. But it wasn't up to me to agree or disagree. I had sabotaged our film career. I wasn't about to sabotage this, too. I thought it would be good for him to be away for a while. To reduce the friction at home. While I wrote, Pradip and Golak spent more than a year building a beautiful stone-and-wood house with a deep veranda that looked straight out into the jungle. It was the beginning of Pradip's long love affair with trees and forests. This turned out to be his real calling. He would go on to become one of India's foremost desert ecologists and tree scholars. Without meaning to, by not writing another screenplay I did him a real favor. Both band members lifted their game.

When he was home, Pradip and I had a deal. I could lock the door of our bedroom, where I had a small writing desk, for four hours a day and work. And we would not talk about what I was doing until it was done. As far as his mother and the girls were concerned, one of us needed to be around. Usually, it was me.

I continued to visit Mrs. Roy every few months. Her asthma was still terrible. Her school was doing better than ever. The extraordinary thing about it was that financially it was entirely self-sufficient. On top of all her other talents, Mrs. Roy had a head for business. Like a local mafia don, she had begun to buy up the plots around her campus. (Making people offers they couldn't refuse.) One recalcitrant man, an out-of-work goldsmith, refused to sell, even though his little house was surrounded by school buildings and the noise of children. Whenever he got upset, he would come out and fire his air gun into the sky. Mrs. Roy made a pig and cattle shed on the border between her land and his. The snorting, the smell, and the shit drove him away.

On the new pieces of land she acquired, she built an auditorium, a swimming pool, small apartments for visiting teachers, and dormitories for senior girls.

Mrs. Roy was convinced that I was doing nothing of any consequence and was frittering away my life. When I told her that I was trying to write a book, she said, "Well then, you jolly well sit down and write it." She loved saying "jolly well." She never stopped treating me like someone who needed to be disciplined and ordered around. All her life she remained puzzled about how I knew anything other than what she had taught me. If I said something that surprised her, she'd say, "How do you know that? Who taught you?" It made me laugh out loud. Which, depending on her mood, would make her smile, or scowl.

*     *     *

Micky Roy meanwhile had lost his job and reappeared in Delhi. I hadn't seen him for about eight years.

He was living with his sister, my aunt. I had begun to contribute what I could toward his expenses. My aunt was a big-eyed, birdlike lady with a naughty sense of humor. She had turned to Christianity and lived with a community of people who helped her to keep an eye on Micky Roy. He had become Christian, too, like his father and his grandfather before him, but was only as serious about it as he was about anything else. Which is to say, not at all. He called them all "Hallelujah People." They didn't seem to mind. They laughed at him and seemed extremely fond of him.

Every now and then Micky hit me with various moneymaking schemes. One of the more memorable ones:

"I say, Orundhuti, I hear you are a famous actress now."

"Not really . . . "

"People say you're a beautiful girl, but I can't see you. I have cataract in both my eyes and I need surgery. But I have no money."

Like a fool, I fell for it and gave him the money. He drank himself into a stupor. Once he recovered, I made him an appointment for the surgery and gave the money directly to the surgeon.

Once Micky's eyes were fixed, he came up with Scheme Number Two. This one I didn't fall for.

The Boxer's Boy was a huge cricket fan, but not a patriotic one. The legendary Australian batsman Donald Bradman, who was still alive at the time, was his god. Micky's love for the Australian cricket team was his true religion. He might have been jailed for that sort of antinationalism in the India of today. I doubt he'd have backed off. He would probably have hobbled into his prison cell and asked his jailer to stop being *muggrah* and arrange for a drink and a TV so that both of them could watch the match.

India and Australia were playing a Test series when he came to see me next.

"I say, Orundhuti, I badly need a TV. I need to watch the match."

"Doesn't Pishi have a TV?"

"Those Hallelujah People . . . they just watch rubbish. Pity poor me sitting there with them and knowing I could just press a button and the match will come on. But they won't let me. I need a TV of my own."

I felt his pain. Pradip and I were lovers of sport, too.

"OK, I'll get you one."

"If you're giving me one, give it now. The match is now. Just give me the money now. I'll go and buy it now."

"No. No money for you, Mr. Micky Roy."

With Pradip's permission I unplugged our TV and put Micky into a taxi with it. He went off happily, the remote control sticking out of his shirt pocket like a rectangular nipple. I was pretty sure he wouldn't trade it in for a bottle. He loved cricket and whiskey in equal measure.

\*　　　\*　　　\*

One morning without prior notice, the railway level crossing opened and the sky-blue Plymouth with the sun in its tail fins sailed through. The architecture of the novel I was writing revealed itself to me. I actually drew it on the back of an envelope. Once I knew what I was doing, I wrote quickly. I developed the habit of taking deep, dreamy catnaps after writing a few paragraphs. After several hundred catnaps, over several hundred days, suddenly one ordinary summer morning that had nothing beyond the blazing heat to recommend itself, the story was told, the book was written. It had taken me more than four years.

With the last of my money, I bought a printer. I printed the manuscript, and without pausing to think about it for even a moment, I printed the title: *The God of Small Things*. Pradip and I went out for a coffee. I sat across the table from him and recited the first few paragraphs.

> May in Ayemenem is a hot, brooding month. The days are long and humid. The river shrinks and black crows gorge on bright mangoes in the still, dustgreen trees. . . .

I knew the whole book by heart.
"Finished?"
"Yes."
I gave him a spiral-bound copy to read. To exact revenge for my having shut him out of what I had been writing for so many years,

he took his time reading it and refused to let me know what he was thinking. I anxiously searched his face for signs; he deliberately kept it completely expressionless. When he finished, he gave it back to me. On the last page he had just written *Oof!* He loved it, but he looked so sad. I thought it was the book. It wasn't. All he said was

"I'm going to lose you."

My cold moth spread her wings. I couldn't tell whether she was preparing to take off or land.

I had no idea what to do next. I felt as though I had crawled out of a bomb shelter and had to face the world. It dawned on me that I had been utterly reckless. My money was finished. I had spent years writing something that probably made no sense to anyone except me and Pradip. I had antagonized the only possible source of funding in our lives as marginal filmmakers. The stress made me break out in hives and my skin started to flake off. I looked as though I had psoriasis. The more skin doctors told me that it was a response to stress, the more stressed I became and the worse I looked.

A friend told me that a young acquaintance of ours, Pankaj Mishra, had taken over as the head of HarperCollins India and that it might be a good idea to give him the manuscript. So, I did. Pankaj told me he was going to be traveling and would read it on his journey. Two nights later he called me from a railway station. (It was pre-cell-phone days.) He was so excited that I couldn't understand what he was saying. Whatever little I did understand, I didn't believe. I thought he was teasing me. He was the first to start ringing the bells. He sent the manuscript to a friend of his, the writer Patrick French. Patrick sent it to his literary agent, David Godwin, who sent it around to some publishers. I had no idea that any of this was happening. Or even what a literary agent was.

On the day the storm broke, I had borrowed Pradip's mother's car and parked it somewhere stupid. It was towed away, and I had to spend hours in a police station to get it back. It was pretty late at night when I got home. Our room was crowded with friends sitting around waiting for me. I mistook their excitement for anxiety and explained what had happened. They told me that the phone had been ringing nonstop. Pradip hugged me so hard my bones nearly cracked.

I couldn't tell one caller from the other. John, Stuart, Philip, David. They were all either publishers or literary agents. Some asked if I had a fax number. I gave them a neighbor's number. Publishing contracts were faxed through. It was pandemonium. The most persuasive caller was David Godwin. He said he was going to fly to Delhi to see me.

"If you don't like me, I'll introduce you to someone else. But please don't sign anything with anyone until we meet."

That night—like the night before I met Micky for the first time—I stayed awake thinking. How could this be happening to me? I could literally feel my skin clearing up, and the blood flowing easy in my body. I was thirty-six. By no means young. As the night sky lightened and the first birds began to call, I fed the squirrels on our little terrace (and blew a kiss to my Ayemenem squirrel, who must have been one of the stars twinkling down at me). I worried about what Pradip had said. What did he mean by "I'm going to lose you"? Would I come to regret having written *The God of Small Things*?

David Godwin arrived in two days. I had suddenly, for no reason, grown suspicious of him. Who was he? Why was he so keen? I decided that if he turned out to be some old colonial "India hand" and patronized me about his love of everything Indian, I would politely thank him and turn him down. Based on absolutely nothing, I began to build up an active hostility toward him. I picked him up from the hotel he was staying in. He was a tall man in a crumpled linen suit. At the time I wasn't aware that was a fashion statement. I almost offered to iron it for him. The first thing he said to me was "I'm terribly sorry but I don't know much about India. I've never been. To be honest, I wasn't even sure whether Arundhati [Aroonditty] was the name of a man or a woman. But when I read the book, I felt as though somebody had shot some heroin up my arm."

We signed up on the spot.

He told me I'd need to go to London to meet publishers and choose who I most liked. For a moment I thought somebody had actually shot some heroin up his arm and that he was hallucinating. But that's how it turned out.

I flew to London. I took David a present. A visiting card. It was a grain of rice set in a glass vial. If you looked at it through a magnifying glass, it said FLYING AGENT, DAVID GODWIN. He turned out to be one of the best things that happened to me. He transformed what could have been a complicated few months into a dream ride.

Within weeks *The God of Small Things* had publishers all over the world. By the end of it all there were more than forty of them. Added up, the advance against royalties was a million dollars. Ludicrous. I felt as though I had ambushed the pipeline that circulates the world's wealth between the world's wealthy, and it was spewing money at me. I didn't tell a soul except Pankaj Mishra, Pradip, and Golak. Golak's response was priceless:

"Good, Roy. Thang God we're rich."

That was the best possible attitude toward money. Share it. And I did. With my mother, my brother, Golak, my other friends, and anybody else who deserved some. I could not imagine hoarding money while those I loved, and those who deserved it, had none. Over the years I would learn that sharing money with love and in solidarity is a delicate process, far more difficult than hoarding it. But until we live in a more equal world, sharing (responsibly) is the best you can do.

205

I was determined that *The God of Small Things* should be published in India first. But within those few months, Pankaj Mishra had given up his job at HarperCollins and more or less moved to London. Most publishing houses in India at that time produced badly designed, shoddy books. Terrible covers, terrible paper, terrible copyediting. I found it painful, disrespectful. Friends of mine, Tarun Tejpal and Sanjeev Saith, got together and started a publishing company called India Ink. I was at the printing press the day the first copies rolled out. I could hardly breathe. To see copies of your first book, piled up in towers—it's an experience that's hard to match.

Readings were planned in Delhi, Bombay, Calcutta, Madras, and Kottayam. Stuart Proffitt, my publisher from the UK, and David Godwin flew in to be a part of the excitement. There were all kinds of reviews. People hated it, loved it, mocked it, wept, laughed. The book flew off the shelves. My friends' nascent little publishing venture could barely keep up. The events in the big cities were exhilarating. People queued around the block to get in.

I was worried about what would happen in Kottayam. The book, and the buzz around it, had increased the complications between Mrs. Roy and me a thousandfold. This despite the fact that she had embraced the character of Ammu, mother of the twins. She called me to say that she had stopped at a wayside stall to buy some fruit, and a woman had had the temerity to ask her if she was Arundhati Roy's mother.

"I felt as though she had slapped me," Mrs. Roy said.

\*       \*       \*

The Kottayam launch of *The God of Small Things* took place in Mrs. Roy's school. It was held down the hill in the nursery that doubled as a stage facing the athletics field. Chairs for the audience were placed in rows on the running track. There was a canvas pandal, in case of rain. Mrs. Roy was both thrilled and upset at the attention I was receiving. Thrilled because I was a former student of her school and that was something to be showcased. Upset because I was her daughter and she felt that I was being given more attention than was good for me, and certainly more than I deserved. (Which was absolutely true.) The Kottayam launch had been her idea, and that upset her even more. She had invited Kamala Das, an accomplished poet and an outspoken, often-controversial writer, to introduce me and the book. Kamala Das had shocked Kerala with her book *My Story*, published in 1973, which was candid and unapologetic about sexual intimacy. Mrs. Roy could not have chosen a better person to be the guest of honor. She greeted me warmly, generously.

The audience of about two hundred people included some of my old teachers and a few journalists. David Godwin and Stuart Proffitt were there, too. They were frayed at the edges after witnessing a series of wild book events across India in which the auditoriums were overwhelmed, and crowds refused to stand in line. The food, the heat, the humidity, and the unpredictability of absolutely everything added to their anxiety.

In Kottayam there were deep undercurrents of local tension that they weren't aware of. The Marxist government in Kerala was unhappy with the book for what it considered to be unacceptable criticism of the party and its legendary leader, E. M. S. Namboodiripad, who was the first Communist chief minister of Kerala. I was an admirer, but not a devotee. The criticism in *The God of Small Things* had to do with the party's attitude to caste. I was denounced as anti-communist (though nothing could be further from the truth), and for a while there was some talk of banning the book.

Five male lawyers in a small neighboring town called Pathanamthitta had filed a criminal case against me for "obscenity and corrupting public morality." They had photocopied the last chapter and submitted it as evidence. They could not have been offended by my description of lovemaking because Malayalam cinema at the time was a citadel of smut and sexism. The last chapter of *The God of Small Things* was a nursery rhyme compared to that. I think what actually offended them was that the woman, Ammu, was a Syrian Christian and her lover, Velutha, a Paravan, a Dalit. A close relative told me that simply wasn't *possible*. She explained that Syrian Christians and Paravans were different species, sex between them was a physical impossibility. She looked at me with wise compassion, as though she pitied me for my ignorance, as though I were some kind of witless alien who hadn't grown up there and didn't understand the ways of local people. The criminal case was serious and required me to appear personally in court. The idea was to humiliate me and to provide entertainment for the press and the public by reading aloud what the lawyers considered to be the obscene portions of the book.

It wasn't just the Communist Party and the moral police—some conservative Syrian Christians were upset with the book, too. So were some of my relatives. The fictional house on the hill in the book wasn't Miss Kurien's house. Its architecture was inspired by a far more beautiful house next door that belonged to better-off relatives who lived in the United States. They disapproved of the book, and I heard they were considering suing me for daring to have unacceptable scenes and false memories played out in a house that wasn't mine, but theirs. (It might have been fun to have a court order on the Legal Limits of Memory.)

All this was swirling under the surface on the day of the launch. Mrs. Roy was aware of all of it and not intimidated by any of it.

But then more trouble arrived. A plump man in a white *mundu* and cotton bush shirt rolled cheerfully down the steep road carrying his copy of *The God of Small Things*. It was G. Isaac. The feud between him and Mrs. Roy was at its peak. She was now back in court seeking his physical eviction from their father's ancestral home, which would mean the end of the Malabar Coast Products. They accused each other of dreadful crimes and said horrible things about each other in their legal affidavits. G. Isaac was forbidden from entering the school campus, but there he was. He wasn't going to miss the launch of his niece's book, even though he knew that his sister was quite capable of calling the police to escort him off her property. Fortunately, Mrs. Roy didn't notice her brother in the crowd. Most people in the audience did—and were braced for trouble. As was I. Imagine your first book launch being disrupted by a brawl between your mother and uncle and being broken up by the police.

Picture me. Rising literary star (supposedly) caught in the cross fire of a battle between a school and a pickle factory.

G. Isaac walked straight up to David Godwin and Stuart Proffitt and introduced himself with a friendly smile, as though everybody ought to know him.

"Hello, I'm Chacko."

His familiarity was completely lost on them. Chacko is one of the main characters in *The God of Small Things*: Ammu's older brother, Rhodes scholar, pickle baron, and uncle to the twins Esthappen and Rahel. G. Isaac was right. He *was* Chacko. Ammu wasn't really Mrs. Roy. But Chacko was definitely very G. Isaac. On the day of the launch, he flipped it around. G. Isaac became Chacko. Life became art. My brother always chuckled about this.

"All of them want to be the people in the book. They'd rather be that than themselves. You've turned all the monsters into nice people."

G. Isaac reeled off some of Chacko's lines from the book, which didn't help to ameliorate the confusion. The moment that is immortalized in my mind is G. Isaac, in my mother's school sports ground, airily quoting Chacko airily quoting F. Scott Fitzgerald with absolutely no context, to my completely bewildered British publisher and literary agent.

"You know Gatsby turned out all right in the end. It is what preyed on him, the foul dust that floated in the wake of his dreams. . . . "

When he didn't manage to initiate an interesting conversation with them, G. Isaac made his plump, cheerful way into the audience and sat in one of the middle rows. Mrs. Roy was already onstage, deep in conversation with Kamala Das, and had still not noticed him. She called the meeting to order as if it were a school assembly. Someone might even have rung the school bell. She introduced Kamala Das, who said some insightful, generous things about the book, and then it was time for me to speak. Conscious that hell could break out at any moment, I decided to do a hurried reading and wrap the show.

The passage I chose was from a chapter called "Abhilash Talkies." Chacko and his seven-year-old niece, Rahel, are sharing a hotel room in Cochin. The whole family has driven up from Ayemenem in Chacko's sky-blue Plymouth. Early next morning they would go to the airport to pick up Chacko's English ex-wife, Margaret, and their young daughter, Sophie Mol (*mol* is a Malayalam term of endearment for a little girl), who were arriving from England. Rahel is extremely worried about the reorganization of love that is about to take place. She anticipates a steep reduction in her quota in favor of her half-English cousin:

"Chacko?" Rahel said, from her darkened bed. "Can I ask you a question?"

"Ask me two," Chacko said.

"Chacko, do you love Sophie Mol Most in the World?"

"She's my daughter," Chacko said.

Rahel considered this.

"Chacko? Is it *necessary* that people *have* to love their own children Most in the World?"

"There are no rules," Chacko said, "but people usually do."

"Chacko, for example," Rahel said, "just for *example*, is it possible that Ammu can love Sophie Mol more than me and Estha? Or for you to love me more than Sophie Mol for *example*?"

"Anything's possible in Human Nature," Chacko said in his Reading Aloud voice. Talking to the darkness now, suddenly insensitive to his little fountain-haired niece. "Love. Madness. Hope. Infinite joy."

Of the four things that were Possible in Human Nature, Rahel thought that *Infinnate Joy* sounded the saddest. Perhaps because of the way Chacko said it.

*Infinnate Joy.* With a church sound to it. Like a sad fish with fins all over.

A cold moth lifted a cold leg.

The cigarette smoke curled into the night. And the fat man and the little girl lay awake in silence.

As I read, Mrs. Roy ran interference. She chatted continuously to Kamala Das in a low voice, holding her mike to her mouth. She planned the launch and then wrecked it, too. She presented me and, in the same breath, undermined me. When I asked if anybody had questions, G. Isaac stood up.

"I don't have a question. I just want to say that when I die and am refused entry at the Gates of Paradise, I'm going to quote from *The God of Small Things*, chapter four, page one hundred eighteen.

See, it says here clearly, 'There are no rules.' You see? It's true. There are no rules."

Mrs. Roy gathered herself up to her full fighting height of four foot ten. But G. Isaac was already making his exit, crab-walking through row five.

"It's OK, Mart. I'm leaving."

He always called her Mart because when she was a child and just learning to write her name, the *y* in her *Mary* always looked like a *t*. He was eight years older than her.

There were no further questions.

Thus ended the Kottayam launch of *The God of Small Things* in Kerala. I was greatly relieved. Things could have been worse. The only thing missing was Micky Roy arriving drunk and demanding the Restoration of Conjugal Rights (which by the way is a real law). For the sake of the children. That would have more or less completed our family portrait.

\*     \*     \*

Micky was very much around though. Still in Delhi. When he heard about the book and the publicity around it, he was not above putting his oar in the water. This time he opted for a cute form of blackmail.

"I say, Orundhuti, some bugger from the *New York Times* called. He wants to do an interview with me."

"You should do it, Micky," I said. "I'm not ashamed of you! Tell them everything."

He giggled. "Don't call me Micky. I'm your Baba."

\*     \*     \*

The rest of that year passed in a blur. I traveled to countries I could not ever have imagined visiting. Finland. Norway. Estonia. I didn't really visit them. I was caught up in that clichéd moment of "fame" that is supposed to be the high point of a person's life—like in the movies. An endless stream of interviews and events and camera flashbulbs. Pradip traveled with me. While I was being interviewed, he would go out and take photographs and show me pictures of the town I was supposed to have visited.

I found to my surprise that I enjoyed reading my book aloud to audiences. I particularly enjoyed doing book signings, where I could get a fleeting moment with individual readers. I was so curious about them—people from countries and cultures I knew so little about, who had found something of themselves in the story of a family from a small village in Kerala. Just that brief meeting of eyes, the exchange of greetings, the myriad variations of "Could you please sign this for my . . . " that revealed something to me about their lives, their loves, their friendships and relationships. It made me realize how literature can join humans in a bond of quiet intimacy the way almost nothing else can. "Your book is about my childhood," my Estonian translator said. "We've all got aunts like Baby Kochamma," a Jewish publisher in the United States drawled. "I can actually smell your book," a Portuguese man told me. At every event I could see Pradip in the audience, looking proud, tearing up when I started to read. But it was difficult for him and stressful for me. All the light shone on me. He, grand, wonderful man, my teacher, lover, and best friend, was made invisible. He didn't mind, but I did. The balance in our relationship was upended. My newfound fame crashed into our little love tent and jerked us around like puppets.

*     *     *

In Kerala the court case gathered momentum. I had engaged a criminal lawyer. He advised me to appeal in the Cochin High Court to quash the case in the district court in Pathanamthitta. When I went to meet him in his office, he explained my legal situation to me.

"Madam, I have read your book quite carefully. The plaintiffs are correct. It is quite obscene."

He took it upon himself to read aloud the sentences and paragraphs that he had marked out as potentially obscene. Each time he read the word *breast* he made an imaginary breast with a cupped hand. To hide my laughter, I had to keep pretending to drop my pen or my papers and duck under the table to look for them. I could only thank my stars that this was taking place in a private lawyer's chamber, and not, as the prosecutors wanted, in a public courtroom with the whole town watching.

"But don't worry. We will argue that their lordships must look at a work of literature as a whole. Not just parts. That is the law."

Finally, after a few adjournments—either because I was traveling, or one or the other side's lawyer wasn't available—we got a date for a hearing. All of us were ready, the prosecution and the defense. In the meantime, I had won the Booker Prize. That changed everything. Even though some communists said that it was all an imperialist plot, people were proud and happy that an Indian author had won a big international award. But to celebrate me wholeheartedly, *The God of Small Things* needed to be depoliticized. It began to be spoken of as a book about children, praised for its lyrical language and stripped of its politics. Stripped of its references to caste.

At the hearing in the High Court the judge said, "Every time this case comes before me, I get chest pains." He kicked the can down the road. Each hearing was postponed for months and sometimes years. Over time my lawyer died, so did the judge. I can only hope that the chest pains induced by my book and the case against it were not the cause. More than ten years later, a new lawyer argued before a new judge and got the case dismissed.

Being accused of "obscenity and corrupting public morality" would be the first of three criminal cases filed against me over the years, by separate, completely unconnected batches of five male advocates. One of which would send me, very briefly, to prison.

# Things Fall Apart

It was thrilling to win the Booker Prize. But the weeks of hysteria around the short-listed authors, the bets that were being laid on us by bookies, the grand banquet at which only one of us would be announced as the winner, made me feel more like a horse than a writer. A racehorse who, despite being coached by G. Isaac, ended up wanting nothing more than to win. I didn't recognize myself. Pradip was drawn into the race, too. For luck, he gave up smoking.

By the time the night of the award ceremony was upon us, we had witnessed up close the workings of the machine in which we were mere cogs; we had heard the purring of the engine and whir of the big wheels turning. When my name was announced and I walked onstage, I could clearly see the outline of a gilded cage. I knew that once I stepped in, it would snap shut behind me. Apart from being happily shocked and having no secretly prepared "in case I win" speech to give, I was a little graceless up there. When I was asked about my next book, I said something like "I'll write another book when I have another book to write. Not because I have won a prize." It was unnecessarily fractious. I shouldn't have done that. I regret my behavior. It was caused by apprehension, by that familiar fear of being trapped. However tantalizing the trap might be, I knew that a trap was a trap. I knew I would have to resist the pressure to sign publishing contracts for books I hadn't yet written. And the pressure to endlessly replicate versions of myself and *The God of Small Things*. I knew that fame could end up being a form of captivity, too. Also, I still hadn't lost that very real, very tangible feeling I had carried around since I was a child—the feeling that each time I was applauded, someone else, someone quiet, was being beaten in another room.

It's easy for me to say this now. Because winning and walking away was of course very different from not winning. The freedom I craved (apart from the freedom of having my buffalo take me home while I lay in my cart singing to the stars) was the freedom to live and to write on my own terms. The Booker Prize helped me to achieve that. I was fortunate that when I won it, I was already one hundred and thirty-seven years old. Had I been any younger, I might have walked into that gilded cage and sung my gilded song for the rest of my days.

*    *    *

The only person I called after the prize was announced was Mrs. Roy. It would have been about 2:00 a.m. for her in Kottayam. She was up, watching the news on TV.

"Well done, baby girl."

An incredible expression of love. I'd caught her on a good day.

That night I dreamed I was a fish. A green hand reached into the water and picked me out. I don't know why it was green. It held me up in the air and said, "Ask for anything. You can have it. What do you want?"

I-the-fish said, "Please put me back in the river."

So, it did.

But as the wise folks say, you can't swim in the same river twice.

My river changed beyond recognition. I had to learn to swim all over again.

*       *       *

When we got back to Delhi, my friends and publishers at India Ink hosted a party to celebrate. I danced with Pradip's mother—admirer of my neck—who had just turned eighty-nine. She wore the silk Tanjore sari that I'd bought her. She had recovered from her husband's death and was (we thought) in excellent health. Her diary was full of social engagements and bridge parties. The morning after our celebration she felt uneasy and a little breathless. We decided to take her to hospital. She supervised the packing of her overnight bag. She insisted she wanted her own sheets and towels. She died in the car, before we got there. It was January 1998.

I ought to have been able to, but I did not anticipate how her passing would change my life.

*       *       *

Pradip's parents left their son all their property. That included the tiny apartment that we lived in on the second floor, the big house downstairs, and an even bigger house next door. All of this in one of Delhi's most exclusive neighborhoods. Their will instructed Pradip to share the rent (which wasn't much at the time) from the big house with his two sisters, who were both much older than him, and to give them a small share of the money if he decided to sell the property. Although Pradip's sisters and their husbands were furious, there was nothing unusual about any of it. It was what all Indian families do. But here was I, daughter of a woman who had fought against this all her life.

What was I to do?

I could not think of myself as a landlady. I could not see myself as mistress of an inherited house and a fleet of servants. There had always been the Upstairs life and the Downstairs life. Two different universes, which Pradip and the girls easily straddled. But not me. I couldn't imagine living the Downstairs life. When I sat on Pradip's mother's sofa in her drawing room, all I could see through the plate glass window was my younger self walking up the spiral staircase for the first time, with the files I had been instructed to bring, chuckling. I could not become the object of my own chuckles. If I did, what sort of writer would I, could I, be? I knew from all the ugliness and quarreling that I had witnessed from the time I was a child that houses—inherited houses—own people and not the other way around.

It's not that I wanted to play Gandhi or live in a slum dressed in the female equivalent of a handloom loincloth. Nor did I want to inflict my politics and my past on Pradip or on the girls, who were grown-up by then, because this was their home, and the only life they knew. They belonged to it. They slipped quickly and easily (like the weather) into their roles as master and young mistresses of the big house, disciplinarians of the fleet of servants. But I didn't. I couldn't. And I did not have the authority—what the twins in *The God of Small Things* thought of as Locusts Stand I—to radically change anything about how the Downstairs life was lived, how things were done or not done. But the seed that had lived nicely, neatly, in its casing had germinated now. It could no longer hide what kind of plant it was. And the searchlight that shone on it was nothing less than the light of literature. That sharpest, most unforgiving light of all.

What was I to do?

I tried not to judge them, the people I most loved, and I failed. Even to explain my dilemma to them was a form of judgment. I made myself miserable with my upside-down inside-out mind. I made everyone else miserable, too. I found myself unable to descend from the second-floor apartment. But even living there was difficult. It was a lovely bohemian space, until we inherited it. For me to live there under the changed circumstances seemed to me a form of high fakery, like building a mud house at the bottom of your rich parents' garden. Added to that snarl of tangled feelings was the fact that by now I *was* the rich parent. The rich parent without any authority or parental rights. An intractable, impossible position.

Pradip had begun work on what would become an iconic book, a field guide to the trees of Delhi. I know nobody like him. Nobody who pays such exquisite, tender attention to the tiniest seed or fern or blade of grass. Nobody who gets more excited by the miracles in the natural world that a change of season brings. But his work was entirely a labor of love. The only way that household, the servants, that lifestyle, and even his research could be maintained and afforded was with the royalties from *The God of Small Things*. He and the girls were not equipped to live in the real world the way I was. I could not let them fall. They knew that I would not. And I did not, for twenty-five years. Until they sold the property and no longer needed my support. Yet, to be the writer I wanted to be, I myself could not live the Downstairs life. That made me principled and hypocritical all at once.

In a country of desperately poor people, I of all people found myself snared in the trap of traps. The cage was made of privilege, money, and property. The bait was love, loyalty, and responsibility. And then it got worse. The turbulence in our personal lives was amplified by political turbulence.

On March 19, 1998, two months after Pradip's mother died, a coalition of political parties led by the BJP came to power. It wasn't just a routine change of government. It was the beginning of what would turn into an ideological coup, the inevitable culmination of L. K. Advani's Rath Yatra that I had watched snaking past me in Bhopal while we were preparing to shoot *Electric Moon*. Advani himself, agent provocateur of the wild mob of Hindu vigilantes that hammered the Babri Masjid into the ground six years ago, was now home minister, in charge of law and order. The prime minister, Atal Bihari Vajpayee, and many of his cabinet ministers were members of the Rashtriya Swayamsevak Sangh (RSS), a far-right, Hindu-nationalist cultural organization founded in 1925 with a militia of hundreds of thousands of trained "volunteers" who believed that India should be declared a Hindu Nation and Hindus should be its first citizens.

My fury at what was happening didn't fit in with the Downstairs life. In that beautiful big house, full of its own acute sorrows, but insulated from the vulgar politics of the outside world, my anger felt a little jarring. Even to myself. I tried to leave it outside the gate each time I walked in. But in that, too, I failed. A chasm opened between us. A chasm that could always be traversed by the drawbridges of love, humor, and years of a shared life, but a chasm nevertheless.

What was I to do?

I followed my instinct, which is the place from where all art and literature comes. It showed me the way. Once again, I made the safest place the most dangerous. Once again, I ran. I moved out. I told the girls that now that they were grown-up, it was time for me to fly away. I rented a two-room apartment with a terrace, a twenty-minute drive from where we lived. On the second floor, of course.

At first, I used my new flat more as a workspace and, like an ant following a chemical trail, would often go back home in the evenings.

There was no quarrel, no ugliness, only a deep, dark, palpable sorrow. Gradually over the years I would drift away and become a visitor to what had been the only real home I had ever known. What ought to have been the happiest, most fulfilling years of my life turned out to be the most forlorn. The price I paid for being Mother Mary's daughter and the writer that I am was not prison or persecution (although there was some of that, too). It was catastrophic heartbreak.

I did not discuss any of this with Mrs. Roy. She was not the kind of mother with whom it was safe to share your vulnerabilities. I knew I needed to keep a safe distance.

It couldn't be that my storm-warning alarms about the approaching tsunami of Hindu nationalism went off early only because I am not Hindu or a patriot or a flag-waver. Plenty of people, Hindus included, reacted similarly. More likely it was my squirrel training from my ledge life in Ayemenem, combined with the slightly warped sense of culpability that comes with sudden fame. As my personal life turned to rubble and I risked coming undone, the outside world smashed in. In a strange way, over the next several years, it was politics—and anger—that held me together.

# Mobile Republic

In May 1998, within weeks of taking office, the new government fulfilled one of the BJP's long-standing desires. It detonated three nuclear devices buried deep in the desert in Pokhran, Rajasthan. India had tested a nuclear device before, in 1974. But the government had gone to great lengths to call it a "peaceful test." In contrast the BJP now gloated, thumped its chest, and did everything short of declaring war. The government of Pakistan responded to this posturing immediately, with tests of its own. Two countries that had fought several wars against each other now had nuclear weapons. They were flaunted as a Hindu bomb and a Muslim one. India's two hundred million Muslims were hostages in this brinkmanship. Kashmir, India's only Muslim-majority state, which India and Pakistan had fought three wars over, was the potential flash point.

After the tests our newspapers and TV channels were saturated with triumphant bombast, much of it couched in the language of masculinity and virility. The most unlikely people, including writers, actors, and artists, joined in the celebrations. A new public language, previously unacceptable, suddenly became acceptable. It became painfully clear that nuclear weapons were lethal even if they weren't used. The idea that India had proudly, openly declared itself a nuclear power seemed to have altered our collective imagination, turned it radioactive.

Because of the Booker, I was sharply in the public eye, on the cover of magazines, splashed across the pages of newspapers. I was regularly trotted out as part of a sort of National Pride parade that segued seamlessly into the celebration of Hindu nationalism. I realized that if I said nothing, it would automatically be taken to mean that I agreed with what was going on. I couldn't tolerate the idea of being so misunderstood.

My first political essay, "The End of Imagination," was published as a cover story by two major magazines, *Outlook* and *Frontline*, simultaneously. It wasn't only the possibility of a nuclear conflict with Pakistan that worried me. It was what India was doing to itself. I could clearly see where we were headed. We were journeying back to the horrors of Partition, when Hindus, Sikhs, and Muslims had turned on one another, slaughtered one another:

Why does it all seem so familiar? Is it because even as you watch, reality dissolves and seamlessly rushes forward into the silent, black-and-white images from old films—scenes of people being hounded out of their lives, rounded up and herded into camps? Of massacres, of mayhem, of endless columns of broken people making their way to nowhere? Why is the hall so quiet? Have I been seeing too many films? Am I mad? Or am I right? Could those images be the inevitable culmination of what we have set into motion?

I wasn't mad. I was right. That's the way things turned out.

The paragraph in the essay that everybody hung their hats on was "If protesting against having a nuclear bomb implanted in my brain is anti-Hindu and antinational, then I secede. I hereby declare myself an independent, mobile republic. I own no territory. I have no flag."

The insults and the outrage that followed—"Get out of India," "Go to Pakistan!"—kicked me off my literary-star, fairy-princess pedestal in a minute. (In my mind they were just more public versions of Mrs. Roy's "Get out of my house!" "Get out of my car!") The most popular accusation was (and continues to be) "Her real name is Susanna. She's hiding the fact that she's not a Hindu."

I wasn't Christian enough.

I wasn't Hindu enough.

I wasn't communist enough.

I wasn't enough.

It came as a relief. It liberated me and set me walking. For years after that I wandered through forests and river valleys, villages and border towns, to try to better understand my country. As I traveled, I wrote. That was the beginning of my restless, unruly life as a seditious traitor-writer.

Free woman. Free writing. Like Mother Mary taught me.

I hadn't just avoided the gilded cage. I had blown it to smithereens.

*     *     *

In the process, like a suicide bomber, I had blown myself to smithereens, too. My life. My home. My love. There were days on which I could actually, physically, feel my heart breaking. I was in a taxi once when I felt I could hear the sound of my blood motoring through my veins. I thought I was going to have a heart attack. Fortunately, I had a friend with me. We rushed to hospital. As I walked through the crowd, my head spinning, I could see heads turning, my name being whispered. The nurse in the emergency ward who took my blood pressure and the doctor who did the ECG got me to sign autographs for them.

"You're fine. It's nothing. Relax," the doctor said, and sent me on my way.

*You're wrong,* I wanted to tell him. *It's everything. Every single fucking thing.*

Not everybody wanted autographs.

When I went for a routine mammogram, once the doctor had me captive, my right breast flattened between the cold plates of his machine, he said, "I found your book, *Children of a Lesser God,* to be quite boring." Then he gave me a lecture on why it was necessary that India be formally declared a Hindu nation, and why we needed nuclear weapons.

The world was too ridiculous for me to remain too sad for too long.

My heart bumped along highways, hung about on the commons, hovered in places it did not belong, and began to take public things extremely personally.

# Rally for the Valley

Less than a year after the nuclear tests, the Supreme Court vacated the legal stay on the construction of the massive Sardar Sarovar Dam, one of four high dams being built on the Narmada River in the state of Gujarat. The dam would submerge endless expanses of ancient, old-growth jungle and displace hundreds of thousands of indigenous tribespeople who lived in the forested hills as well as relatively prosperous farmers who farmed the silty, fertile plains. The reservoir of the dam, the size of a city-state, would flood villages, towns, marketplaces, monuments, mosques, and temples, a whole ancient riverine civilization. I had, for some years, followed the anti-dam movement in the valley. The Sardar Sarovar was already half built, but each meter it rose meant that much more area submerged, that many more villages drowned.

When the court order came, the Narmada Bachao Andolan (NBA)—Save the Narmada Movement—started to mobilize to reignite the resistance. One of the activists, Himanshu Thakkar, encyclopedia of all things dam, called to ask if I would consider going to the Narmada Valley. I think he called because, after the publication of "The End of Imagination," the NBA had me marked as someone who would not be intimidated by the aggression of its critics. At our first meeting, another activist, Nandini Oza, said, "When we read *The God of Small Things*, we knew you would be against Big Dams." I was delighted by that single-minded extrapolation from a literary novel. For my part, I wanted to test myself, to see whether I could find a language, a writer's language, to write about the Narmada and the tragedy that had befallen it in the way I had found a language to write about Ayemenem and the Meenachil. Could I write about irrigation, agriculture, displacement, and drainage the way I wrote about love and death, or about characters in a novel?

Visiting the Narmada Valley was the intellectual and emotional equivalent of visiting a chiropractor. My skeletal structure was realigned. My brain turned around. The intellectual rigor, the profound ecological understanding, and the gentle militancy of the NBA predated today's climate protests by decades. For all the battering, both physical and psychological, that Indian women, particularly in rural areas, are subject to, this movement was led by women. Their fight against Big Dams in the Narmada Valley remains one of the world's most spectacular battles. I was privileged to be a part of it. Though we lost, I would not, for anything, have wanted to be on the side of those who won—those who look at a river and want to stop it, tame it, own it, pour concrete and garbage and sewage into it. Kill it.

I traveled along the river through towns and villages in the hills and plains that were slated for submergence by the dam reservoir. Some of the villages I went to were still pristine, thickly forested, sleepy. Kilometers downstream, villages closer to the dam were already underwater. The process of dam building was so slow that it was hard for people to imagine in advance the devastation that awaited them. It was a contradiction in terms, a slow-motion explosion.

\*　　　\*　　　\*

My essay "The Greater Common Good," once again published in *Out-look* and *Frontline*, argued that Big Dams were ecologically disastrous, economically unsound, and politically undemocratic. That planners and engineers inflated their benefits and minimized their real cost. That they could never deliver what they promised to on paper. Before I wrote it, I had a conversation with Medha Patkar, the charismatic leader of the NBA, about what the consequences of my writing it might be. The battle the NBA was waging was fierce. Ideologically, legally, and politically. Even physically. Every chink in its armor, every misstep, was seized upon by the opposition. We had to think ahead, consider every possibility.

Medha and I were as different from each other as two women could be. She was a Gandhian, a tireless activist, who had worked in the valley for years, walking from village to village mobilizing people, explaining how the dam would destroy their lives. She lived an impossibly frugal life, wore rough, handwoven khadi saris and appeared to have renounced all kinds of delicious pleasures including romance. I could not hold a candle to her when it came to righteousness, dedication, and commitment.

To carry people along in a place like the Narmada Valley, women activists had to blend in as far as possible with the other women. They had to conform, outwardly at least, to traditional expectations and then go a step further. Gandhian women activists wore no jewelry, no flowers in their hair, no beads. They were as austere as nuns, or monks. None of them had children. They knew their lives were too unpredictable for that.

My brief was different. My commitment was to writing. To being a writer, not a leader or an activist. To do that I could not be weighed down by the burden of a "following," or of fulfilling people's expectations. I had to have the right to be unpopular. I had to have the choice of probing the boundaries of acceptability, of not fitting in, of standing alone. And most important, even though I considered Gandhi a visionary in some ways and admired many things about him, I was not a Gandhian. I was a critic. A skeptic. To put it mildly.

Medha and I talked about this. We both understood that when my essay was published, attempts would be made to exploit the difference between us, to pit us against each other. (Good Woman versus Bad Woman.)

"The Greater Common Good" unsettled many people's notions of what a writer's role in society should be. What *was* this essay? Was it journalism? Was it academic? Was it literary? Was it a travelogue? The pro-dam lobby raged against it and called it fiction. But even people who claimed to be on our side were uncomfortable. I was publicly lectured by men who thought of themselves as progressive about how to write, what tone to take, and what subjects I was allowed to address. Their manly vanity allowed them to be unselfconscious about the quality of their own writing and their feeble grasp of the facts. They passionately called me names for being passionate about what I was advocating. They advised me to be quiet and nuanced, when all I wanted to do was to shout from the rooftops.

More annoyed than all of these men was the most revered institution in India. The Supreme Court. The court that had been good to Mrs. Roy was less impressed by her daughter. A three-judge bench held hearings in which they deliberated on whether I should be charged with contempt of court—a criminal offense that carried a six-month prison sentence. They were aggravated by my criticism of their order that allowed the building of the Sardar Sarovar Dam to recommence. The bench was advised by a senior lawyer appointed as a "friend of the court," known as an *amicus curiae*. They argued about whether the opening passages of "The Greater Common Good" "scandalized and lowered the dignity of the court." This is how the essay began:

I stood on a hill and laughed out loud.

I had crossed the Narmada by boat from Jalsindhi and climbed the headland on the opposite bank from where I could see, ranged across the crowns of low, bald hills, the Adivasi hamlets of Sikka, Surung, Neemgavan, and Domkhedi. I could see their airy, fragile homes. I could see their fields and the forests behind them. I could see little children with littler goats scuttling across the landscape like motorized peanuts. I knew I was looking at a civilization older than Hinduism, slated—*sanctioned* (by the highest court in the land)—to be drowned this monsoon when the waters of the Sardar Sarovar reservoir will rise to submerge it.

Why did I laugh?

Because I suddenly remembered the tender concern with which the Supreme Court judges in Delhi (before vacating the legal stay on further construction of the Sardar Sarovar Dam) had enquired whether Adivasi children in the resettlement colonies would have children's parks to play in. The lawyers representing the government had hastened to assure them that indeed they would, and what's more, that there were seesaws and slides and swings in every park. I looked up at the endless sky and down at the river rushing past, and for a brief, brief moment the absurdity of it all reversed my rage and I laughed. I meant no disrespect.

During the hearings the exasperated brother judges passed copies of *Outlook* and *Frontline* to each other pointing out the sentences they were unhappy about. "Saying that you mean no disrespect doesn't indicate respect. It's the opposite. She thinks we don't understand English." They debated the legal and criminal ramifications of sarcasm. They often referred to me as "that woman."

They probably did not mean it in the way I understood it, but "that woman" took me back to Mrs. Roy's raging at me in her school dining room the day Baker visited—the day I decided I would never return home. It remined me of insults by our relatives X,Y,Z that she had endured on my behalf and relayed to me: "mistress," "keep."

I began to refer to myself as the Hooker who won the Booker.

*        *        *

Another part of "The Greater Common Good" the judges were partic- ularly exercised by was my suggestion that giving cash as compensation to displaced people who belonged to indigenous tribes—people who lived outside the money economy and had, in the official resettlement policy, been explicitly promised "land for land"—was the equivalent of paying Supreme Court judges their salaries in fertilizer bags. After a few hearings the bench handed down an order. They let me off with a stern warning written in such elaborate prose that I needed a dictionary to decode it.

*        *        *

As the monsoon approached, villagers and activists in the Narmada Valley declared that when the water level in the Sardar Sarovar res- ervoir rose to submerge their villages, they would not move. They would stand in the dangerous currents of rising water to register their protest.

A group of us put out a call asking people to join us on a journey through the valley to understand what Big Dams did. We called it the Rally for the Valley. Hundreds of people responded. They came from cities across the country. Pradip, Golak, and Arjun Raina (who had played Annie) were there, too. A big contingent of journalists, some supportive, some hostile, joined the rally. We traveled by train, bus, road, and on foot. Thousands of villagers arrived to greet us, travel with us, and participate in the public meetings that the NBA organized.

The NBA activists were brilliant public speakers. I was mortified each time I was called onstage to speak. I had no idea how to address such massive audiences. I wrote a line for myself that I repeated like an idiot at every meeting: *Main lekhika hoon. Main sunne ke lie aayi hoon, bolne ke lie nahin. Narmada ghati Zindabad,* "I'm a writer. I'm here to listen, not to speak. Long live the Narmada Valley." Although my Hindi had improved vastly from my *Subah uthke dekha to kutiya mari padi thi,* "When he woke in the morning, he saw the bitch was dead," days, speaking it in public was a different matter altogether.

It would take me a few years to lose this diffidence.

*       *       *

I was soon being called a *writer-activist*, a term I found absurd because it suggested that writing about things that vitally affected people's lives was not the remit of a writer. That needed an additional appellation. To me *writer-activist* sounded a bit like a sofa bed.

My non-Gandhian, nonactivist behavior often embarrassed my Gandhian activist friends. Sometimes terribly so.

I had written an essay called "Power Politics," about India's New Economy, the opening of previously protected markets to unregulated

Capital, and the dangers of indiscriminate Privatization and Structural Adjustment. The essay dwelled in some detail on the disastrous Maheshwar Dam, which was the first dam upstream from the Sardar Sarovar. It was being built by a private corporation.

The NBA had called a press conference in the town of Indore at which I was to be one of the speakers. Some of the journalists definitely seemed more like attack dogs who had been sent by the private corporation than real journalists. They tried to derail the press conference by suggesting (screaming) that I had an illegal mansion in the jungle built on land stolen from an indigenous tribe and therefore had no right to speak about the environment. They were talking about the house that Pradip and Golak had built on the edge of the forest in the village near Pachmarhi. It wasn't illegal, of course, and it wasn't mine. I was disgusted. Here was our great society ("This is India, my dear") in which it was perfectly right that men should inherit everything, and also perfectly right that women should be blamed for what wasn't even theirs. I asked the attack dogs if they wanted an answer from me or had only come to howl. They quietened down. What I did next was, I think, the equivalent of Mrs. Roy's exhibiting her bra and explaining its uses to the boys in her school assembly.

"Let's for the sake of argument assume that I am a very bad person. Let's say that I have an illegal palace in the forest, stuffed with drugs, and that I use indigenous people as bonded labor. *And* I'm not a virgin. OK. But why build the dam?"

It just came out that way. I hadn't thought it through. There was a small, shocked silence. The conference dispersed pretty quickly. The accusation of my illegal palace in the forest followed me around for years though. It had a longer life than the private corporation that was building the Maheshwar Dam. That corporation has collapsed and the dam remains abandoned, half built. A monument to greed and irresponsibility.

*       *       *

"The Greater Common Good" was the first of several essays I wrote on the Narmada dams. I traveled up and down the river. Sometimes by road, sometimes in the boat the NBA had bought with the money that came with the Booker Prize. My travel companion on these journeys was often Sanjay the Neat, who had begun to shoot a long documentary—*Words on Water*—about the anti-dam movement. I was glad to be able to support him, just as I supported Pradip, so that they could take their time to write their books and make their films the way they wanted to—the kind of films and books that no funders or publishers would easily back. I wanted everybody to be able to do the kind of work that funders wouldn't easily fund. Because all of us realized that big money always tended to soften edges and support the status quo. Sometimes brazenly, and sometimes in sophisticated, roundabout ways. Small money is always more subversive.

Not even in my dreams could I have imagined that a single book could earn the kind of money that *The God of Small Things* did. (I mean this relatively, from my point of view, not from a rock star, movie star perspective.) As I traveled in the Narmada Valley, meeting people whose lives, lands, and histories had been or were going to be submerged, desperately poor people facing complete erasure, I felt a little guilty and embarrassed that my book was selling in millions around the world and my bank account was burgeoning. Being a well-known and now-wealthy writer in a country of very poor people, most of whom do not or cannot read books, was troubling. What did it mean? What was the meaning of being me?

Like many women, I became almost apologetic about myself and my so-called success. At times it seemed as though every tender moment in *The God of Small Things* had been traded in for a silver coin. And that if I wasn't careful, I would turn into a cold silver figurine with a cold silver heart.

*       *       *

Once again, but for completely the opposite reason—too much, not too little—money had begun to preoccupy me more than it should. I was disoriented. I began to give it away as quickly as I could. Having grown up with Mrs. Roy and her taunts about being my "banker," I promised myself that I would never attach strings to what I gave away. My motto was "Give. And forget about it." But that didn't work out too well either. Because the art of receiving is just as complicated and requires the same amount of grace as the art of giving. I learned the hard way that too much feminine self-effacement can lead people to slump against you with a callous sense of entitlement and serious disrespect. There are few things in my part of the world that people (which includes women in my part of the world) love more than a self-effacing, invisible woman. At times I felt like the most visible invisible woman in the world.

I was glad to be financially independent. But I had more money than I needed for myself, for Pradip and the girls, for my friends. For anyone who was doing beautiful work, for anyone who needed help. I was sickened by the idea of being seen as a saintly benefactress. Nor did I want to be that virtuous, invisible, self-sacrificing woman. It was a maddening but interesting conundrum.

I muddled around in this ethical quagmire for a long time before I found my way through it. A group of us, which includes activists and lawyers, started a trust into which I put a portion of my royalties every year, as they come in. The trust does not bear my name and does not raise or accept money from anyone else. It is solely devoted to sharing my crazy royalties. The money goes out to journalists, activists, teachers, lawyers, artists, and filmmakers who have the courage to stand up against the tide. To people who understand the politics of corporate NGOs and international foundations and refuse to take money from them. To people who don't know how to or don't want to make smooth proposals that massage the NGO machine. As trusts go, it's tiny, but it is not removed or in any way distant from the people with whom we share our money. And we share it in the spirit of solidarity, not as charity. All of us who are part of the trust know that our work has to be done with the greatest care. Because money can be liberating, but it can also be debilitating and as destructive as nuclear waste. When my books stop selling and the money runs out, our trust will shut down. Like Laurie Baker's architecture, it's not meant to last forever. But for now, we have borrowed our tagline from Golak:

"Thang God we're rich."

*     *     *

In case I'm giving the wrong impression here—I wasn't being self-sacrificing and generous. I believe in the axiom "Beware of the person that sacrifices." (Because they soon become insufferable and extract a price far greater than what they sacrificed.) I had my nonapologetic moments, too. I faxed my bank statement to our relative Mr. Z and asked him if he would like to be my keep, now that I could afford him. I recognized a sense of defiance in myself when I would walk into a shop and buy something without asking the price. I confess to returning from trips with suitcases bulging with clothes and shoes for Pradip and the girls and me. I remember Mrs. Roy had those hinge moments as well—particularly when she graduated from penury into solvency. I was witness to some of them when, as a child, I went shopping with her in Kottayam. Particularly in sari shops.

*I'll take these . . . Yes. All five. And the green one, too.*

# More Trouble with the Law

In 2001 hundreds of villagers from the Narmada Valley traveled to Delhi and converged on the Supreme Court to protest against its judgment that allowed the construction of the Sardar Sarovar to continue. They sat outside the gates for days, singing songs, shouting slogans. I was not present at that protest, but five male lawyers (Batch Number Two) went to the police saying that Medha Patkar, Prashant Bhushan (lawyer for the NBA), and I had physically attacked them. They accused me of trying to strangle one of them with my scarf. It was so silly that even the police, who were present on that day and knew I hadn't been there, refused to register their complaint.

Batch Number Two approached the Supreme Court directly. The Supreme Court is not only strict but very often punitive about being approached directly by petitioners who try to circumvent legal procedure by hopping over district courts and high courts. It has a backlog of tens of thousands of decades-old cases. Hundreds of thousands of undertrial prisoners are packed into crowded jails awaiting their last chance at justice. For them the Supreme Court is almost as out of reach as heaven itself. So, we were shocked when we received summonses asking us to appear personally before the Court and explain our attempts at daylight murder with only our garments for weapons. To this day I do not know what moved the judges of the Supreme Court to act on the five lawyers' outlandish petition.

For our first hearing, I did not hire a lawyer and drafted my affidavit in reply myself. The judges let off Medha and Prashant, but took offense at what I said in my response, and this time charged me formally, on its own behalf, with contempt of court. I was asked to apologize, but I couldn't see what for. I was told that I wasn't behaving like "a reasonable man." Transitioning from being "that woman" to an (un)reasonable man in the eyes of the law was progress of some sort I suppose.

The case became the subject of national debate. A well-loved former judge wrote a piece in the newspaper censuring me for disrespecting the Court. In his next piece he wrote a critique of the Narmada dams in which he lifted paragraphs, sentence for sentence, from something I had written. He was a great man and an excellent judge. But I wished he would choose between patronizing and plagiarizing me. Both together were a little confusing for my pretty little head.

Once the hearings were completed, the Court was adjourned. The sentencing was scheduled for early March 2002.

By then, the world had changed.

Again.

*       *       *

The War on Terror, whatever that was supposed to mean, had begun. U.S. troops had invaded Afghanistan. U.S. hypernationalism was punching the whole world in the face, making our local Indian brand look like a shabby hand-me-down. Any effort to suggest that the 9/11 attacks, tragic though they were, had not taken place in a vacuum but had a historical context was pilloried as a justification of terrorism.

The essay I wrote, against the advice of those who loved me and wished me well (which made it more difficult), "The Algebra of Infinite Justice," was published in papers all over the world except in the United States. The title of the essay was drawn from Operation Infinite Justice, which was what the U.S. invasion of Afghanistan was initially called. It was later changed to Operation Enduring Freedom. We used to joke that it was like the man whose name was Arthur Stinks who went to a great deal of trouble to have his name changed to John Stinks.

International Islamophobia arrived like a gift from God to Hindu nationalists in India. When President George W. Bush said, "You're either with us or with the terrorists," the BJP government could barely hide its glee.

As if somebody had thrown a switch, India was convulsed with a series of "terrorist" attacks. Each of which was immediately labeled "India's 9/11." With terrifying regularity young Muslim men began to be arrested or shot dead in what the police called "encounters." The stupidest, most often repeated remark in political circles in India was "All Muslims aren't terrorists, but all terrorists are Muslims."

*     *     *

Mrs. Roy followed my writing closely, never missing a thing. She subscribed to both *Outlook* and *Frontline* and didn't need me to alert her about what I was up to. To me that felt like love. She was extremely worried, I knew, because she would tell Kurussammal (who was quite old now and had begun to look like a little raisin wrapped in a sari) and some of the teachers in the school, who would tell me when I visited. To me she never expressed any anxiety and acted as though she were completely indifferent. The comments she made about my essays ran along the lines of

"You're just deliberately being nasty."

But she never asked me to back down.

She hovered over me like an unaffectionate iron angel. The metallic swoosh of her iron wings spurred me to pick the big fights, not the small ones. When I went home to Kottayam to visit her—wait, let me rephrase that—when I went to Kottayam to visit her in her home, she would ask me to speak to her older students about what I was doing. Sometimes what I said made their parents uneasy. She ignored them.

Her students were still almost all Syrian Christian. Their parents lived insular, comfortable lives and had insular, comfortable dreams for their children. On one of the occasions when I spoke to the senior students, I said that I was a little tired of hearing from the parents of ex-students about how their children were in Oxford or Harvard or Johns Hopkins University, and that I was waiting for a proud parent to say that their son or daughter was in jail for standing up for something they believed in, for fighting for something other than their own careers, their families, or themselves. That crossed the red line for a few parents. There were some complaints. Mrs. Roy heard them out and then told them that she agreed with me.

The more I was hounded as an antinational, the surer I was that India was the place I loved, the place to which I belonged. Where else could I be the hooligan that I was becoming? Where else would I find co-hooligans I so admired? And who among us supposed equals had the right to decide what was "pro" and "anti" national?

When my grandmother fell ill and was admitted to hospital for what was clearly going to be the last time, she begged her daughter to visit her. Mrs. Roy refused. She was as iron winged with her own mother as she was with me. It had been years since she met her mother, even though they lived a fifteen-minute drive from each other. Mrs. Roy blamed her for supporting her eldest son through the years of the court case, for signing everything he asked her to sign even if that meant the character assassination of her daughter. My mother had never forgiven my grandmother for accompanying G. Isaac when they came to Ooty all those years ago and tried to turn us out of the only shelter we had. Since then, my grandmother had grown into a blind, browbeaten old lady, caught in a firefight between her volatile daughter and her eccentric, entitled son. Her only comfort was her violin, but her violin-playing days were over.

When she died, my brother and I went to her funeral. Mrs. Roy did not.

My grandmother's funeral was like a short story I might have written in my youth. As the bishops stroked their wiry beards and stood over my grandmother's open coffin, preaching mechanically about her wonderful life of music, sacrifice, and food processing, a tiny old lady about as high as my shoulder, white hair plaited into a tight rat's tail, burrowed her way through the crowd and appeared at my side. Our conversation, between the *Amens* of the congregation, was unforgettable.

"I really loved your *God of Small Things*."

"Thank you."

"Shall I tell you which part I liked most?"

"Afterwards maybe?"

"Farting under the water! We all have done it."

When I turned to look at her, the little gnome was gone. I never found out who she was.

Soon after my grandmother died, Mrs. Roy filed an appeal in court to have G. Isaac evicted from the Imperial Entomologist's ancestral home. When the eviction order came, she sat in her car on the main road while the police forcibly threw him and his wife, Soosy, out. When I heard about it from my brother, I reacted with admiration, but sorrow, too. Admiration for Mrs. Roy's steely perseverance—few women would have had the nerve to see it through. Sorrow, because I loved G. Isaac.

Immediately after his eviction he moved into a rented flat in town. Eventually he built himself a small house on the edge of a paddy field, a few kilometers out of town, where he lived with his wife, his mother's old piano, and the oar he had won for being on Balliol's rowing team. The Malabar Coast Products had to be shut down. The old family house was sold, the money divided between the siblings. (And spent.) The new owners demolished it and built an ugly multistory shopping mall in its place. I avert my eyes when I drive past.

*    *    *

While countries were being invaded and rivers were being dammed, while the earth was spinning faster than it should and I was on trial for not behaving like a reasonable man, Micky Roy went missing.

My cousin, daughter of my aunt with whom Micky was living, called me one morning to say that he had disappeared. He had been gone for some days.

"He'll die if we don't find him."

I surprised myself by being distraught. I thought I had trained myself to feel nothing. Micky was not the only person close to me who was addicted to alcohol or drugs. By then I had learned the hard way that every emotion, relationship, good intention—theirs as well as mine—would be trumped by the addicts' craving for whatever they were addicted to. I knew that the only thing to do was to withhold judgment, and, if possible, hope, but to try never to withdraw love, or affection. Of course I knew. But what we know isn't always in line with what we feel, or what we do.

I rushed to Noida, where my aunt lived, on the outskirts of Delhi. My cousin and I walked around the neighborhood for hours asking every cigarette-seller, cobbler, and taxi driver if they had any idea where he might be. They all knew him, and each face crinkled into a smile when we mentioned his name. Micky was their letter writer, form filler, and drinking buddy. By evening we tracked him to a building site. He was living there with a Bengali rickshaw-driver friend in the midst of bags of cement, heaps of sand, and steel reinforcement rods, in a temporary shack made of spare building material covered by a tin sheet. Both he and his housemate were completely sozzled. Micky, swaying in the doorway, told us cheerfully that they were long-lost brothers and were saving money to move back to their village in West Bengal.

I managed to trick him into the car, and we drove him to a hospital, where he was admitted for a few days to dry out. He won over the young doctor who was looking after him by punching the air with his matchstick arms and saying, "Come here, you! Let me box your ears." It reminded me of my brother as a four-year-old in Ooty, punching the air around me saying, "I'm Cassius Clay!"

Once Micky was able to walk straight and wasn't reeking of alcohol, I flew with him to Madras, where I had booked him into a rehabilitation center for eight weeks. (Thang God for royalties.)

I had no idea what I would do with him after that. My aunt said she wouldn't have him back. I had no home of my own where I could look after him.

My brother (who had lost some of his early enthusiasm about his father) and I found a little cottage we could rent for him in a place called Hosanna Mount in Kerala. It was a beautiful campus with half a dozen independent cottages, a palliative-care hospital for poor patients, and a study center with facilities for organizations to host seminars and conferences. The owner promised to keep it quiet and to look after Micky in every possible way. He said he would make sure that Micky had no access to alcohol. It was risky having Mr. and Mrs. Roy both living in Kerala only a couple of hours apart from each other. Anything could happen. The world could end. But since I had no options, I decided to risk it.

Once eight weeks had passed, I went back to Madras to pick Micky up. He was in his room, lording it over a gathering of glue sniffers, cough-syrup junkies, drug and alcohol addicts, nurses and doctors, all of them hanging on his every word, laughing uproariously at his jokes. They seemed to love him and were a little annoyed with me for taking away the life and soul of their party.

I traveled with him to Kerala and settled him into Hosanna Mount. It wasn't easy for him to adjust to solitude after the camaraderie and brotherhood of his co-addicts at the rehabilitation center. I visited him often with every bit of Don Bradman memorabilia I could lay my hands on—cricket caps, badges, signed photographs, and Bovril, which, according to Micky, the Don loved—it didn't help. Micky got lonely and unhappy there. He couldn't speak Malayalam, which meant he couldn't easily woo the people who looked after him or persuade the neighborhood cigarette sellers and shopkeepers to smuggle in alcohol for him. He never asked about his former wife. He lasted in Hosanna Mount only for a few months. He longed to return to Delhi.

Fortunately, his kindhearted sister forgave him and allowed him back into her home and into his own room (where he had his own TV).

His own daughter, meanwhile, was preparing to go to jail.

# Jailbird

On the day of my sentencing, before going to court to present myself, I called Mrs. Roy to say goodbye. I was expecting the maximum sentence for contempt of court—six months.

"Bye, baby girl."

That meant that to her this was just as big as my winning the Booker. To me it was bigger.

The entrance to the courtroom was blocked by a wall of policemen. A crowd of journalists and hundreds of people, many of whom had traveled all the way from the Narmada Valley to demonstrate their support, had gathered outside. I knew what it took—the money, the logistics, the organizing—for so many people to travel such a long distance. It brought tears to my eyes, tears that I hastily brushed away because, in the glare of the cameras, they would be mistaken for fear or regret. I had to go into the courtroom alone. I was given one last chance to be a Reasonable Man and apologize. I politely declined. I was sentenced to a day in prison and ordered to pay a small fine, failing which I would have to remain in jail for six months. It was really quite sweet. Some people advised me not to pay the fine and to stay on in jail to make a political point about the farcical subsection of the contempt-of-court law ("scandalizing and lowering the dignity of the court") that I was being charged with. A law that more or less excluded courts from public criticism. It was a good point, but I thought I had already made it.

Even though my punishment turned out to be more or less symbolic, it still made headlines. It didn't deserve to because something far more serious was happening. The old black-and-white film footage I had written about in "The End of Imagination," the scenes of mass murder and mayhem, of fleeing people being herded into refugee camps, was being reprised. Our present was indeed running toward our past.

In the days leading up to my sentencing, in the state of Gujarat, mobs of men who belonged to vigilante Hindu organizations, proudly wearing saffron headbands to announce their ideological affiliation to the BJP and the RSS, were rampaging through the streets, slaughtering thousands of Muslims in broad daylight. It was carnage on the same scale as the 1984 pogrom against Sikhs in Delhi. The difference was that the massacre of Sikhs by Congress Party workers in 1984 was a political vendetta—at odds with the official, stated ideology of the Congress Party. Legally and morally both massacres were equally reprehensible. But ideologically, they were very different. What was happening in Gujarat was straight out of Hindu nationalism's ideological playbook. And it was being livestreamed on national television. The mobs had stockpiles of gas cylinders and cadastral lists of Muslim homes and businesses. Muslims were being beaten, raped, and burned to death. The police were refusing to intervene. Hospitals were refusing to treat the injured if they were Muslim. More than two thousand people were slaughtered. Tens of thousands had to flee their homes and were living in refugee camps.

All the killing was happening under the cold, unblinking gaze of Gujarat's new chief minister, whom the BJP had paradropped into office three weeks after the 9/11 attacks in the United States. His name was Narendra Modi. (After assuming office unelected, he won a by-election by a narrow margin.) He had been a member of the RSS for all of his adult life. His party clearly knew what he was made of. He was the man they chose for their carpe diem moment. From their point of view, they couldn't have made a better choice.

The massacre had begun a few days prior, at the end of February 2002. People were being murdered even as I was being driven to jail.

The killing was justified as "Hindu" revenge for a terrible tragedy that had taken place on February 27. A coach of a train returning from Ayodhya was burned in Gujarat, at the Godhra railway station. Fifty-nine passengers were scorched to death. They were Hindu devotees, *kar sevaks*, returning home after donating symbolic bricks for the new temple to be built on the ruins of the demolished Babri Masjid. Before a preliminary investigation had been done to ascertain even basic facts, L. K. Advani, the clairvoyant home minister, announced that it was a terrorist attack. The bodies of the pilgrims were put on public display, and Modi gave speeches full of suggestion and innuendo that inflamed public sentiment. The slaughter followed.

It turned out to be the first stepping stone of his glorious political career.

\*       \*       \*

Although I knew I was going to be in jail only for a day, the sound of the prison door slamming shut behind me was unnerving. Clearly I was entering a parallel universe and would be vulnerable as long as I was in there.

The ward where I spent the night was a single-story building, with the cells arranged around a courtyard. Prisoners were only locked into their cells at night. As I entered, the women crowded around me trying to gauge my crime. They weren't interested in the details. They only wanted to know which section of the criminal penal code I had been arrested under. Most of them were charged under one of four categories: harassing their daughters-in-law for extra dowry, prostitution, economic offenses, and murder (of either their husbands or their daughters-in-law). They had me down as a husband killer.

"Section 302? You killed your man?"

It wasn't the time to get into a discussion about my complicated marital status.

"No, no . . . he's alive. He's outside."

For a moment they lost interest in me.

"He's outside? What work does he do?"

"He's writing a book on trees."

They looked a little disappointed. What good was a man who wrote books on trees?

"So why are you here then?"

"They say I insulted the court."

"*Insulted?* . . . They deserve much more than just insults."

You can't call incarcerated people a disinterested party on matters concerning the judiciary. The only other person I knew who had a similarly unshakable bias against the courts, for similarly personal reasons, was G. Isaac. Whenever we went to see him (after he lost the case to Mrs. Roy), my brother and I would lay bets on how soon the conversation would turn to the structural flaws in the Indian judiciary. The options were two minutes, three minutes, and seven minutes. Seven minutes was rare.

*          *          *

In the course of that one day in prison I met Afsan. She had been arrested along with her husband, Shaukat, and two other Kashmiri men as a conspirator for the attack on the Indian Parliament that had happened a few months ago, in December 2001, which of course the BJP prime minister Atal Bihari Vajpayee immediately compared to the 9/11 attacks and blamed on Pakistan. The hundreds of new private television news channels (gone were the days of the staid old single news channel, Doordarshan) had already pronounced Afsan and the others who had been arrested guilty. They broadcast unsubstantiated information from police charge sheets as though it were the absolute, indisputable truth. One channel went to the extent of making and showing a feature-length film based entirely on the police version and calling it the "truth." The prime minister endorsed the film. An enraged public was demanding that the "terrorists" be hanged immediately. Within days of the attack, half a million Indian soldiers were moved to the Pakistan border. Fearing a nuclear war, foreign embassies in Delhi were evacuated. Hysteria was at fever pitch.

To compare the attack on the Indian Parliament to the 9/11 attacks and to what had happened in the United States was disrespectful to the scale and carnage of what happened there. In Delhi, on the morning December 13, 2001, five armed men had driven through the gates of Parliament House in an old Ambassador car, jumped out, and opened fire. They killed eight security guards and a gardener before being killed themselves. The sticker manifesto on their windshield explained their motives in clear, idiotproof language:

INDIA IS A VERY BAD COUNTRY AND WE HATE INDIA

WE WANT TO DESTROY INDIA AND WITH THE GRACE OF

GOD WE WILL DO IT GOD IS WITH US AND WE WILL TRY OUR BEST. THIS EDIET WAJPAI AND ADVANI WE WILL KILL THEM. THEY HAVE KILLED MANY INNOCENT PEOPLE AND THEY ARE VERY BAD PERSONS THERE BROTHER BUSH IS ALSO A VERY BAD PERSON HE WILL BE NEXT TARGET HE IS ALSO THE KILLER OF INNOCENT PEOPLE HE HAVE TO DIE AND WE WILL DO IT.

Within a day of the attack, the Special Cell of the Delhi Police said it had "cracked" the case. The "conspirators" were arrested the day after that. The "mastermind" according to the police was a young Kashmiri professor of Arabic who taught in Delhi University, S. A. R. Geelani. The media made him out to be a cold-blooded killer who had spent his life indoctrinating others to become terrorists. All four of the arrested were in Tihar Jail in Delhi at the same time I was.

When I met Afsan in prison, she was several months pregnant. Her eyes were glazed, her pupils dilated. She seemed to have no idea why she was in jail. She was lying on the floor, unhinged and wailing. Most of the other prisoners shunned her as a terrorist. Her distress and confusion seemed genuine to me. I asked her if she had a lawyer and if there was anything I could do for her after I was released. She looked at me blankly and said, "Do you have a towel? I don't have a towel. I've lost mine."

I sat with her until it was time for us to be locked in. I was given the option of having a cell to myself, but the other prisoners dissuaded me, saying that staying alone was a bad idea. I spent the night in a cell the size of a double bed packed together with three undertrials who were accused of burning their daughters-in-law to death so that their sons could remarry and bring in a second dowry. We slept on the floor with the light on. The courtyard was pitch-black. Late at night we heard men's voices. Someone shone a torch at me through the bars. The new acquisition in the zoo was being inspected. I couldn't see my inspectors. I was glad not to be alone, and grateful for the company, heinous though it might have been. The next morning, I was released into the arms of hundreds of my comrades from the Narmada Valley who had spent the night outside prison waiting for me to come out.

*     *     *

Afsan had her baby in jail. She and her co-accused were tried in a "fast-track" court. The men were sentenced to death, and she to ten years of rigorous imprisonment. Despite the bloodthirsty din being drummed up by the media, some people did realize that a terrible miscarriage of justice had taken place. The police story was shot through with gaping holes. Nothing added up. Nandita Haksar, a well-known human rights lawyer, stepped in. She put together an All India Defence Committe for S. A. R. Geelani—the alleged mastermind of the Parliament Attack. Her thinking was that if she could prove that the mastermind was innocent and had been framed, the whole case would fall apart. Both Sanjay and I, along with a few others who were prepared to face down the anger and hatred that was sure to come our way, agreed to be on the committee. (He, like Nandita, was a Kashmiri Hindu. For Kashmiri Hindus to step up to defend Kashmiri Muslims was unusual. It helped to cut through some of the lies.)

Nandita, assisted by a team of young activists, ran a formidable campaign.

In 2003, after having spent two years in prison, Afsan and Geelani were acquitted of all charges. The sentence of Afsan's husband, Shaukat, was reduced to ten years.

So now we had a conspiracy with no mastermind. That didn't turn out to be a problem. The fourth person, who had so far been cast as a minion in the police script, was quickly promoted. Afzal Guru became the new mastermind. The High Court handed him a double death sentence and several life sentences. *Somebody* had to be punished. In its final 2005 judgment, the Supreme Court said it had no "direct evidence amounting to criminal conspiracy," but went on to say, "The incident, which resulted in heavy casualties, had shaken the entire nation, and the collective conscience of [the] society will only be satisfied if capital punishment is awarded to the offender." A man's life was prescribed as medication to soothe a maddened nation.

Even though she had been acquitted, I could not get Afsan's expression of numb incomprehension out of my mind. I became obsessed with the case. When he came out of jail, I met S. A. R. Geelani, the Delhi Police's first choice for the role of mastermind. He told me how they had all been tortured, beaten, forced to drink urine, and asked to sign confessions. He had refused, but Afzal, who had a young wife and son in Kashmir, succumbed. He allowed the police to videotape not one, but several confessions, each of them spinning a different story. Because the police needed some choice, some shoulder room.

I filled a suitcase with all the legal documents that I could lay my hands on and flew to Goa. It was at the height of the monsoon, so the tourists had moved out. I sat alone in an empty open-air restaurant on the beach with towers of paper taking the place of friends I should have been eating and drinking with. I did not emerge from that reading with a conspiracy theory about the Parliament Attack. I still don't know who did it. But I believe that it isn't who they said it was, and that we had been lied to on every front.

I did one more thing in Goa. I met my old sweetheart JC, who still lived there. It had been twenty years since we were last together. I was thrilled to see him. I don't think he felt the same. He was calm and a little guarded. Understandably. He was happily married with two children. And I was drifting on dangerous currents, messing around with court documents and terrorist attacks.

# My Seditious Heart

The more I learned about the Parliament Attack, the more intrigued I was by the story of Afzal Guru and his long relationship with Davinder Singh, a senior police officer whose fingerprints were all over the case. (He was jailed years later in another case, accused of double-dealing, playing both sides. It somewhat vindicated what Afzal had said about him during his trial. But it was too late.) I decided that it was time to go to Kashmir.

If the Narmada Valley realigned my skeletal structure, the Kashmir Valley spun my heart around. Nothing that you read or watch in the Indian newspapers and television channels prepares you for the reality of Kashmir. I could not believe the range, the depth, the depravity, and the sheer inventiveness of the cruelty that was being perpetrated on a people, all in the name of democracy. "Demon crazy," people there called it, and demon crazy it surely was. Human nature is a permanent exhibit in the Kashmir Valley. Its wickedness as well as its resilience.

Tens of thousands of young Kashmiri men had lost their lives when the struggle for self-determination turned into an armed insurrection in 1990. The valley was dotted with graveyards, almost every village had one. The villagers in the ones that didn't had trouble explaining themselves to other villagers. But apart from the stories of the killing and the dying, apart from learning about those who had been maimed physically and psychologically by unimaginable torture, apart from meeting some of the mothers and "half widows" of the thousands who had "disappeared," apart from the stories of betrayal, collaboration, and inter-militant sub-wars, what shocked me was the way ordinary Kashmiris were expected to live their lives, the routine humiliation they were supposed to accept as normal.

Soldiers were everywhere; they locked down streets, markets, hospitals, highways, villages, forests, and the mountain roads that looked down on the valley. Everything was in their crosshairs. They poked the snouts of their guns literally as well as figuratively into the most private recesses of everyday life. They regulated every inhalation and exhalation of the population.

My first reaction to what I saw was "This looks like a military occupation!"

I was traveling with Sanjay, who was shooting a new documentary. He shushed me. His father was a retired Indian army officer. In Sanjay's family those words would have been nothing short of blasphemous. They were Kashmiri Pandits (Brahmins)—the tiny, privileged Hindu minority, almost all of whom had fled the valley when the Pakistan-backed, overtly Islamist insurrection began. As a community, during the uneasy years since Partition in 1947, and the first public demands by the Muslim majority in the Kashmir Valley for the right to self-determination, most Kashmiri Pandits had aligned themselves with the Indian state. This became more true, steadfastly, bitterly so, after more than two hundred Kashmiri Pandits were killed by militants in the early years of the insurrection, triggering the exodus of the whole traumatized community from the Kashmir Valley. By the time Sanjay finished shooting his film—*Jashn-e-Azadi*, "how we celebrate freedom"—having seen what he saw and learned what he learned, his views, as well as those of his family (beloved son that he was), changed drastically. His heart turned around. He became a scholar of the politics of modern Kashmir. Both in his writing and in his speech, he is more cautious, more circumspect, more empirical, than I am. Still, most Kashmiri Pandits denounce him as an apostate.

Every piece of news that comes out of the Kashmir Valley is censored or twisted around to suit the Indian government's narrative. Every Kashmiri Muslim journalist is on notice. People are blackmailed, intimidated, or bribed into spying on one another and becoming informers. There are double agents, triple agents, quadruple agents. A whole society schooled by experience not to trust itself. The system of incentives, rewards, and promotions seemed only to enhance the brutality meted out by soldiers to Kashmiri civilians.

It is in these malign, shadowy grottoes that Afzal Guru existed (not lived) and tried to survive.

The first of the series of essays I wrote about the Parliament Attack was called "'And His Life Should Become Extinct.'" I borrowed the phrase from the Supreme Court judgment that sentenced Afzal to death. It was the only time that Vinod Mehta, the editor of *Outlook*, asked me to reconsider my decision. "It's ugly out there," he warned me. He was right. Even though the BJP had lost the 2004 elections and a Congress government was in place, the climate of ultranationalist Hindu supremacism was gathering below the surface, building up to a critical mass. After the essay was published, a letter to the editor said, "Spare Afzal Guru and hang Arundhati Roy."

\*　　　\*　　　\*

I was troubled by even the most casual conversations I had in Kashmir.

I could see cold anger and resentment being bottled up by people like money is banked in a capitalist economy. I felt their rage would mature with interest. Somehow. Someday.

The only shield Kashmiri Muslims seemed to have against the systematic cruelty of those who governed them was the solace of religion and the shelter of their close-knit families. Families are close-knit in India, too, of course. The family unit is the rope on which the whole world swings. But in Kashmir it had a different import altogether. Grief, loss, anger, fear, shame—families were drawn close by these threads of acute suffering. That closeness then brought upon itself further punishment. The security establishment often treated Kashmiri Muslim families as though their members were interchangeable. A brother could be arrested or killed in place of another. A father could be tortured till he gave up his son. A whole family could be punished in a variety of ways for what one of its members may or may not have done. All suffering in Kashmir was borne, chronicled, memorialized, quantified, calculated, and assessed—by the perpetrators as well as their victims—along the grid and latticework of family relationships.

For me, who flew another kind of flag, to witness the intensity of familial love and the untethered grief that stems from that love was unsettling. Perversely, it made me feel forlorn and terribly lonely. It made me worry that the unsanctioned ways in which I loved and lived were too precarious, too fragile to withstand real adversity. Even though I knew I was too far out at sea and that for me there was no turning back, it made me question myself, the decisions I had made, the sanctuary I had given up on, the ways in which I had behaved. I talked this over with one of my closest friends, Shohini. She was the only person I knew who I thought might understand what I meant.

She smiled and hugged me. "I'm queer and you are qwicked."

When Qwicked traveled in Kashmir, she was like a private conflict zone wandering through a public conflict zone. And she wondered about queer and qwicked people in Kashmir. Who sheltered them? Who mourned them? Who prayed for them? Who sanctified their unsanctioned grief? Someone did for sure.

To visit Kashmir as an Indian citizen who has even a sliver of conscience is to be unhomed. Because after encountering Kashmir, you cannot return to old conversations, old jokes, harmless fun. Most Indians' deliberate, cultivated, amoral innocence about what is happening there, what is being done there in their name, becomes hard to bear. Almost without my being aware, my circle of close friends changed. I changed. My humor changed. It became a little Kashmiri—bleaker and blacker.

Over the years deep attachments formed. Those friendships are the best kind of royalty a writer could ask for. A Kashmiri journalist asked if I was going to write a book about Kashmir. I told him that I would never presume to write a book about Kashmir, but that Kashmir would be in all the books that I wrote. Because in that ethereally beautiful valley, the souls of everybody, on all sides of the conflict, mine included, were being constructed and corroded simultaneously. There was no innocence.

That soul stuff is what drew me to the valley.

It turned my writing into a high-stakes gamble, a chancy waltz on a mined dance floor.

Fortunately for me, Mrs. Roy had a startlingly refreshing opinion about Kashmir. She had never been there. She knew just as much or as little as most Indians; she had been fed the same propaganda. But she didn't buy it.

"If they don't want us, why are we forcing ourselves on them? It's so vulgar."

# A Home of My Own

To be guarded and diplomatic about what I was seeing and learning in Kashmir wasn't easy. Anything that I said, casually or formally, in writing or in speech, invited violent responses. Police cases were filed. Politicians called for my arrest. Public meetings at which I spoke were attacked. Goons affiliated with the BJP and RSS would march around chanting, *Arundhati Roy gaddar hai, Pakistan ka yaar hai,* "Arundhati Roy is a traitor. She is a friend of Pakistan." I learned to expect trouble the minute I recognized the faces of crime-beat journalists and certain professional provocateurs who came to events at which they knew I would be present. Disrupters always alerted their friends in the media in advance. It wasn't enough for nationalist anger to be expressed. It had to be performed.

Sometimes small mobs and vans full of journalists turned up at Pradip's house thinking that I still lived there. I realized it was just a matter of time before I became a liability to the landlords of my rented apartment. I began to look around for an apartment of my own.

The one I found (on the second floor of course) was on the tree-lined road I used to cycle down on my way to work from the

Nizamuddin dargah. From my terrace I could wave hello to my younger self cycling past. At first, I found the idea of owning an apartment, a beautiful apartment in a beautiful part of Delhi, a little difficult. I have grown used to the idea now and I love my home. My royalty home, bought wholly with the proceeds of literature. A dangerous place of my own. One from which nobody can order me to get out. Every now and then I kiss the walls and raise a glass and a middle finger to my critics, who seem to think that to write and say the things I do I must live a life of fake, self-inflicted poverty.

I was lucky to have found my new apartment while it was under construction. I was able to design most of it myself.

Pradip, who had become an expert on wood and wood polishing, helped me put in my doors and windows. As a gift for my new home, he carved me a fabulous Salvador Daliesque wooden clock—a nonclock—with wavy wooden hands that put the time permanently at ten to two. It was a reference to the little plastic toy wristwatch that seven-year-old Rahel wore in *The God of Small Things*. On her watch, the time was always ten to two.

His field guide, *Trees of Delhi*, had just been published. It garnered him a community of almost reverential admirers. Our girls (whose Noonie I was) were in their mid and late twenties. They still lived with their father. Still quarreled with him and with each other like teenagers. I was still earning indecent sums of money, still supporting the Downstairs life financially. In some strange ways Pradip's clock was right. In parts of my life time stood still. It was always ten to two. Reassuring and unnerving simultaneously.

I made sure that my apartment building had a lift so that Mrs. Roy could visit me. Although I wondered how I would survive such an event. She never did come because by then Delhi's air had turned putrid, almost fatal for a person with asthma as severe as hers. Micky

Roy the Boxer's Boy never made it to my new home either. G. Isaac did. Although he wasn't happy that I no longer lived with Pradip, toward whom he felt an extra tug of kinship because Pradip was a fellow Balliol man.

When I moved in, the lady who lived downstairs came up and complimented me several times for being "brave." I knew she wasn't a reader so I had no idea what she meant. It turned out that she meant I was brave because my front door opens directly into the kitchen and dining space—there was no place for hidden-away, out-of-sight servants. So, according to her, my apartment would have a low resale value. I couldn't believe it. The utter shamelessness of the upper classes in "India, my dear."

# Utmost Happiness

An abandoned baby, her skin smooth and blue-black as a newborn seal's, appears late at night on a pavement in New Delhi. She is swaddled in a crib of litter and is watched over by a column of mosquitoes. Who is she? Whose is she? Whose will she become?

That was how my second novel, *The Ministry of Utmost Happiness*, began to form in my head. Like *The God of Small Things*, it, too, came to me first as an image.

Why did fiction return to me? I honestly cannot say. But it felt like benediction.

I started writing *The Ministry* sitting at my dining table during a summer storm. The wind howled around my apartment. I watched the magnificent neem tree that filled my home with dappled green light oscillate like a metronome, dipping in and out of view. The amplitude of oscillations increased alarmingly. Then the tree dipped and did not reappear. I found myself in tears. I went out into the storm and saw it, lying on its side like a beaten animal, its roots torn out, taking the soil with it. Was it a curse? A curse on my new book and the story I was trying to tell? The curse of the second novel?

When the storm settled, instead of a tree, my home was full of sky. Instead of something comforting, something specific, something with a clear form and shape, I had something indeterminate, risky, moody, open-ended. Something waiting to be described. A young gray hornbill swooped in and sat on my balcony. It shrieked at me like Mrs. Roy. "If you're writing a book, then you jolly well sit down and write it."

So, I obeyed.

It was peacetime. Or so they said.

All morning a hot wind had whipped through the city streets, driving sheets of grit, soda-bottle caps, and bidi stubs before it, smacking them into car windshields and cyclists' eyes. When the wind died, the sun, already high in the sky, burned through the haze and once again the heat rose and shimmered on the streets like a belly dancer. People waited for the thundershower that always followed a dust storm, but it never came. Fire raged through a swath of huts huddled together on the riverbank, gutting more than two thousand in an instant.

Still the amaltas bloomed, a brilliant, defiant yellow. Each blazing summer it reached up and whispered to the hot brown sky, *Fuck you.*

She appeared quite suddenly, a little after midnight. No angels sang, no wise men brought gifts. But a million stars rose in the east to herald her arrival.

The storm I wrote about wasn't the one I had just witnessed. The new storm jogged my memory of an old one—my first Delhi dust storm, which I watched as I sat inside the inverted arch of the brick sculpture on the lawns of the School of Architecture hostel, high on my first spliff.

The chapter was called "The Nativity." It ended up being the third chapter of the book. The young gray hornbill came almost every day that summer, to shriek at me, to get me going, and to supervise my progress. I called her Mart. I took her chiding as a blessing. As I did Mart Sr.'s.

*The Ministry of Utmost Happiness* evolved as a conversation between graveyards. One graveyard is the beautiful valley of Kashmir, often referred to as *jannat*, "paradise," which is overlaid with graves. The other is a graveyard just outside the walled city of Delhi, where Anjum, one of the main characters, lives and gradually begins to enclose graves to build the Jannat Guest House, in which each room has a grave of its own.

Anjum, CEO of the Jannat Guest House (and CEO of the novel, too), was born to a Shia Muslim family in Old Delhi. Brought up as a boy—Aftab—she transforms into Anjum and leaves home to live with others like herself in the Khwabgah—the House of Dreams. They call themselves Hijras—bodies in which a Holy Soul resides. In 2002 Anjum and her father's friend Zakir Mian travel to Ahmedabad in Gujarat, where they get caught up in the Gujarat massacre. Zakir Mian is murdered but Anjum is spared because the Hindu vigilantes doing the murdering believe that killing a Hijra would bring them bad luck. Traumatized and unable to return to her old life at the Khwabgah, she moves with her few possessions to live in the graveyard where members of her family are buried.

It takes Anjum a long time to regain her fierce spirit, but when she does, she begins to build the Jannat Guest House, which, over the years, turns into Jannat Guest House & Funeral Services—a place where derelicts, vagrants, and those who have fallen out of India's strict grid of caste, religion, gender, and ethnicity are buried, where all kinds of prayers are said, all kinds of poems read.

The Jannat Guest House is not a dream or yearning for another world. It *is* that other world. It is that subversive revolution hidden in plain sight that goes on every moment of every day. To see it, to know it, you only have to pay attention.

*The Ministry* folded me into itself. It was the city I lived in. The river I swam in. Its characters crowded into my home and refused to move out. When I traveled, they came with me and made their own connections and affiliations, came to their own conclusions.

I was in no hurry. Nor were they.

Lucky.

Because it would be ten years before I was able to finish writing it.

# Madam Houdini and the Nothing Man

As Anjum and I mounted our stealth operation in the Old Delhi graveyard, bribing and cajoling municipal officers, building our guest-house a room at a time, a grave at a time, I continued to make trips to Kottayam every three or four months to see Mrs. Roy. It was the one place where I always went alone, without Anjum. Because she was a match for Mrs. Roy, temperamentally and otherwise. I couldn't see them getting along. I couldn't risk them meeting.

Mrs. Roy was now in her mid-seventies. She was slowing down, getting visibly more fragile. My brother's wife, Mary Roy Jr., had taken over a lot of the administrative responsibilities. She lived warily in her mother-in-law's house, doing what she could without putting herself in the way of her mother-in-law's wild temper. In an odd, convoluted way, for everyone who worked with Mrs. Roy, her behavior with me served as a consolation: *If she's like this with her own daughter, then maybe we shouldn't be too upset by the way she is with us.* I boosted their tolerance levels. Inadvertently I gave my mother more latitude to misbehave with other people. We all hung on to that old trope, the life raft on which battered wives, mistreated children, and abused employees stay afloat: *It's only because she loves us.*

The worst casualty among us was Mrs. Roy's loyal secretary, Mercy GeeVerghese, who had been at her side through every crisis—all her court cases and other confrontations. Mercy had, for decades, worked night after night, way beyond the call of duty, taking dictation, preparing documents for whatever high-wire drama Mrs. Roy was currently involved with. It was hard to watch the way Mercy was treated. And impossible to intervene because her three children were on scholarship in the school, receiving the best possible education, which their mother did not want to disrupt. Even now, so long after she has retired, I visit her, only to find her sitting on her sofa, staring into space, tears rolling down her cheeks, unable to forget how she was humiliated, year after year. But sometimes, when we're together, we act out some legendary Mrs. Roy scenes and those tears turn into helpless laughter. We compete to see which of us can shout "Get out!" louder. Mercy is one of the funniest women I know.

\*     \*     \*

A naturopath who Mrs. Roy had begun to consult had radically changed her diet and inhaler protocol, which seemed to help a little. He made the mistake of offering her some nonmedical counsel. He told her that *The God of Small Things* was written for her, *to* her, and that if she wanted to get better, she should consider having a serious conversation with her daughter about the past. I heard about this from Mary Roy Jr., who had accompanied her to the naturopath. I wasn't flattered by his reductive view of literary fiction. But Mrs. Roy had an entirely different version of the conversation.

"My new doctor says that all my sickness is because of you."

A superb maneuver. Even Bruce Lee would have applauded.

Her new diet and inhaler protocol controlled the frequency and intensity of her asthma attacks. But her lungs were getting weaker and losing their elasticity. If she caught even the slightest chest infection, they were unable to cope. Her oxygen saturation levels would plummet and the carbon dioxide level in her blood would shoot up. This caused inflammation in her brain, which affected her coherence and made her hallucinate. At the first sign of incoherence, she had to be rushed to hospital. Each time she was admitted, we were prepared that she might not survive. She was lucky to live in Kerala, where there are small hospitals with excellent doctors and nurses in almost every town and village.

Her stock was high in the hospital she went to in Kottayam. It was owned and run by two of her former students. The doctor who looked after her, Dr. Rajesh, had children in her school. They all adored her and tolerated her tantrums with infinite patience and good humor. She had the whole establishment wrapped around her little finger. From the moment she was admitted she would begin to raise hell, throwing the whole place into a spin, agitating to be discharged. Often I would fly down from Delhi and drive straight to the hospital from Kochi. Standing outside the ICU, I could hear her yelling.

"I'm Arundhati Roy's mother! Let me out! I'll file a police case!"

But when she saw me, she would glower and become paranoid.

"All these people here, they're only interested in you, not me."

If she was moved to a private room, she raised havoc there, too. She developed random but intense likes and dislikes of hospital nurses and her own staff. She would so charm the ones she liked that they'd virtually be prepared to lay down their lives for her. The ones she disliked would leave her room weeping. It was exactly how Anjum behaved with guests at the Jannat Guest House in the graveyard.

Some would be welcomed and allowed to live there for months for no charge; others would be turned away with an unearthly roar. I wonder where she got that from. Maybe Mr. Mary Roy c/o India My Dear. My mother once told me with a laugh, but with unmistakable pride, that people thought she had achieved *purushaprapti*—the status of a man. Her journey was, in a way, the reverse of Anjum's.

One morning Dr. Rajesh dropped in to her hospital room to see how she was doing. He was a sweet, shy man with an endearing lisp. He often visited her at home and knew her medical history well. She was sitting up on her bed, dressed in her hospital gown, when he walked in. She flashed him her winning smile. She had dimples you could drown in.

"Dr. Rajesh, do you love me very much?"

Even though he was used to her, this really embarrassed him.

"Yes, Mrs. Roy. Everybody loves you."

Her expression suddenly changed. "Oh, that's nice, because I *hate* you! Let me out of here!"

When she was finally discharged, I wheeled her down the hospital corridors, past groups of patients who often rose to their feet out of respect for her and all that she had done for the town. She rolled past scowling, refusing to acknowledge them, twisting her head around to address me instead.

"It's all about you, isn't it?"

All that the spectators saw was a loving mother and her caring daughter.

I was in Kottayam one Christmas Eve when she had just come home from a short stay in hospital. She told me that she wanted a commode—a portable WC—near her bed. She had some precise specifications for the kind of commode it should be. My sister-in-law made some calls, and in a few hours, several salesmen were laboring up the hairpin bend with every possible type of portable commode. Once they had all assembled, Mrs. Roy sent for me. She was sitting at her little round rosewood table in the room next to her bedroom where she watched TV on a huge flat-screen. To her left was a crescent moon of men with portable commodes. To her right, another, of bankers, shopkeepers, and wholesale stationery suppliers who had brought her Christmas cake. She beckoned me to her and whispered loudly enough for all of them to hear:

"This is what you call woman power."

It was. But it was also what you call class power. And all kinds of other abstruse power.

Each time I went to Kottayam, I made a point of visiting Ayemenem. I needed to say hello to the fish in the Meenachil and to the trees on her banks. It wasn't nostalgia that took me back so much as the desire to exorcise some of my old ghosts by looking them in the eye, and to hang on to others, to tell them of my great escape. That, I learned, is impossible. We either house all our ghosts as I do, or unhouse them all, as my brother does. There's no bargaining with ghosts. On my visits I often dropped in to pay my respects to the old Rotary Club too. I was attached to it in the way some people are to their grandparents.

The car workshop downstairs is no longer there. Neither is the grease. The club has moved, the halls are locked up. But they haven't changed at all. The same rough concrete floors that made me sneeze, the same row of baby washbasins outside. When I peer through the dim windowpanes, time seems to have stood still. (It's ten to two.) The shrieks of happy children still hang in the air. I can see Mrs. Mathews's quivering outrage and hear ChellappenBhavani keeping the staccato beat with a baton on a piece of wood—*ttha tthaiy thirakitta ttheem*—for our unchristian bharatanatyam classes. I can see myself sitting on a low stool at a trestle table, pretending to concentrate on my lessons, but worrying instead about the cold sweat trickling down the back of my legs, wondering if that meant that the Kottayam Santa had made me pregnant. I can hear the sound of the slow ceiling fan, informing me of my impending doom.

*　　　　*　　　　*

Mrs. Roy's big health crisis came in July 2007. I was forty-seven. It was, as always, a scorching summer in Delhi. Perhaps as some sort of premonition, I had developed low-grade asthma. It disappeared when that horrible year ended and hasn't reappeared since. I will never understand or get over the fact that Mary Roy and Micky Roy, who hadn't seen or spoken to each other for forty-five years, were both admitted to hospital on the same day. He in Delhi, she in Kottayam. Neither knew about the other. I was with him and my brother was with her.

After years of being rescued from his various deeds and exploits, Micky had gone back to the Yellow Stuff and the Orange Stuff that he had warned me against the day I first met him. The high quantities of varnish in the batch of bootleg liquor he drank burned through his intestines and turned them to lace. He was hemorrhaging internally. The doctors said it was peritonitis. And that it was the endgame for him. Micky found a reason to be cheerful about that, too. He couldn't speak because he was on a ventilator. Blood traveled from his abdominal cavity through a tube and filled a bottle that hung behind his bed. He indicated that he wanted to write. I gave him a pen and an envelope.

*What's wrong with me? No lies.*

I told him he had peritonitis.

*Bradman died of peritonitis.*

And then:

*Can you give me fifty chips? I have to tip the nurses. I'll be getting out on Wednesday.*

I could see that he was sinking. A day later my brother called and said that it looked as though Mrs. Roy was sinking, too. It was an awful choice to have to make. Fortunately my aunt and cousins were in the hospital with Micky. I said goodbye to him and left for Kerala. I knew I would never see that beloved rogue again.

By the time I arrived at the Kottayam hospital, Mrs. Roy was almost comatose. I was about to enter her room when my cousin messaged to say that Micky had died. He became just another statistic in what newspapers like to call a "hooch tragedy." I didn't have a moment to mourn him. Within twenty minutes of Micky dying, Mrs. Roy was being wheeled into the ICU to be put on a ventilator. It was hard not to read some deep, esoteric meaning into the timing of all this.

Micky's doctors in Delhi had told me that for elderly people to come off a ventilator was rare, if not impossible. My mother was almost seventy-four. The doctors said her chances were slim. I felt as though I were dying myself. My valiant organ-childhood flooded back. I tried to breathe for her. I admit that I prayed. To the only God I knew, the God of Dogs, the God of Fig Wasps, the God of Striped and Spotted Things . . . *Please, God. Please please please* . . . The corridor outside the ICU was full of people crying for her. G. Isaac, more than eighty years old by now, was there, too. For his little sister, Mart.

Someone heard us. Something worked. Within a few hours Madam Houdini opened her eyes. We were allowed in to see her.

When she realized that she was on a ventilator, her rage was uncontrollable, and all of it was focused on me. I was used to her anger, but this time I couldn't decode it. Her blazing eyes followed me around, drilled into me wherever I went. In them I saw not only anger, but unmasked hatred. I was mystified. I couldn't understand what I had done, or what she thought I had done.

Only months later did the school office give me a letter she had written to me long ago in which she said that she did not want to be put on life support and that it was her daughter's responsibility to see to that. Only then did I understand that her rage against me came from a feeling of betrayal that I had no idea about. Over the next few days, the doctors tried to wean her off the ventilator and failed. Her lungs did not have the strength to exhale on their own. We decided to shift her to a bigger hospital in Cochin.

In the big hospital she stayed on the ventilator for three weeks. Her suffering was indescribable. To watch her, this powerful woman, our crazy, unpredictable, magical, free, fierce Mrs. Roy, reduced to abject helplessness, was its own form of suffering. We longed for her to get out of bed and send us scattering. She was pumped with steroids through a port in her neck. Her arms had turned a dark purple from being jabbed by needles. On certain days she became so violent that she had to be strapped down. But Dr. Mohan Mathew, a veteran of critical care at the hospital, had no doubt at all that she would recover. He said that her unmanageable anger showed a fighting spirit that wasn't anywhere close to giving up. He was right. Miraculously, one morning she came off the ventilator.

Except I wasn't sure whether it was her or someone else. The doctors didn't warn us that the side effects of the steroids she was being given and her prolonged stay in the ICU could induce temporary psychosis. Although she was breathing by herself and her oxygen saturation levels were steady, she was completely disoriented. Her pupils were dilated, but suddenly they would narrow and her eyes would turn sly and cunning. She was paranoid and restless. She believed she had been kidnapped and held hostage by my brother and me, that we were trying to take over her school and that I was the mastermind of the operation. She trusted nobody. She didn't sleep for days at a time and was suspicious of her medications. She tried to bribe the nurses to help her escape. She offered to sign over all her property to them.

The day she was moved from the ICU to a room of her own, the hospital lifts were not working, so she had to be carried up the stairs on a stretcher. It was like a scene from Werner Herzog's *Fitzcarraldo*, in which a group of men carry a small ship over a mountain. The hospital stairwell looked like the last, difficult leg of a punishing pilgrimage. Four people carried the stretcher at a steep, dangerous angle with angry, suspicious Mrs. Roy strapped to it. They were followed by a procession of staff from her school carrying her clothes, her sheets and pillows, her crockery, her curtains, her inhaler and steamer. Bringing up the rear was somebody carrying a large jar of jujubes. She had become obsessed with jujubes.

Being in a room of her own did not calm her down. She wasn't sleeping at all. The doctors were reluctant to prescribe sedatives for somebody with such a serious pulmonary disorder. Had I known it was psychosis and that it would pass, I might have found it easier to handle. Since I didn't, and nobody had thought to show me her letter, her heightened hostility toward me seemed like a display of her actual feelings, which she was too ill to mask anymore. Her undisguised hatred wore me down. She developed another strange fixation. I couldn't tell whether it was real or her way of needling me. She wanted to know the religion and the caste of every doctor, nurse, and cleaner who looked after her. She kept up a running commentary: *He's not a real Syrian Christian. He's from the fisherman caste. She's a Chowathi. Those men are all Parayas. . . .* (Parayas are considered to be the bottom rung of the ladder of all the Dalit castes in Kerala.) I couldn't believe it. I couldn't understand it. It was completely unlike her, and it so enraged me that I found it hard to be around her.

She sounded like the people from our childhood who would whisper about my brother and me not being blue-blooded Syrian Christians. Their whispering made her protect us fiercely. But sometimes she would relay the insults to us:

"Do you know what they call you? *Address illathu pillaru*—'the children without an address.'"

It probably hurt her more than it hurt us because we were too young to understand what it meant. The slur had less to do with our having no paternal home, no address, than it did with our having no father, no dynast with a proper family name and a rubber, coffee, or spice estate for my brother to inherit. After all, who knew who our father was? Certainly not us, except for the photographs in the gray album, which we examined closely whenever we got a chance. So, *address illathu pillaru* could, at best, be taken to mean "those little hybrid mongrels" and at worst "those little bastards."

The fury building up in me about her running commentary in hospital wasn't just political or altruistic. It was personal.

Lack of sleep deepened her disorientation. A psychiatrist prescribed a mild antidepressant. It had no immediate effect. Hospital infections were also a constant worry. After three more weeks of hardly any sleep, the doctors felt that she might recover better if she was in a familiar environment. They decided to discharge her, but asked us to keep her in Kochi in my brother's flat and watch her for a few days before taking her back to Kottayam.

The hospital nurses had been relentlessly cheerful and professional. It was hard for us to manage her in the flat without them. We were all worn to the bone because we had to be at her beck and call, attending to her endless requests—*Put on the fan, Put it off, Draw the curtains, Open them, Take off my socks, Put them back, Change my diaper, Change it again*—night and day. It was all a part of the mania, but we didn't know that. We tried to take shifts, but she wouldn't let us. She wanted all of us on call all the time. She asked for me constantly and would get furious if she heard I was sleeping. I wanted to go back to Delhi, but my conscience wouldn't allow me to leave my brother and sister-in-law to deal with the nightmare. It might have turned out better if I had.

One night I was woken up and summoned to her room. She was lying in bed with her eyes open. She barely acknowledged me. She didn't need anything, she just wanted me to stand around. I felt I was on the verge of a breakdown myself. Suddenly she said in an unnaturally loud voice, "Tell those Parayas to come in here and clean me."

Without realizing what I was doing, I picked up the chair near her bed and smashed it down. Her body jerked. I could literally see the sound traveling through it. It was the first and only time in all my life with my mother that I had reacted spontaneously. And what a terrible reaction it was. I thought I had killed her. But I hadn't. I had only killed something in myself.

She was used to complete subservience. Nobody had ever responded to her like this before. The shock made her momentarily lucid. She seemed to return to her old self. She sent for my brother. When he arrived, I left the room. She told him that she would not under any circumstances live in the same house as me, and if he didn't ask me to leave, she would leave. My brother told her that she was free to go.

Our mother was old and very sick. But so were the rocks that weighed down our souls. They sometimes made it impossible for us to do the right thing, or even to know what the right thing was. She summoned her personal car, the school car, and two more hired ones.

Her convoy (with jujubes) left at dawn. LKC and I, terribly worried, followed at a safe distance.

When I think back to that night, those knotted feelings, all that twisted, matted anger, the fetid threads of caste and feudal hierarchy that slither into our souls even in our most intimate moments of insanity, vulnerability, and mortality, my mind shuts down. Do we have to kill our own mothers to exorcise this horror that lives inside us? What if she had died? What if I had killed her? How could I, valiant organ-child who had spent my childhood breathing for her, have continued to live? Maybe she had always known that I would be the one to kill her. Maybe that is why she was the way she was with me.

When she got back to her school, members of the cult lined the road from the hostel right up to her home to greet her. Short of waving palm fronds, they did everything. My brother and I drove in quietly, after the hosannas were over, and slipped into the house. Mrs. Roy was put to bed. Her things were unpacked and put away. Her jar of jujubes sat next to her nebulizer on her bedside table. It was raining heavily. The voltage flickered, the lights were dim. Within a couple of hours her oxygen level began to dip. She became restless. She couldn't recognize anybody, including my brother. I slipped into her room and went to her. She looked at me but didn't seem to know who I was. She said there were Chinese people in the room. And a whole lot of roosters pecking at her furniture. She threw her head back and began to howl like a wolf. I sat next to her and put my arm around her.

"Why are you doing that?"

She smiled at me blankly. "Isn't that what dogs do?"

I called Dr. Mohan Mathew in Cochin. I will never be able to repay him for what he did. He got into an ambulance and drove like a bat out of hell to Kottayam. Once he arrived, he sat and watched her without saying a word for about twenty minutes. Then he called for the stretcher, loaded her into the ambulance, and was off.

The convoy followed. With the sheets, pillows, towels, inhalers, curtains, clothes, and the jujubes, of course. At the head of it, just behind the ambulance, in a separate car, a pair of murderers. My brother and me.

We were driving in the dark. The monsoon was at its peak. The Kerala monsoon always made me feel that God was speaking to us directly, with no intermediaries. The sky was thunder. The air was water. Rain smashed down. We could hardly see anything except our windshield wipers and the blurred taillights of the ambulance ahead of us. Our hearts were racing about five hundred times faster than the cars were moving. Every time the ambulance stopped or slowed down to navigate a pothole, we thought it was all over. For us she died as many times as the number of potholes on the Kottayam–Cochin highway. When we got to the hospital, we drove with the ambulance to the back entrance of the emergency ward. The sound of the rain hammering down on the tin roof of the hospital porch was like the soundtrack of a cheap horror film. But inside the hospital it was deathly quiet. We were braced for the whole story to repeat itself. Ventilator, steroids, psychodrama. Fortunately that didn't happen. They put her on a BiPAP machine, the pulmonary equivalent of those little side wheels on children's cycles. With carefully calibrated pressure, it helped her lungs to go about their business of inhaling and exhaling. In a few days she was out of the ICU and in a private room of her own. Two weeks later she was home.

I stayed close by, but out of her way. I finally read the letter she had written to me asking me to make sure that she wasn't put on life support. I was grateful that I hadn't seen it earlier and followed her instructions, because she lived for fifteen years after coming off that ventilator. It took her months to get well, and though she never recovered completely, she lived a full life.

She needed oxygen for several hours a day. The doctors suggested that she use a BiPAP machine at night. We bought one, but she flat out refused to use it. Mainly because we had bought it. She was still suspicious and paranoid. It was a task to get her to take her medicines. She had no memory of the weeks she'd spent in hospital, of having been on a ventilator, of being taken to Cochin. The only thing she was clear about was that I owed her an apology. For something. She was a little fuzzy about what. Or why.

I couldn't do it. I decided to return to Delhi and wait for her to calm down. We hadn't yet told her about Micky. We thought we'd tell her when she got better. We needn't have worried. When we finally did, it hardly seemed to matter to her.

She just murmured absentmindedly, "Poor fellow. He was such a Nothing Man."

*     *     *

Back in Delhi I went looking for Micky's grave. He ought to have been buried in Anjum's graveyard. Then we could have made a room around his grave and I could have lived there with him, in Anjum's Jannat Guest House. Instead, he was buried in the Indian Christian Cemetery in Burari on the outskirts of Delhi. It was a wild, unkempt place with small creatures scurrying through the tall grass. There were hundreds of graves, most of them makeshift and unpretentious. The graves of poor people. There was no chance of my being able to find Micky's grave by just looking around. Since I knew the date on which he died, I went to the tiny office at the entrance and asked for the logbook. There he was, in the tattered book, right under the late Ms. C. Betty—Rajib Michael Roy, son of Paresh Roy.

Micky Roy the Boxer's Boy.

The man who worked in the office walked me to the grave. My cousin had made him a green marble gravestone. It said JUST AS I AM. She really loved him. I sat with Micky for a while. I tried not to be *muggrah*. I couldn't hold him and my mother together visually in the same frame. It was the first time that he didn't ask for money for a drink. I wished he had. I wished I had brought him some good whiskey. As I walked away, I could have sworn he stood up on his toothpick legs, made a pair of binoculars with his hands, and peered through them at me.

"Ta-ta then. Bye-O. Don't be good."

*          *          *

It took months for matters to improve between Mrs. Roy and me, but eventually they did. I broke the ice by calling her and playing "Old Man River" and her other favorite, "Hi-Lili, Hi-Lo," to her on the phone. She would try to sing along.

> *The song of love is a sad song*
> *Hi-lili, hi-lili, hi-lo*
> *The song of love is a song of woe*
> *Don't ask me how I know*

It's hard to describe how her singing tore through me.

She had stopped going down to her office. She held most of her meetings at home. Although she could walk, she had stopped walking altogether and insisted on using a wheelchair. She often hosted lunches and dinners for visiting relatives or groups of old students. She would always disappear in the middle of the meal—or not appear at all. Her guests would be served by the staff. If they became too relaxed or had too good a time, chits would be delivered to them from the bedroom: *Please lower your voices.*

I began to visit her again. In her new, housebound life, every morning and evening she sat out on her tiny front porch in her wheelchair and watched the children walk past her, up and down the hill, for their dance classes, swimming lessons, theater practice. It had been years since she had taught a class herself, so for the new generation of students she was just a barnacled rock, or a monument of some kind, to be regarded with awe and not a small amount of fear. On her birthdays she would appear on her balcony like Evita Perón or a Bollywood movie star. The children assembled below and sang for her. They called her Mary Ammachi, "granny." *Mrs. Roy* had been canceled along with English medium instruction in the junior classes. The children learned Malayalam now, and English only in their senior years. No more punishments.

Mary Ammachi was in her eighties learning to read and write Malayalam, too. On the days when the sun was sharp, she wore a pair of stylish Christian Dior sunglasses that I had been gifted when I was on the jury of the Cannes Film Festival. With those magnificent sunglasses on, she looked as though she could tackle the whole world single-handedly. Hindu god-men, Muslim maulanas, Christian bishops, Communist apparatchiks, corporate robber barons—no sweat. On the wall behind her was a poster with a black-and-white ink drawing of a huge, malevolent mosquito with a vicious proboscis and a children's poem about mosquitoes written in Malayalam, which she would read aloud falteringly to show off her prowess to teachers and old students who visited her. There's not a person I know who wasn't floored by the charm of that performance.

*Mooli pattu paadi varunnoru*
*chora kudiyan kurukomban . . .*

Here he comes with his harmless hum,
that bloodsucking evil little tusker . . .

Until the day she died, she never stopped learning, never stagnated, never feared change, never lost her curiosity.

One of her first students published a book, *Brick by Brick*, about her life. She edited it herself, slashing through whole pages mercilessly, excising paragraphs that even tangentially praised other people, rewriting sentences as if it were a holiday assignment that her student (who would have been in his mid-fifties) was turning in. Her one-page introduction to her own hagiography, which she had signed below, as though she was issuing a check, was entirely in capital letters:

NOTHING CAN BE MORE REWARDING THAN TO WIN THE TRUST OF YOUNG PEOPLE. TO TEACH THEM, TO LEARN FROM THEM AND TO USHER THEM INTO SOCIETY AS ADULTS, READY TO USE THEIR SKILLS TO MAKE THE WORLD A BETTER PLACE TO LIVE IN.

She had done that for generations of her students. Without a doubt. But when my brother read it, he threw his head back and laughed his delighted laugh.

"It's true, it's true."

She tested my brother's and my love for her by giving us shopping lists for the most unlikely things. Mostly clothes and shoes. When I brought them for her, she would put them all on at once. On one of those occasions, I found myself sitting next to her on her high bed. She was perched on the edge, looking thrilled, swinging her legs like a schoolgirl, wearing her oxygen nasal cannula, her diamond earrings, a size 44DD lilac lace bra, adult diapers, and a pair of high-top Nike basketball shoes—"for stability," she explained.

I remember thinking, *What chance do I have at anything that vaguely resembles normality?*

She loved herself. Everything about herself. I loved that about her.

*　　　*　　　*

I was particularly pleased with the bra. It had been hard to find because she had exact specifications. I had bought it for her in Italy, in Ferrara, city of the Finzi-Continis, whose story I wanted to gift the Kottayam collector who had banned *Jesus Christ Superstar*. I was there for a small festival hosted by the city. The main attraction for me was that my beloved friend John Berger, one of the most tender, attentive, beautiful writers I have read, was going to be there, too. So many of us had grown up reading his *Ways of Seeing*. Soon after my essays on the Narmada dams were published, I got a letter from him, a fax actually, written in his graphic handwriting: *Your fiction and non-fiction—they walk you around the world like your two legs.* He was one of the few people who didn't pit my fiction and nonfiction against each other as though they were antagonists.

After the festival, I was going to spend some time with him in his village in the French Alps. Before we left Ferrara, John Berger and I spent half a day looking for bras for Mrs. Roy. Each time we entered a shop, I hung back to experience the sheer delight of watching this extremely handsome eighty-something man say in his British-accented Italian, "Excuse me, could you show us what you have in size

44DD?" I loved that he was helping me to buy my mother's lingerie. I occasionally allowed myself these weird, secret games.

The first evening we spent together in his home, after dinner and after we had washed the dishes, John turned to me still wearing his kitchen apron and said, "I know you're writing something. I want you to read it to me."

I hadn't so much as hinted that I was writing a book and was taken aback at that calm instruction. I find it hard to read from a novel that I am in the process of writing. I worry that if I do, it will just stand up and walk away. But with John Berger, it felt like the most natural thing to do. In the quiet of that mountain night, I read to him from *The Ministry of Utmost Happiness*. I started at the beginning, with Anjum.

She lived in the graveyard like a tree. At dawn she saw the crows off and welcomed the bats home. At dusk she did the opposite. Between shifts she conferred with the ghosts of vultures in her high branches. She felt the gentle grip of their talons like an ache in an amputated limb.

John Berger could have written a book called *Ways of Listening*. He listened with his whole body. As though my words were rain, and he was the earth. He absorbed everything, gathered every drop, missed absolutely nothing. His listening eyes were lakes in the high mountains. It was love, there's no other word for it. I don't think that stillness, that quality of attention, is even possible in digital-age humans, who suckle on mobile phones from the moment they're born. It's a generational thing. Lost forever, I believe.

When I finished, he said, "I want you to promise me that you will go home and finish this book. You will do nothing other than finish writing this book. If anything happens to upset you, remember that

I'm standing right behind you like an old elephant, flapping my ears to cool you down."

That might be the most beautiful thing that anybody has ever said to me. Until he said it, I didn't realize how badly I needed an old elephant. From then on, I called him Jumbo, and he called me Utmost. I made him a solemn promise but went home and broke it almost immediately. I had to. He understood.

# Walking with the Comrades

It was 2010. True to my promise to John, I was working hard on *The Ministry of Utmost Happiness* when a sealed envelope was pushed under my door. It was an invitation from the Communist Party of India (Maoist)—the Naxalites—to go into the Dandakaranya forest in Bastar, where a bloody war was raging. It was a new war, but an old, old story. About mining companies, money, lies, soldiers, guerrillas, vigilantes, barbaric violence, and the vandalism of the earth. An old story that must be told and retold because it challenges the meaning of progress, happiness, and civilization itself.

The Congress government in power in Delhi at the time had signed hundreds of memorandums of understanding handing over the protected homelands of indigenous tribes to corporate mining and infrastructure companies. The fight against mass displacement and environmental desecration was no different from the fight in the Narmada Valley. Except that in those villages deep inside the jungle, people were not fighting rising water. They were fighting flying bullets.

To clear the land for the corporations, the government had flooded the forest with tens of thousands of paramilitary soldiers. It had raised a vigilante army, the Salwa Judum, "purification hunt," recruited from the very population of indigenous people that was being evicted. The Salwa Judum, weaponizing old rivalries and blood feuds, had gone about its mission by raping, murdering, and burning down hundreds of villages. The official name for the eviction drive was Operation Green Hunt.

Inside the forest, the Maoist People's Liberation Guerrilla Army, the PLGA, was seeing unprecedented recruitment. It had responded to Operation Green Hunt with killings, land mine blasts, and ambushes on convoys of security forces. The Congress prime minister, Manmohan Singh, called the Naxalites India's single largest internal security threat. He was right. Extreme poverty was, is, and ought to be India's single largest internal security threat.

The note inside the envelope asked me to be at the Maa Danteshwari Temple in Dantewada, Chhattisgarh, at any of four given times on two given days. I felt that if I wanted to make even the smallest contribution toward breaking the lying, bullying consensus being built up in the media, I'd have to go in.

I remembered my first introduction to the Naxalites—the photograph of the beheaded landlord on the front page of the papers the day we got our first telephone in our hostel-home in Kottayam. The day my mother called me a bitch. I knew that if I went into the Dandakaranya forest, it wouldn't be a picnic. Or, as Chairman Mao famously put it—a dinner party. I also knew that the comrades inside knew that I (not Hindu enough, not Christian enough, not communist enough) was not uncritical of their idols, neither the Great Helmsman nor the Red Tsar. Nevertheless, they invited me. Nevertheless, I decided to go.

I smiled to myself at the idea that Pradip would be wandering around in a similar forest, not far from where I was. He was researching and taking photographs for his next monumental book: *Jungle Trees of Central India*. Our worlds were so close and yet so far apart.

Mrs. Roy called the day before I left. She had not the slightest inkling of what I was about to do. Perhaps buried somewhere deep in her byzantine soul she still had a mother's instinct:

"I've been thinking . . . what this country really needs is a revolution."

How could I not love her?

How could I ever pretend to understand her?

\*　　　\*　　　\*

I flew to Raipur, drove the ten hours from there to Dantewada through dense fog, and arrived at the Maa Danteshwari Temple on time. I was dressed—disguised—as a God-fearing Hindu pilgrim in a white salwar kameez, a bright yellow dupatta, and fat, fake pearl earrings. I have never looked more ridiculous. I was accompanied by my old letter reader, father of the bride, and now well-known maker of extraordinary long-form documentary films, Sanjay K. He didn't know it, but Anjum came along, too. Neither knew the other was there. They were my consiglieri. We carried what we needed on our backs. We knew that the most dangerous part of the expedition would be getting into the forest and getting out. On a previous visit of mine to Dantewada, a senior policeman had pointed out the flat, white sandy banks of the Indravati River. "Across that river, ma'am, is what we call Pakistan. Out there, my boys shoot to kill." We had an international border in the heart of our country.

At the Maa Danteshwari Temple we met our greeter, whose tattered T-shirt said CHARLIE BROWN, NOT YOUR ORDINARY BLOCK-HEAD. Probably flood-relief material, like I once wore. After he had guided us safely into the forest, we realized that for all his put-on simple-village-lad demeanor, he was a trained guerrilla fighter and could handle an AK-47. An internal security threat for sure.

Over the next few weeks, we walked through the Dandakaranya forest with a squad of Naxalite guerrillas. We slept under the stars. We would camp and then have to move at a moment's notice if the lookout raised an alarm. We walked through village after village that had been burned to the ground. Thousands had been displaced by the war. For months people had slept out in the forest because the paramilitary and the Salwa Judum usually attacked their villages at night. We heard testimonies of unthinkable violence, not surprisingly, and most especially against women. As a result, almost half the armed guerrillas in the PLGA were women. Furious women. When they were caught, they were not just killed, they were savagely mutilated. Some were raped and beaten and then sent back to tell their comrades what they had suffered.

The women guerrillas walked shoulder to shoulder with the men, carrying an equal amount of weight. Huge cooking vessels, fresh vegetables, sacks of rice and flour. Bags stacked high with documents. And their own belongings and weapons. We ate red-ant chutney and rice, fruit, and occasionally fresh fish or chicken, cooked on the fly. I bathed in the river, guarded by female guerrillas. Sometimes I'd be overwhelmed by the kind of women bathing with me. We were farmers, soldiers, writers. We were singers and dancers, too, members of the cultural troupe. The high point of those weeks inside the forest was the celebration of the anniversary of the 1910 Bhumkal rebellion, in which the Koya tribe rose up against the British. *Bhumkal* means "earthquake." Thousands of villagers arrived for the celebration, each village with its own troupe of performers. Their drumming filled the night. The stories they told moved seamlessly between white colonizers and the new brown-skinned company men who had arrived to once again take their land from them. The dancing went on through the night and well into the following day.

Those were the most intense, extraordinary weeks of my life. Anjum's, too.

In the forest, when the comrades greeted each other with a Lal Salaam, "red salute," Anjum, unseen by them, always replied with a Lal Salaam Aleikum. She was expressing a unique kind of solidarity that ought to exist but does not. All this was a secret between her and me.

Far away in the French Alps, an old elephant was waiting patiently for that story to be written.

\*       \*       \*

Coming out of Dandakaranya was as tricky as going in. These are the last few paragraphs of "Walking with the Comrades," the book-length essay I wrote after I returned to Delhi:

> At dawn, I say goodbye to Comrade Madhav and Joori, to young Mangtu and all the others. Comrade Chandu has gone to organize the bikes and will come with me to the main road. Comrade Raju isn't coming (the climb would be hell on his knees). Comrade Niti (Most Wanted), Comrade Sukhdev, Kamla, and five others will take me up the hill. As we start walking, Niti and Sukhdev casually but simultaneously unclick the safety catches of their AKs. It's the first time I've seen them do that. We're approaching the "Border."
>
> "Do you know what to do if we come under fire?" Sukhdev asks, as though it was the most natural thing in the world.
>
> "Yes," I said, "immediately declare an indefinite hunger strike."
>
> He sat down on a rock and laughed. We climbed for about an hour. Just below the road, we sat in a rocky alcove, completely

concealed, like an ambush party, listening for the sound of the bikes. When it comes, the farewell must be quick. *Lal Salaam, comrades.* When I looked back, they were still there. Waving. A little knot. People who live with their dreams, while the rest of the world lives with its nightmares. Every night I think of this journey. That night sky, those forest paths. I see Comrade Kamla's heels in her scuffed chappals, lit by the light of my torch. I know she must be on the move. Marching, not just for herself, but to keep hope alive for us all.

The editor of *Outlook* turned over a whole issue to "Walking with the Comrades." There followed the usual calls for me to be arrested, hanged, shot, and so on. I was also caught in the flight path of the entertaining insults with which various sects and factions of Communist parties denounce one another. That high-minded debate was necessary of course. But that forest was necessary, too. Without the Naxalites, whatever anybody thought of them, there would be no forest.

Writing about vexed, contested things rarely ends with just the writing. My dreams were full of all that I had seen and heard in the forest. A few of us began a campaign against Operation Green Hunt. We spoke at universities, in press clubs, we held public meetings all over the country. We earned ourselves the epithet Urban Naxals—intellectual "terrorists." One of the people with whom I often spoke at public meetings as part of the campaign was my friend G. N. Saibaba. He taught literature at Delhi University. He came from a poor family in rural Telangana. An attack of polio in his early childhood had left him paralyzed from the waist down. Saibaba became a special target of the media and the government. He was accused of being a Naxalite and a member of an overground front of the underground

Maoist Party. Over the next three years he was regularly threatened and intimidated, his house was raided, and he was subjected to hours of questioning by the police.

We were approaching a dangerous time. The general election was coming around. The two main political parties chose their villains and the turf on which they would pitch their strident campaigns. The Congress, weakened by a massive, populist, and for the most part brainless anticorruption movement, showcased economic growth and targeted "antidevelopment" Urban Naxals, personified by people like G. N. Saibaba. The BJP promised it would turn back the clock on centuries of Muslim oppression and return India to its glorious Hindu past. The villains who blocked this path to glory were, of course, "Muslim jihadis," personified by Afzal Guru, the main accused in the Parliament Attack, who had, by then, been in prison for eleven years. One of the BJP's election slogans was *Desh abhi sharminda hai, Afzal abhi bhi zinda hai*, "Our country hangs its head in shame. Afzal is still alive." Hoping to defuse the mounting hysteria, and the wave of Hindu nationalism building in the BJP's favor, on the night of February 9, 2013, in a display of unforgivable pusillanimity, the Congress government secretly hanged Afzal Guru. His family was not informed. Later, the former Congress home minister, a senior lawyer himself, admitted, "The case may not have been correctly decided."

They hanged a man to win an election.

A little more than a year on, it was Saibaba's turn. He was on his way home from college when the police stopped his car. He was virtually abducted, put on a flight, and taken to Nagpur Central Jail. On cue, in exactly the same way it had for the Parliament Attack, the media ran a relentless campaign, branding him a dangerous terrorist "think tank." Five others, including a young student from Jawaharlal Nehru University were also arrested. To bolster their case against Sai, whenever he was taken to a hospital or to the courts in the towns where he was supposed to have committed his heinous crimes, they broadcast images of him being driven in a convoy of vehicles full of armed police. In hospital he was chained to his bed with an armed guard standing over him. How else do you turn an almost-paralyzed professor into a dangerous terrorist?

Hanging Afzal Guru and arresting Urban Naxals didn't help the Congress to win the election. It was swept aside by the BJP. In May 2014, Narendra Modi was sworn in as prime minister. He made a point of flying from Gujarat to Delhi in the private jet of a major mining company whose logo, ADANI, was emblazoned across the aircraft. It signaled that Hindu nationalism and corporate capitalism had blended into a new alloy. One that would tear through the social fabric and the very idea of India.

*     *     *

On the first anniversary of Saibaba's incarceration, I wrote an essay called "Professor POW." For the third time in my life, five male lawyers (Batch Number Three), confident that they now had a sympathetic government, approached the Nagpur High Court asking that I be charged with criminal contempt of court and arrested. One of the accusations was that I had called a magistrate a "small town man." This was the offending sentence: "On 12 September 2013 his [Saibaba's] home was raided by fifty policemen armed with a search warrant for stolen property from a magistrate in Aheri, a small town in Maharashtra."

I was summoned to Nagpur to appear personally before the High Court. The courtroom filled with people who had come to jeer and ogle. My main accuser, leading light of Batch Number Three, wore so many rings and chains that he looked as though he had burgled

Arundhati Roy

a jewelry store. He had two hairstyles—his hairpiece and his own hair peeping out from under it, both completely different textures and colors. He was so pleased with himself for successfully dragging me into court and putting me on display that he presented me with a bouquet of flowers while his friends stood around gloating. Fortunately, the judge exempted me from having to appear personally for subsequent hearings and gave me leave to appeal to the Supreme Court, where, all these years later, my case still remains. One more in the massive queue of pending cases.

On the day I appeared in the Nagpur High Court, in a town close by, a glittering literature festival that was sponsored year after year by corporate mining companies and a hyper-Hindu-nationalist TV channel that worked as their bullhorn was hosting a star-studded panel of international writers, who spoke eloquently and movingly about the dangers of censorship and the importance of free speech.

The trial court sentenced Saibaba to life imprisonment. In his one-thousand-page judgment the judge expressed regret that the sections of the law under which Saibaba was charged did not permit him to pronounce a death sentence, which he would have liked to do. Had they permitted it, my friend Sai might have been hanged like Afzal Guru to "satisfy the collective conscience of society." We would then have had those familiar, detailed reports in the press about what sort of rope was used, how good it was, where it came from, who the hangman was, how many children he had, how he felt about his job, and how he dealt with his emotions.

\*       \*       \*

We were well into the dark years of Hindu nationalist hell: public lynching of Muslims, videos of public lynching, public floggings, videos of public floggings, mass murder, videos of mass murder and sword-wielding mobs marching through our streets calling openly for the genocide of Muslims. A group of students in Jawaharlal Nehru University in Delhi decided to hold a protest to mark the third anniversary of the hanging of Afzal Guru. It was another of those moments of mainstream media hysteria. Screaming anchors on television channels aired doctored videos with fake soundtracks. They singled out students one by one, hounded them, lied about them, and called them Pakistani agents. They reserved a special brand of hysterics for Muslims, particularly Kashmiris. The police entered the campus and made arrests. One anchor took to addressing me directly on his prime-time news show, looking straight into the camera: "Arundhati Roy, we think you are disgusting." Night after night he would rave, "Why has she not been arrested? Why is she free?"

By then I was only weeks away from finishing *The Ministry of Utmost Happiness*. The thought of going to prison at that particular moment was devastating. An almost-complete manuscript can make a writer paranoid and fearful. I felt responsible for Anjum and all the other characters in the book. If I went to prison, they would be locked up with me. I thought it was my duty to usher them into the world, to make sure that their chatter mingled with other conversations on living bookshelves. To protect them I did what I never thought I ever would. I fled. I bought a ticket to London. I have never felt worse about myself. I woke up in a horrible hotel room with racist paintings of African dancers with real straw for skirts. I sat in the breakfast room and cried for myself, for my country, for everything that was going up in flames. Within a day I knew I had to return. Because I was a tree in Anjum's graveyard. If I was transplanted in another forest, my leaves would fall. I was back home within a week.

Why was I not arrested while so many others were? Who knows. Maybe my readers protected me. Maybe my iron angel did.

\* \* \*

It was a task to shut out the noise and the heartbreak of having so many friends in prison and return to writing *The Ministry of Utmost Happiness*. By the time I finished it, John Berger, my Jumbo, was sinking. I flew with my manuscript to Paris, where he had moved to be with his longtime companion, the Russian writer Nella Bielski. It was the last book he read before he died. I like to think of him—his earth, my rain, and then we switch roles—in Jannat Guest House, too. He doesn't need to be alive to flap his ears for me. All I need to do is to concentrate, and I can feel that cool breeze, the kind that only an old elephant can generate.

\* \* \*

*The Ministry of Utmost Happiness* was published in 2017.

In the signing queue at the launch in New York was Nishrin Jafri, daughter of Ehsan Jafri, former member of Parliament. Ehsan Jafri had been murdered—hacked to death—by a Hindu mob during the pogrom in Gujarat in 2002 when Modi was chief minister. Weeks before he was murdered, he had campaigned against Narendra Modi in a by-election, which Modi just barely won. Sixty people—friends and neighbors—whom Jafri had sheltered in his home had been murdered, too. Nishrin's mother, Zakia Jafri, had, like Anjum, survived the ordeal. The murderers were later caught on camera boasting about how they had dismembered Ehsan Jafri with swords and then burned him. Before he was killed, Jafri had made hundreds of phone calls asking for help. Nobody from any political party helped. The police stayed away. As an eyewitness to the massacre Nishrin's mother spent years in court trying to hold not just the murderers but Modi and his administration accountable. She failed. Instead, the people who helped her were jailed.

I signed Nishrin's book. I felt ashamed of our country.

Back in India, Saibaba, locked up in the notorious *anda* cell—egg cell—in the Nagpur prison, wrote a letter to Anjum:

Dear Anjum,

How are you? I hope you are doing well along with the entire Ministry in Jannat Guest House. . . . I would have written to you as one of my best friends but indications from your latest life show you are getting busier and busier with your team ever growing. I suddenly felt that you are the only person in the world who would really take my letter seriously and do something concrete for my freedom.

Anjum wasn't the letter-writing sort, so I replied on her behalf.

Saibaba was only one among hundreds of people who were being arrested and imprisoned. Many of them, activists, lawyers, students, journalists, were beloved friends. Saibaba would remain in prison for almost ten years before eventually being acquitted of all charges by the Nagpur High Court. The judge who acquitted him said, "There was nothing in the matter." *Nothing.* Nothing that even merited a trial. Nothing that merited even a day's imprisonment.

Only seven months after he came out of prison, my friend Sai died. He developed an infection after a gallbladder surgery. His body, weakened by ten years of incarceration, did not have the strength to fight it. His wife and daughter, who had lost ten years of their lives fighting for him, were left with nothing. *Nothing.* Not even an apology.

All I am left with is a bottle of mango pickle that he specially made for me. I might keep it for as long as I live.

A week after he died, I read an account of the killing of Comrade Niti (Most Wanted), who had walked with me during those weeks I spent in Dandakaranya. She was one of the eight people who had, at the end of our journey, escorted us across the Border up to the road and waved goodbye. The report said she was among thirty people who had been killed in the forest by the paramilitary. One of the women had been dragged over the rough, stony roads by her hair until her scalp came off her skull. I couldn't tell whether she was Comrade Niti or someone else. Comrade Niti did have long, beautiful hair.

# "Her Birth Certificate Was an Apology from God"

Around the time *The Ministry of Utmost Happiness* was published in India, a well-known Hindi-movie actor, who was also a BJP member of Parliament, angered by something he claimed I had written or said about Kashmir (it turned out to be a figment of his, or some fake-news vendor's, imagination), suggested that I be tied to a jeep and used as a human shield by the Indian army in its operations in Kashmir—a privilege reserved exclusively for local Kashmiri Muslim civilians. He was referring, approvingly, to an incident in which this had actually been done to a local Kashmiri tailor.

TV anchors debated the matter hotly. Was the actor within his rights to hold this view? Should I or should I not be used as a human shield? Thrilled by all the attention he was getting, the actor decided to land the knockout punch: "When she was born, her birth certificate was an apology from God."

Imagine his joy had he known that my own mother might have agreed with him. Imagine his sorrow had he known that I had the equivalent of Navy SEAL training on this subject and that his exertions didn't move my needle even a micromillimeter.

\*        \*        \*

Mrs. Roy had often told me about how miserable she was when she learned that she was pregnant with a second child. Me. She described how lonely life with Micky was on the tea estate in Assam. How she would stand for hours on the veranda of their house watching wild rhinos grazing in the grassland just beyond the fence, feeling nauseated and apprehensive about the life she had chosen. Her first baby was only nine months old, and she already had another coming.

When I was old enough to understand, she described to me the various ways in which she had tried to induce an abortion. The least horrifying was eating lots of green papaya; the most horrifying involved a wire coat hanger. It wasn't a nice thing for a mother to tell her daughter, but I sensed that she was warning me about drifting into a life of marriage and children without thinking it through carefully. I felt terrible for her. Even now when I think about it, I am not entirely on my side. I imagine her alone and ill, isolated on an inaccessible tea estate with a drunk husband, a small baby, and another on its way. Although the rhinos tilt the balance somewhat in my favor, I understand the attraction of green papayas and coat hangers. I am the outcome of their failure to deliver on their promise as abortion inducers. From that failure came the litany of "I wish I had dumped you in an orphanage," "You're a millstone around my neck," "All my sickness is because of you," and, of course, "Bitch."

Each time she told me about her unsuccessful attempts at aborting me, I felt relieved that I had been more successful in my own endeavor during the *Massey Sahib* shoot. And grateful that I hadn't had to subject a human that I had brought into the world to the kind of anger and resentment my mother often felt for me.

Years later, her story about her misery at her second pregnancy was backed up by Jane, her British sister-in-law. Jane was married to Micky's oldest brother. The only sober one. She and my mother hadn't met since my mother left Micky. When I met Jane, she had moved to Delhi. She was nearly ninety and dementia was setting in. She was funny and laconic, but seemed to live in the past, in her Calcutta days. She greeted me as though I were my mother, pregnant with me.

"I know you don't want that baby, Mary, but, really, it's too late for anything now. What does the doctor say?"

I ought to have been disturbed by it all, I suppose, but by then I had put up with so much and had moved so far away from the notion that mothers are meant to be some sort of haven of love and protection that I just felt, *Well, it's too bad, ladies. I'm here now.*

*     *     *

Mrs. Roy wouldn't have agreed with the Hindi-movie actor about much else. She was unwell and in bed with a severe attack of asthma when a group of BJP workers entered her school campus belligerently demanding a cash donation for their party. The teachers were intimidated. Although Kerala had not yet given the BJP even the smallest foothold, the teachers knew that the chain of command of the people who had entered the campus went all the way up to Prime Minister Narendra Modi, who did not take even the smallest rebuff lightly. The school was extra-vulnerable because it was a "minority institution," a Christian school. The teachers decided to invoke their own chain of command. They trudged up the hill to Mrs. Roy's house and timidly presented the problem. She sat up in bed, ramrod straight.

"*Never!*"

*        *        *

Although she still made a point of reading the papers, Mrs. Roy found it hard to read for long stretches. She tried to read *The Ministry of Utmost Happiness*, but couldn't. She was too frail to organize the Kottayam book launch and then sabotage it. Her memory had begun to play tricks on her. She insisted that Edward Snowden, the fugitive American whistleblower who had escaped to Russia, had visited her in Kottayam. Sometimes she said it was "that Julian fellow." Julian Assange, she meant. She would set her jaw and fly into a rage if anybody tried to persuade her otherwise. She was mistaking Snowden for my friend the actor John Cusack, who had indeed visited her a few years ago in Kottayam when Cusack and I were working on our little book, *Things That Can and Cannot Be Said*, about our visit to Snowden in Moscow and to Assange, who had been given political asylum and was holed up in the Ecuadorian embassy in London. We had gone to Moscow with Daniel Ellsberg—Snowden of the seventies—who leaked the Pentagon Papers and played a major part in stopping the Vietnam War.

Cusack and my brother still go into paroxysms of wheezing laughter when Cusack imitates what he calls "the look of naked terror on the face of the fearless Arundhati Roy when her mother asked us if we would like to have a cup of tea with her."

G. Isaac, on the other hand, read *The Ministry* so many times that he knew it by rote. The unexpected, unimaginable new development during those years was that G. Isaac and his baby sister, Mart Roy, had become inseparable buddies. He visited her at least twice a week.

He would hold her hand and they'd sing old songs together, she with her oxygen cannula in her nostrils. She couldn't really sing anymore, but she tried to. They had both blown up the money they'd received from the sale of their father's house. He on repaying his massive debts. She, buying more land for her school. For a larger sports ground. It was as though they had fought each other all their lives only because they respected each other as opponents. Because nobody else would have made the battle entertaining or worthwhile.

*   *   *

From being housebound Mrs. Roy had become more or less room-bound, although she regularly went out on evening drives in the school car, visiting people. When she arrived at their homes, she sat in their driveways, or outside their gates, wearing her sunglasses, like a gangster, and spoke to them through the car window or with the door open. Her visits lasted just a few minutes. She had stopped entertaining as much as she used to. She still sat on her porch every morning and evening. But her home had become a little bleak and very quiet. Children's excited voices floated through the windows, but inside, no human sound was permitted. Everybody had to whisper and tiptoe around.

The house was badly in need of attention. There were dangerous cracks in Laurie Baker's filler slab; the steel was exposed and rusted. Termites had attacked the window and door frames. To hide the cracks in the cement, the floor had been covered with some terrible, peeling vinyl. Nothing could be done about any of this because Mrs. Roy could not tolerate dust and noise. She had withdrawn completely from the school. My efficient sister-in-law was in charge of administration. The new principal was an old student.

It was a poignant moment in the history of the school, a mix of sorrow and relief, when an old student of Mrs. Roy's sat on Mrs. Roy's chair in Mrs. Roy's office, which had lain empty for a long time. The framed anticipatory bail order from the *Jesus Christ Superstar* days still hung on the wall behind her, reminding everybody that whoever ran the school needed her predecessor's steel spine.

The handover was smooth, the school carried on without breaking stride. It remains an excellent institution, missing only that unpredictable, irreplaceable spark of mad genius.

# Retreat

Her retreat from the school had no effect on Mrs. Roy's temper. If she didn't like the food she was served, she still hurled plates and dishes across the room. If she was annoyed with someone, she still demanded that they return any gifts or money she may have given them long ago. Occasionally, she expressed something like regret.

"I've been a little nasty today."

My beloved Kurussammal, whom I had known since I was five years old, wasn't there anymore. She had retired and moved back to Ooty to live with her family in an apartment she had bought with her life's earnings. From her home she could look out at where the Imperial Entomologist's cottage used to be. Where she once bathed my brother and me with a pot of hot water and dressed us in the sweaters she had knitted. Kurussammal had learned well from her mistress and dominated her children and grandchildren like a little mafia don. I visited her two days before she died. When she screamed at the people around her, she and I exchanged secret smiles. We lay next to each other on her bed and shouted out a roll call of all the dishes she had cooked for Mrs. Roy.

Rasam!

Thairu sadam!

Date chutney!

Fish pie!

Parippu payasam!

Mrs. Roy's old whipping horse, Ammal, now lived with her sister Mariamma in a small house just outside the school grounds. Ammal would, like a version of her beloved mistress higher up on the hill, stand on her porch and watch the comings and goings all day long.

Ammal had long ago been replaced by a team of four women who provided round-the-clock care for Mrs. Roy. Two attended to her in the day and two at night. Jessie-the-gentle and Reena-the-stern were sisters, Indira was a former nurse, and Annamma was also a former nurse, who seemed to have the ability to slow sound down. She always heard things a few seconds after they had been said. The four looked after Mrs. Roy with a dedication and love that was a great comfort to me. They knew how suddenly and without notice an attack of asthma would begin, like a phantom fist squeezing down on her lungs. They had learned to drop everything, wherever they were in the house, day or night, and rush to her room when they heard the call bell. There was a bank of bells behind Mrs. Roy's bed. Some sounded like birdcalls. She also had a small, old-fashioned brass bell to use when there was a power cut, or what was called load-shedding, which often lasted for more than an hour. Of late it hadn't mattered so much because a diesel generator kicked in automatically. The bell she used most frequently played the tune of "Are You Sleeping, Brother John?"

Her days seemed just as busy as when she was running the school. Just as tense and unpredictable. It was only that the roster of activity was somewhat different. Mrs. Roy's morning bath and postbath grooming had become an elaborate affair. Jessie, Reena, Indira, and

Annamma knew her body perhaps better than they knew their own. They knew how to sit her down on the built-up cement seat in the bathroom with her back resting against the wall while the big steel bucket was filled with piping-hot water, how to lift her breasts and soap underneath them, how not to lift her arms higher than shoulder level. (Her way of expressing pain or discomfort, however slight, was to roar. Loudly. *Aaaargh! Owww!* Like a character in a comic book.)

A reverse-bathing lesson for the one who had taught scores of children how to bathe.

On Sundays, if one of the women wanted to go to church, then a fifth person, Brinda, who worked down the hill in the office, would come in to assist the bathing team. Brinda was small, only as high as the door handles, with a braid of black hair that was almost as long as herself. Her father was a goldsmith and had made his daughter exquisite jewelry scaled to size, which she always wore to work. Her toe rings, tiny bangles, and *jhumka* earrings glinted in the dim bathroom. She wore a Brinda-size rubber apron over her kurta and salwar. (Malayalis had taken to this Punjabi attire with immeasurable enthusiasm.) The amber cake of translucent Pears soap looked as big as a brick in her hands. For her to lift and hold up my mother's breasts was something of an endeavor, and all the women, including my mother, would laugh about it.

If I happened to be visiting, Mrs. Roy often sent for me.

"Would you like to watch your mother being bathed? Why don't you take a photograph?"

"OK, I promise not to show it to anyone."

"Then what's the point?"

It was beguiling, but it was more than that. Toward the end of her life, Mrs. Roy's bath became a ritual, a kind of sacrament, a signifier of certain milestones. It was a proclamation of her triumph over all her enemies real and imagined who peopled her past, who had tried to break her, keep her down. (Here she was now, Cleopatra being bathed in ass's milk.) It was an assertion of authority over the women who looked after her. It was her way of telling me that other people were doing what ought to have been my duty. (Sometimes I waded in and joined the bathing team.) Most of all it was her way of dealing with chronic ill-health. She had learned early what a powerful weapon physical vulnerability could be if it was properly deployed.

The bathing and grooming generated a bond of intimacy between her and those who looked after her that was deeper, clearer, surer, and less thorny than mine with my mother. She looked after those who looked after her, too, with generosity and concern. On those occasions when I was summoned to her bathroom, I could see that although there was apprehension and strain in that soapy, steamy room, there was also love.

Mrs. Roy's bath ritual, the polar opposite of mine with the comrades in the forest, always made me think of the story of the old patriarch in a nearby village who would be taken down to the river to be bathed. His vastness spoke to his prosperity and breeding, a matter of pride, not shame. His family once dominated the cinnamon—I think it was—trade. His servants would have to precede him down the steps and pour buckets of hot water into the river to soften the shock to his system before he deigned to immerse himself. Once he was in, standing firmly on a mossy underwater platform, he would be soaped and scrubbed like a baby elephant, while small fish nibbled at his nipples. On one such occasion, the story goes, one of the servants found a key lodged inside a fold of fat. There was an outbreak of spontaneous celebration and happy splashing because it was the key to his money safe, which had gone missing some days ago. The servants had been accused of stealing it.

I had learned that the best way to minimize the chances of conflict between Mrs. Roy and me was to visit her often, but only for a few days at a time. I learned to enter her orbit like a clever insect negotiating a spider's web—to fold my wings and minimize my surface area as I stepped in, and when I left, to retreat along the path I had cleared when I entered, taking every possible precaution not to entangle myself in the filaments of her web. I made a hobby of twisting old adages to suit my situation.

*Where there's a will, there's a way out.*

*I'm an escape goat.*

She still did her best to needle me, but I had become more skilled at subverting her provocations than I used to be. Some of our conversations were hilarious. This one, for example, about her revised views on marriage:

"I think the way you are living is terrible. I think marriage is a wonderful idea."

"For me or for you, Kochamma?" I had started calling her Kochamma, "little mother," by then, same as the rest of the bathing team.

"For me of course."

"So, what would be different if you were married right now?"

"There'd be a man around here."

"Doing what?"

"Oh . . . you know, those man things."

She said this airily, disdainfully, as though it were too obvious to have to explain. It's one of the few times I have ever known her to be vague.

The thing that upset and frustrated her most of all was being unable to walk around her beloved campus. Every inch of it was mapped in her head. She could issue unnervingly accurate instructions about what needed to be done:

*Has the leak in the dining-hall roof been fixed?*

*Have you changed the washbasins in Dorm Three?*

*Tell Achoo to trim that long branch of the old mango tree in the sports field.*

*Ask Jophin to see me about the physics lab.*

It was as though while her body was confined to her bed, her spirit still made regular inspection tours.

She didn't like seeing other people taking charge of what she had spent her life building—yes, brick by brick. She said as much to me one night when we were sitting out on her porch together.

*I feel jealous of everybody.*

Sometimes she withdrew into her shell for weeks at a time. Not speaking, not eating, sleeping all day. The doctors prescribed an anti-depressant.

*I'm taking a medicine for sadness.*

When COVID swept over us, I was locked down in Delhi and couldn't go to her. I didn't believe Mrs. Roy would make it. Her life was already full of oxygen cylinders, oximeters, and BiPAP machines. Over those nightmare months, while Delhi ran out of oxygen and crematoria ran out of space, I dreaded the phone call that would tell me she had COVID. Everybody around her got it, including Jessie, Reena, Indira, and Annamma. But not her. Madam Houdini triumphed again. What nearly killed her, though, was her silent school campus. Empty swimming pool, empty auditorium, empty dormitories. She couldn't understand what online classes were.

*They say it's all been moved to some sort of a cloud now.*

She couldn't believe that people thought education was just about lessons in classrooms. She was convinced that the era of real brick-and-mortar schools was over. Her baby was dead. Her life's work was obsolete. It would just be a little chapter in the onward march of human history. *Once there were schools where little humans learned things. . . .*

I wanted to hug her and reassure her that everything would be OK. But you can't hug a porcupine. Not even over the phone.

There are few things I am more grateful for than that Mrs. Roy lived to see her school reopen and the children return to campus.

# A Declaration of Love

It was January 2022. I was in Sanjay's little apartment in Delhi. He lived alone. Like me. We were having dinner with two of our close friends from Kashmir when I got a message on my phone. It was from my mother. They, all men, each of them, including Sanjay, beloved by their besotted mothers, must have noticed the blood drain from my face and wondered what had happened. How could I explain to them that what had scared me was that I had got a message from my mother saying that she loved me.

Mrs. Roy was too imperious to use her phone herself; she dictated her messages to her staff. This meant that her phone messages were never casual. They were declarations. Statements of policy. The one I received that night said, *There is no one in the world whom I have loved more than you.*

Despite everything that had happened between us, somehow I knew that to be true. My lifelong refusal to stop loving her no matter what had finally breached her barriers. Along with a rush of happiness, I felt the cold moth of my childhood land on my heart. I sensed that her end was near. My fingers were shaking as I typed out my reply.

*You are the most unusual, wonderful woman I have ever known. I adore you.*

I was capable of making declarations, too. Mine, too, like hers, was true.

It was January. Freezing in Delhi. I was soaked in sweat.

After that I became permanently fretful, permanently apprehensive. Every time my brother called me, he would cackle like a witch at the anxiety in my voice when I said hello.

"She's OK, Kuriakose, she's fine. Relax. That's not why I'm calling."

For no reason that either of us knew, he had started calling me Kuriakose and I called him Kuttappen.

And then one day in September he called and didn't laugh.

\*     \*     \*

At the last dinner I had with Mrs. Roy there was cake. It was a student's birthday and a small chocolate cake had been sent up from the school kitchen for her. She demolished her slice at high speed and fixed her eyes on mine. I slid it across the table to her. And then she was ready for another. Her final score was three large slices. I was delighted. I thought the return to gluttony meant a new lease on life, a few more years at least. She smiled at me, her lovely, naughty smile.

"You know of course, Kochamma, that people with dimples can get away with anything."

The smile vanished and she fixed me with her cold glare. Her father's eyes. The Imperial Entomologist's eyes. Those cold eyes that stared out of his photograph in the family album—the famous portrait he had had taken in a Hollywood studio. I have never stopped wondering what made him do the things that he did. Because I know it's the key to understanding why she did the things she did.

Even up to my very last day with her I never managed to get used to or anticipate the sudden shifts, the sunlight and shadow, the precipitous climate changes in her moods. But I had learned to stand just outside the range of their clawing, lashing fury. Or so I thought. I often miscalculated. In truth I am constructed from its debris.

The next morning, just before I left for Delhi, she sent for me. She smiled and tapped her dimple.

"Take a photograph."

I did.

That was my last photograph of her. When I look at it now, I can see that the camera lens picked up what my naked eye had not. Her lush, healthy hair was brittle, dead. A fine fretwork of veins, like the map of a hidden city, lay just under her almost transparent skin. She had started her journey. The chocolate cake was rations for the road.

Two days after I got back to Delhi, on the first of September, she changed (was changed) into fresh clothes, ate a good breakfast, and then lay down on her bed and died. Her face was peaceful. Not a flicker or a grimace, not a trace of suffering. It was a perfect death. Miraculous, given her medical history. Nobody would have known she was dead if she hadn't been lying on her back. She never lay on her back, only on her side, against a high wall of pillows.

Finally, that mighty, troubled heart had stopped beating.

*       *       *

It was late at night by the time I arrived in Kottayam. She was laid out in a temperature-controlled glass-topped coffin in the dining room. A small group of people, including some press photographers, were there. Her whole life would be condensed into a few sentences in the papers the next morning.

She had always been adamant that she did not want to be buried on the campus.

"They'll say my ghost haunts the school."

"But we want you to haunt us, Kochamma. Haunt us forever."

I showed her a picture of Heathcliff lying on Cathy's grave from an old illustrated edition of *Wuthering Heights*.

"See . . . I'll be like this."

She wasn't impressed. We both knew that our conversation was theoretical. It was illegal to bury anybody on private property. And there was no place for her—divorcée and challenger of Christian law—in the church cemetery. She said she wanted to be cremated. She had marked out two jackfruit trees that were to be cut down and used as firewood. That she believed it would take two gigantic trees to send her off was a measure of her undiminished self-regard. Fortunately cutting down trees turned out to be unnecessary. The very civilized Kottayam municipality had a mobile crematorium. It was like a coffin with chimneys, fired by gas cylinders. Since the school was closed, she could be cremated on the campus. And we could immerse her ashes in the Meenachil.

I wasn't happy with that. I felt that cremating her and immersing her ashes was not enough. I wanted something more for her. What could that something be?

We sat with her all night, telling stories about her that made us laugh and cry. At dawn we took her down the hill in a beautiful hearse covered with flowers, to the hall in the new junior school building, where people could come and say goodbye to her. Kunju-mol Kochamma, the first parent to entrust her children to the care of Mrs. Roy all those years ago when the school was in the Rotary Club, was among the first to arrive. She stayed to the end. Others streamed in—relatives, parents, teachers, students, old students, old teachers, students whose children were now in the school, women she had sheltered, orphans whom she had given scholarships to, everyone who worked with my brother in his Kochi office. My friend the owner of the A-1 Ladies store at the Kottayam bus stop. These were all people who loved her. I wasn't surprised to see them there. But as the day wore on, what happened was just extraordinary. People began to come in from all over Kerala. People who had once worked for her, people she had quarreled with, people she had fired, doctors who had looked after her thirty years ago, rival labor unions, construction workers, local politicians and shopkeepers, journalists who had trashed her, priests who disagreed with her.

I think Dido my Alsatian was there, too, with a bullet hole in her skull. I wonder what she would have thought about the message of condolence that came in from an old student who worked as a senior special effects technician in Hollywood: *She was more than just a school principal to me. She was in equal measure a mother . . . she let me have a menagerie of animals in school . . . not a single school I know today would allow that.*

Maybe Dido would have chuckled like my brother and said, "It's true, it's true."

Ammal hobbled in, beating her chest, lamenting loudly, her eyes blurred with grief. G. Isaac, the only person in the world who called Mary Roy by her first name, came with his wife, Soosy.

Tulasidharan, Laurie Baker's master mason from more than fifty years ago, came all the way from Trivandrum, in a bright pink shirt with the newspaper that announced her death rolled up under his arm. He had laid the foundation stone for the school along with Baker and Mrs. Roy, when the property was still *motta kunnu*, "the bald hill."

"There was nothing here you know," he said to me. "Absolutely nothing except snakes and lizards, and skeletons of birds. We used to think this place was haunted. We were scared to live here at night. She made all this from nothing. She was an amazing woman. I saw how she worked. What she did. What she created. All alone."

"I know."

"She had two children who were always running wild. Where are they?"

"Here's one. In front of you."

"But aren't you that writer? Arundhati Roy?"

"Even writers were children once."

There was an open mike for anybody who wanted to speak. Many did. Joe Ikareth, an old student, came with his guitar. He had been cast as Judas in the *Jesus Christ Superstar* that was sabotaged by the Kottayam collector. Joe decided to sing Judas's opening song, "Heaven on Their Minds," but to replace *Jesus* wherever he appeared in the song with *Mary*. I don't think he had thought it through:

> *Mary!*
> *You've started to believe*
> *The things they say of you,*
> *You really do believe*
> *This talk of God is true*

Once he realized, he stopped. With a shy smile.

Some people spoke about the Travancore Christian Succession Act and her brave battle against it. I was grateful that G. Isaac was almost completely deaf (except if you spoke directly into his good ear). The speeches washed over him as he smiled a beatific smile.

He said he wanted to sing for her. On his way to the coffin, he asked me, "What is the name of the whiskey Garson Hobart likes?"

"Cardhu."

"Ah yes."

Garson Hobart, whose real name was Biplab Dasgupta, is a decadent but brilliant Indian intelligence officer in *The Ministry of Utmost Happiness*.

G. Isaac stood by the coffin and sang "The Lord's My Shepherd." For his little sister, Mart. It broke my heart. In exactly a year's time, he would die, too. He who enriched my life in such quirky, magical ways. There will never be another pair like them. Mart & G. Isaac.

(He would be buried in his church cemetery. His marriage to an "outsider," his divorce and early years of Humbert Humbertism, didn't matter of course. Because he was a man and this was India, my dear.)

As the time came to take her up the hill to the back of the house to cremate her, the Kottayam collector arrived. A very different kind of collector from her spiteful long-ago predecessor. She brought along the Kottayam Police Band. They played "Day Is Done, Gone the Sun" on their somewhat leaky bugles.

That tune. It always made my heart do a little shuffle. The boys' band in our military boarding school would play it every year for the Beating of the Retreat during our Founder's Day march-past. LKC, tiny fellow in Class VII who played the bugle, was the designated Echo. He had to stand far away, unseen, on the diving board of the swimming pool and play back the tune with a couple of seconds' delay. Since then, whenever I hear "Day Is Done," it makes me smile. Kuttappen the Echo. The Echo who had become a fat-cat businessman with two grandchildren and three guitars.

The Kottayam Police Band marched alongside the hearse as it drove slowly back up the hill. Before the mobile crematorium was fired up, they gave Mrs. Roy a twenty-one-gun salute. The last time the police had entered the campus was thirty years ago, on a raid to find the video of the *Superstar* dress rehearsal and arrest her.

My mother's funeral was a novel that I would not have had the imagination to write.

I'd been thinking since the morning about what kind of a memorial we could make for her. While the flames consumed Mrs. Roy's mortal remains and turned her to ash, I got it. I suggested to my brother that we should make her a grove instead of a grave. I said I would design it. It had to be a living space, with fish and frogs and plants. A place where we could go and talk to her. Say the things we needed to tell her while she was alive but never could. Thinking about it, trying to imagine it, took the edge off my grief.

Once everybody left, her lawyer announced he was duty bound to read out her will in the presence of her heirs. I had already signed away my share in everything. As a person with a target on my back, I had worried for a while about my mother's school as well as Pradip and the girls being attacked by our vindictive government as a way of punishing me. I had resigned from the partnership that owned a part of the land on which the school was built and had suggested to Pradip that we get divorced with the same lack of seriousness with which we got married, so that he and the girls (and their property) had no legal connection to me. It has to have been the sweetest divorce of all time. At our court appearance, as we sat around waiting for our turn, our lawyer admonished us for playing the fool and laughing too much (at some silly Pradip joke). She was worried that the judge would get offended. The order granting us a divorce had been delivered to me the previous morning, at the very moment Mrs. Roy died. So, I, free woman, free-falling, was heir to nothing at all. But I was curious about our great will-making mother's will.

We sat around her dining table—the school accountant, the lawyer, my brother and sister-in-law, and me. There was more than one will in the envelope. We had to find the latest one. It lived up to my expectations of our great will maker. It was a precise, clear, thoughtful document, worthy of someone who had been obsessed by wills all her life. She had left something to every single person, no matter how small, who had looked after her. My brother and sister-in-law were now the controlling partners in the partnership that owned the land on which the school was built. The school itself was run by a society with a governing body. Once everything had been clarified, my brother announced that he had something to say to me.

"You are not going to be allowed to drift away from us like a smoke ring."

I said I had no intention of drifting away.

"You have to have something here. Something that is yours."

He insisted he was going to mark off Mrs. Roy's house and its compound from the rest of the school and have it registered in my name. Even though his wife, Mary Jr., lived in it, and visiting teachers and other guests stayed in the spare room, he wanted the house to be mine. My brother was our mother's son. He didn't want to be the man who inherited everything. In fact, neither of us really wanted to inherit anything. I was reluctant for a number of reasons. Beautiful as it was, I was a little scared of the house and the memories it held for me. I didn't see myself living there. I knew that my brother, still haunted by our past, was reluctant to spend even a night there. Anjum leaned over and whispered in my ear, "If we're building a memorial for her, then it's going to be like our Jannat Guest House. Only we can do it. And look at this house, it's falling down. Who's going to repair it? Who's going to love it?" She was right. I looked around the table. Already there was more noise and chatter in the house than there had ever been. It felt like the kind of profanity that was long overdue.

"You mean this place is now mine?"

Everybody nodded.

"Well in that case . . . *get out of my house!*"

Our laughter floated into the night. Mrs. Roy got the joke and smiled, too. I could almost hear her say, "I've been a little nasty today. I just upped and left."

That first night in a Mrs. Roy–less world, I spun unanchored in space with no coordinates. I had constructed myself around her. I had grown into the peculiar shape that I am to accommodate her. I had never wanted to defeat her, never wanted to win. I had always wanted her to go out like a queen. And now that she had, I didn't make sense to myself anymore.

A friend in Delhi who hadn't ever met her sent me a couplet in Urdu that comforted me more than anything that anyone said. It allowed me to see her happy, liberated from a body that had limited her so severely. I saw her walking through her campus once more, breathing easily, bending to smell the flowers, looking up to count the jackfruits and coconuts, inspecting every corner of it in a way she hadn't done in years.

> *Aaj ki raat mein ghoomunga khuli sadakon par*
> *Aaj ki raat mujhe khwabon se fursat kuch hai*
>
> Tonight I will wander on open roads
> Tonight I have some time off, even from my dreams

We decided that we would put some of her ashes in the Meenachil River, some in the ocean, and some we would bury at the base of the clump of tall bamboo behind her house, where I would make the Grove.

I don't understand why putting her ashes in the ocean haunts me in the way that it does. Watching the waves take her away was wrenching. I cannot seem to get over it. I see her clearly, all the time. She's walking on the water. But she's using a walker. She's all alone, under the stars. There's nobody to carry her inhaler and her other paraphernalia. Nobody to put on her socks, take them off, put on the fan, put it off, switch on the light, switch it off. Nobody to carry her jar of jujubes. I want to do that for her. But I can't get to her.

I decided to start renovating the house and building the Grove simultaneously. I consulted some fellow architects who were acolytes of Laurie Baker. They thought the house was in terrible condition and not worth trying to repair. They advised me to take it down and rebuild it. I could not countenance that idea. I would rather it collapsed on its own. If it did, I would have cherished the ruins. But there was no question of taking it down. I wanted to take a chance and try to restore it. I called Golak, to back me up on my decision. He came, and we both agreed that it was the right thing to do. So many years after having abandoned the profession that I was trained in, I returned to it. I began the process of surgery—the architectural equivalent of a triple bypass. I hoped the restoration would also honor her spirit and heal mine. I wanted it to be a house in which Kuttappen could sleep peacefully and play his guitar loudly. A house where friends could come and stay. A sort-of guesthouse in a sort-of graveyard.

The architectural triple bypass took us the best part of a year. We had to cut away the rusted steel inside the filler slab and replace it, had to repair the cracks and waterproof the whole roof, take out the door and window frames and replace them, take out the whole floor and replace it, replace all the pipes, all the wiring. We had to do all this to a fragile, exposed-brick structure. The house ended up being like the Ship of Theseus—the same house, but with every single part replaced. Laurie Baker might not have approved because the expense was very un-Baker-like. But Anjum knew that there was more than architecture going on there. There was witchery. And spirit work.

We built the Grove at the base of a clump of towering bamboo that I think had been there from the *motta kunnu* days. It was speaking bamboo and seemed to have a lot to say, many stories to tell. It moaned and creaked, rustled, whistled, and sang all day and all night long. We raised a low platform of unpolished black granite, the size of a small room, with four old, rough stone pillars at each corner supporting a teakwood trellis. We trained creepers to grow over the trellis. Around that little structure we planted all the things she loved: banana trees, ginger, chili, pepper, ferns, and orchids. On the center of the granite platform we placed an antique stone trough fitted with a motor to oxygenate the water so that fish and frogs and water lilies could live in it. A square slab of rough stone, supported from behind, slanted into the long side of the trough like a headstone. Along the length of the stone trough (with a nod to Toni Morrison) we carved:

*B E L O V E D.*

On the headstone it said:

*Mary Roy,*
*Dreamer Warrior Teacher*
*07.11.1933 – 01.09.2022*
*Founder Pallikoodam.*

It did not occur to either my brother or me to say the usual things: Mother of (Kuttappen and Kuriakose), or Wife of (the Nothing Man).

She wouldn't have liked that. Those were not the stripes she had strived to earn.

Once the house was repaired and the memorial completed, a wave of grief crashed over me again. I felt as though the only way to stave it off would be to keep working on the memorial, to keep tinkering with it forever.

"Kuttappen, what shall we do now? Shall we put surround-sound speakers on the pillars and play Black Sabbath?"

"No, Kuriakose! She'll jump out. She'll jump out."

"I want her to. I want her back."

"No. Enough now. Let her be."

We're old now (like Carlo), but sometimes we behave like children who are living the childhood we never had.

I still see her clearly. All the time. She's walking on the high seas. Through storm and stillness, through sunshine and rain. She's walking when the tide is high, she's walking when it's low. She's walking when I wake up. And when I drift into sleep. She takes small, unsteady steps, but she keeps going. She stops only to watch ships pass. Or to grimace at the continents of garbage bobbing by. She's always alone. She's on the Red Sea. She's in Morocco. She's off the coast of Scotland. She's in the Galápagos. Still watching. Still learning. Still practicing her Malayalam mosquito poem. Still plotting her next move. She isn't dressed very well. She's in a white salwar and a soft, oversize tea-brown T-shirt. And her high-top basketball shoes.

For stability.

Every now and then she stops as though she's looking at herself in her bedroom mirror. Then she straightens her shoulders and walks on. The way she always did.

As for me, I stand on the shore and look at her through the binoculars I've made with my hands.

The wind is picking up. I must straighten my shoulders, too. Because

> (a) Anything Can Happen to Anyone.
> (b) It's Best to Be Prepared.

Bye-O, Mart Roy.
I'll be seeing you.

# Acknowledgments

My brilliant editors: Simon Prosser, who sensed from the beginning how hard it would be for me to write this book, without whose encouragement I never would have written it, Nan Graham and Kathryn Belden, who guided it through some fairly choppy waters, Sarah-Jane Forder, who streamlined it, and Manasi Subramaniam, who brought it home.

Antoine Gallimard, Luigi Brioschi, who have published every word I have ever written.

Hans Balmes, who's always there.

Lisette Verhagen and Anthony Arnove, cherished friends who happen to be my literary agents too. Without you two, I'd drown.

Mayank Austin Soofi and Carlo Buldrini, whose hearts I own and whose photographs of me, old and young, are on the cover.

Aditya Pande for the hours spent in his design studio doing more than just work, and Kaushik Ramaswami for his expertise on everything to do with paper and printing.

Ashok Kumar and Krishna for keeping me afloat.

Begum Filthy Jaan and Maati K Lal for their love and harkat.

Acknowledgments

Finally, my beloveds whose names aren't in this book, but without whom my life would be desolate: Aijaz Hussain, Aradhana Seth, Deepa Verma, Jawed Naqvi, Jiten Yadav, Naomi Klein, Nikhil De, Parvaiz Bukhari, Prashant Bhushan, Rebecca John, Saba Naqvi, Shah Alam Khan, Sharmila Mitra, Shripad Dharmadhikari, Suman Parihar, Sushrut Jadhav, Tarun Bhartiya, Upasana Garnaik, and V.

And finally, finally, Pia and Mithva. Flown away. Free.

# About the Author

Arundhati Roy is the author of *The God of Small Things*, which won the Booker Prize in 1997, and *The Ministry of Utmost Happiness*, which was long-listed for the Man Booker Prize in 2017. Both novels have been translated into more than forty languages. Roy's works of nonfiction include *The End of Imagination*, *The Doctor and the Saint*, *My Seditious Heart*, and *Azadi*. In 2023 she was awarded the prestigious European Essay Prize for lifetime achievement, and in 2024 the PEN Pinter Prize for telling "urgent stories of injustice with wit and beauty." She lives in Delhi.